THE LITTLE BOOK OF ROCK PAINTING

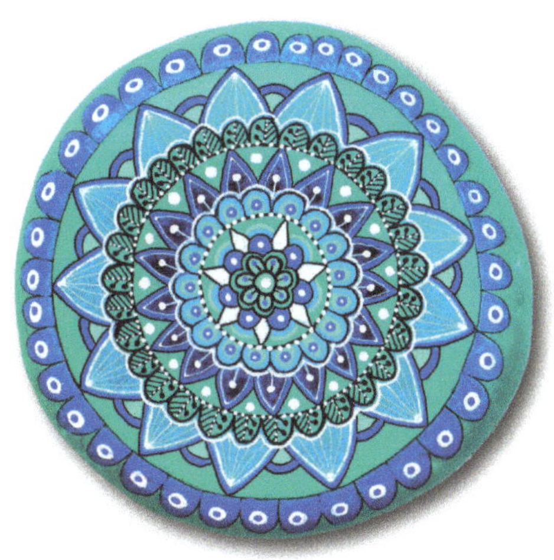

MORE THAN 50 TIPS AND TECHNIQUES FOR
LEARNING TO PAINT COLORFUL DESIGNS AND PATTERNS ON ROCKS AND STONES

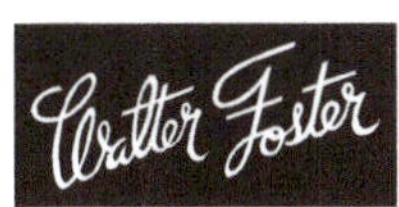

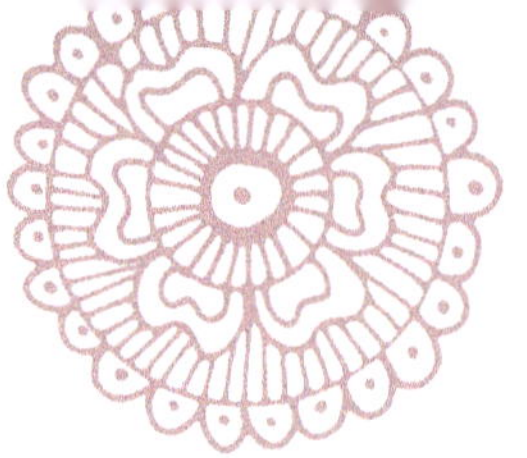

Quarto.com
WalterFoster.com

First published in 2019 by Walter Foster Publishing, an imprint of The Quarto Group.
26391 Crown Valley Parkway, Suite 220, Mission Viejo, CA 92691, USA.
T (949) 380-7510 **F** (949) 380-7575

EEA Representation, WTS Tax d.o.o.,
Žanova ulica 3, 4000 Kranj, Slovenia.
www.wts-tax.si

ISBN: 978-1-63322-731-6

Digital edition published in 2019
eISBN: 978-1-63322-732-3

TABLE OF CONTENTS

INTRODUCTION

Every rock is a unique canvas, and each three-dimensional shape can be transformed with paint to produce brilliant results. For example, imagine a carrot-shaped rock, with the hint of organic imperfections already on the surface; all you need to make it come alive is to brush on the colors! Follow along as this book demonstrates a number of basic techniques for painting a variety of rocks. You'll also find useful shortcuts and easy ways to create exciting special effects. Once you've begun your journey in rock painting, don't be surprised to find yourself eyeing every rock in sight for possibilities!

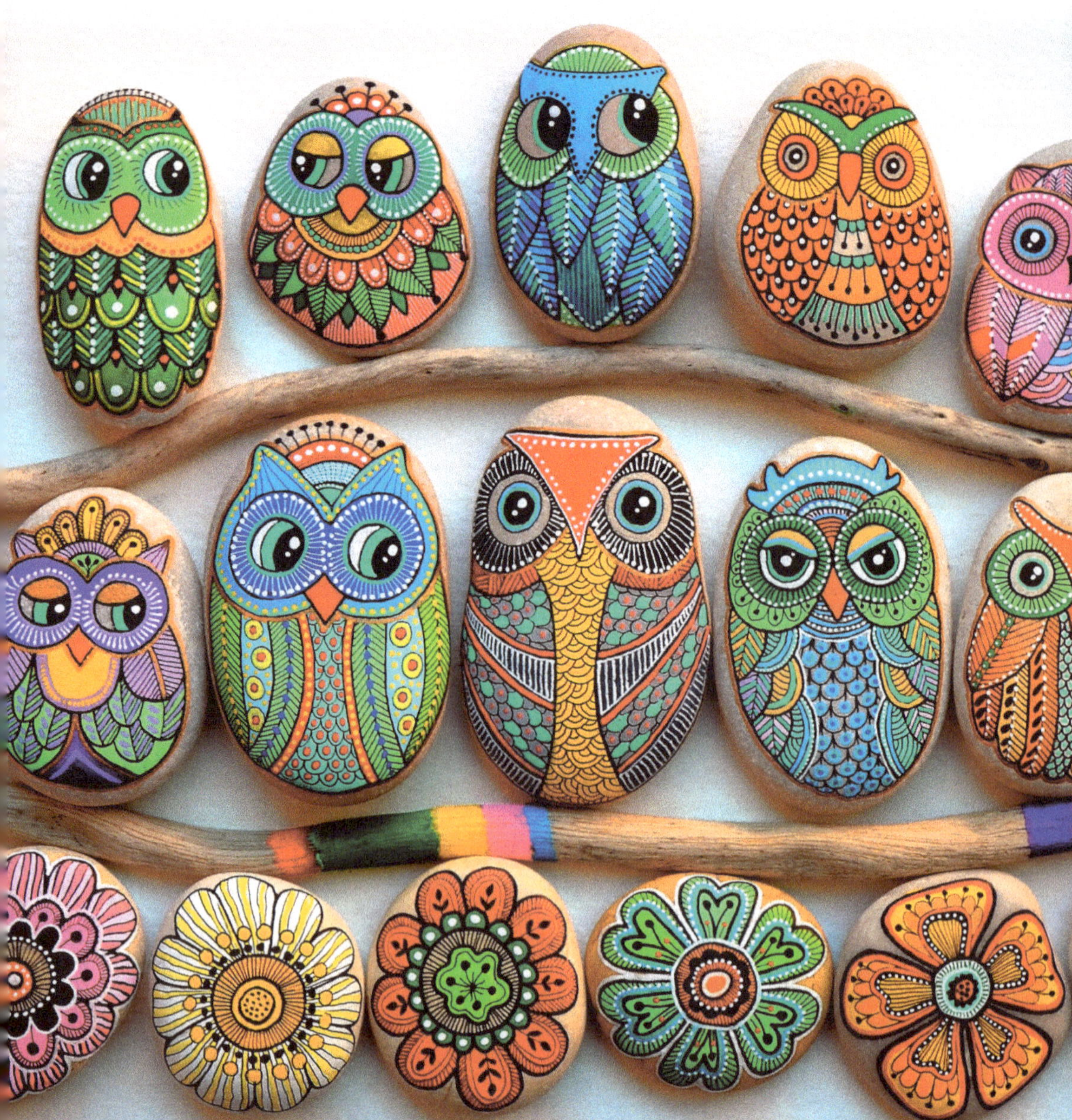

PART I: GETTING STARTED

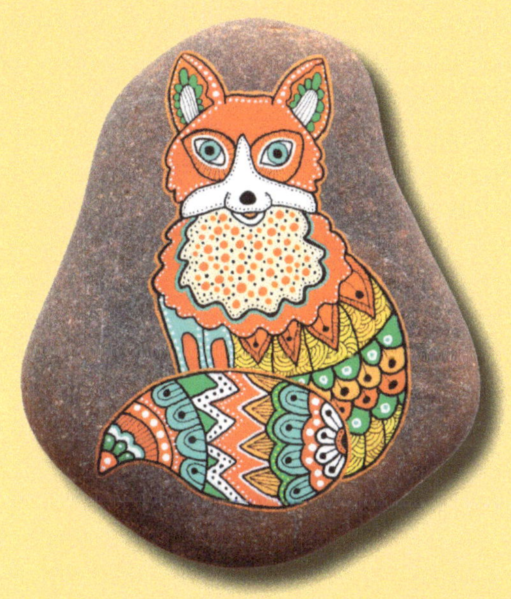

TOOLS & MATERIALS

Before you begin painting your stones, you need to have the correct materials and tools. Most of these items can be found at your local art and craft store. In time, as you paint more stones, you can decide which materials work best for you.

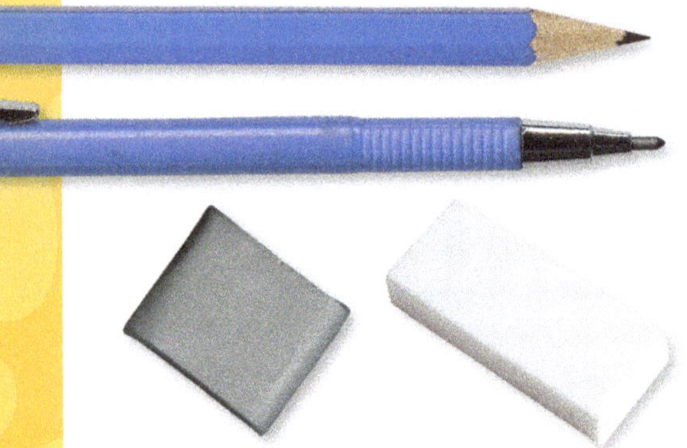

Pencils & Erasers

First you need hard lead pencils (at least 2H) to sketch your designs onto the stones. To correct any errors on your sketch, use soft art erasers. You can use a compass for basic circles in mandala designs.

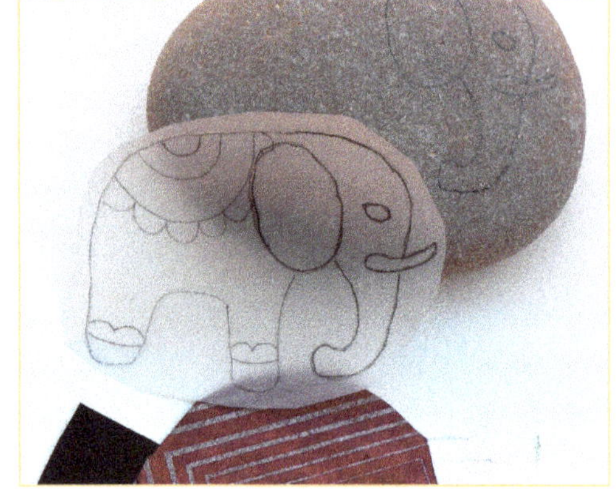

Transfer Paper

There are different levels of transfer paper for light-surfaced stones and dark-surfaced stones. Use them with caution, as it can be difficult to remove transfer lines with an eraser.

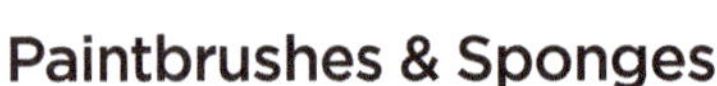

Paintbrushes & Sponges

You will need synthetic round brushes with different sizes to begin. Use tiny ones (sizes 0, 00, 000) for details, and sizes 14, 16 for larger areas. Always wash your brushes with soapy water after use. Use sponges to create bright backgrounds and special effects.

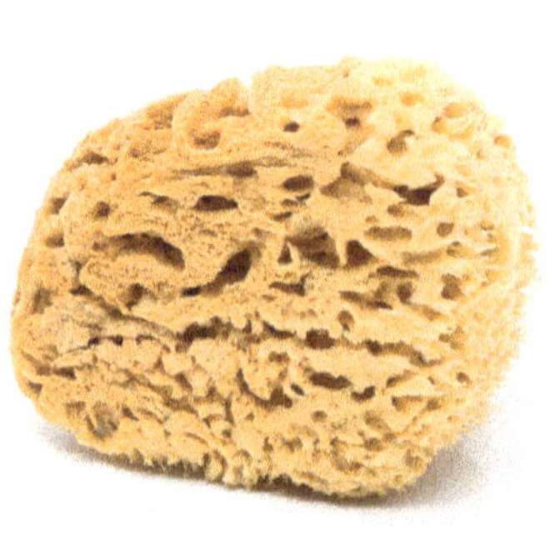

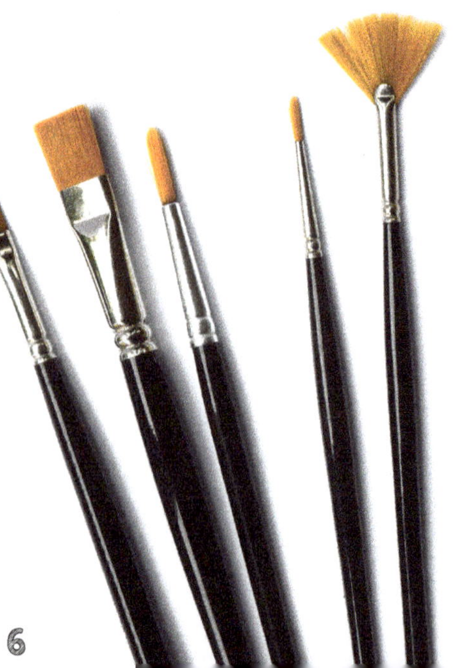

Paints

Acrylic paints are the best choice for stone painting. They are easy to apply, have brilliant colors, and cover the surface easily. You can find them in tubes, jars, or plastic containers. These paints dry very quickly, so keep their containers closed when they aren't in use. Alternatively, you can use water-based craft colors.

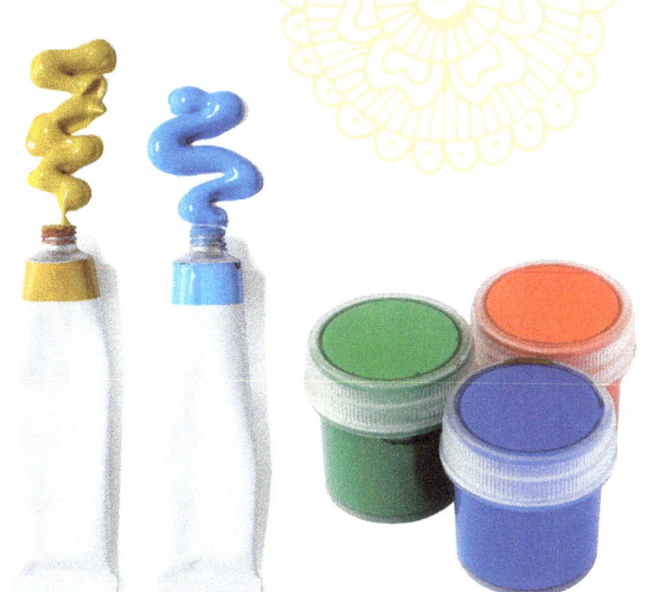

Inks & Dip Pens

You can use acrylic inks on your stone paintings, as they are highly pigmented and have intense colors. Inks are very good for fine details if you use them with a small brush or dip pen.

Varnishes

Use acrylic varnishes to protect your painted stones. You can use glossy or matte varnish according your taste.

Paint Pens, Markers & Fine-liner Pens

When you want to draw or paint more detailed designs, you can use water-based paint pens and markers. Fine-liner pens are useful when you want to detail designs on your stones or pebbles. They have archival indelible ink, and extra-thin sizes are useful to work with tiny details.

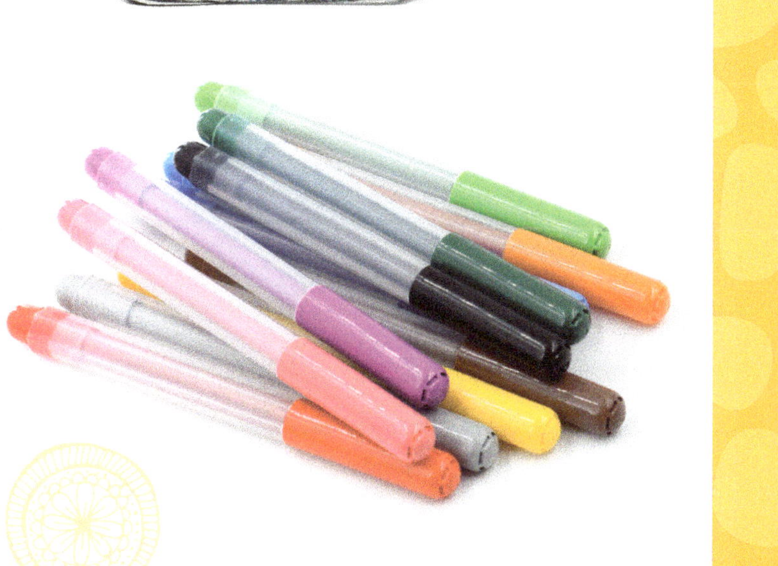

SELECTING & PREPARING ROCKS

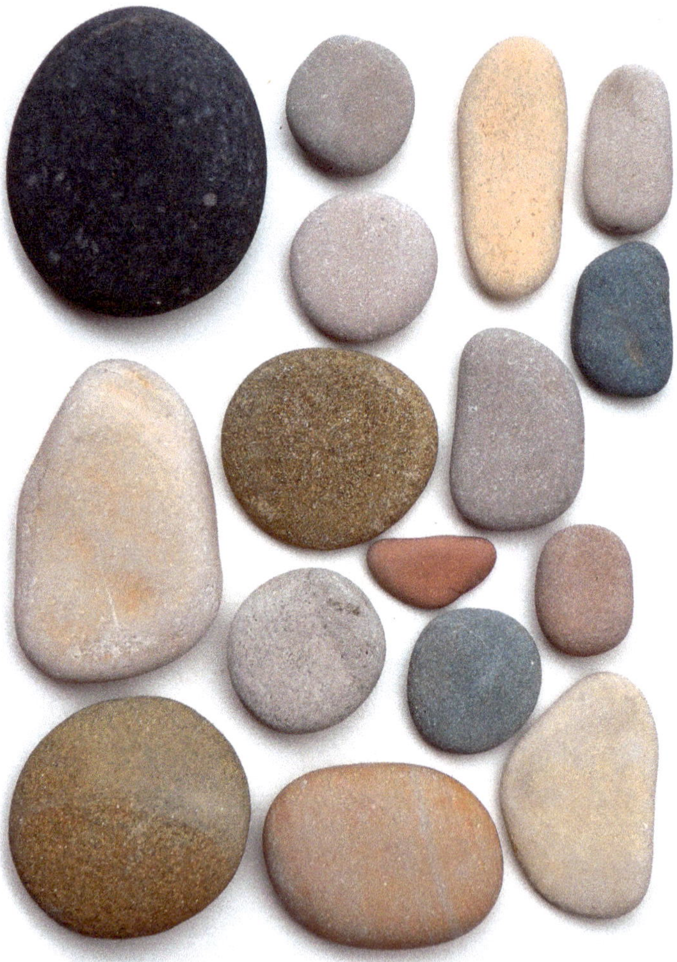

When you want to paint rocks as a hobby or for your craft projects, first you need to search for the right rocks. Along the shores of beaches, you can find stones of different sizes, shapes, and forms. Rivers, riverbeds, or lakes are also wonderful places to collect stones; but take care, it is often illegal to remove stones from public beaches, rivers, or lakes. Be sure to ask permission before removing any stones from their natural environment.

As an alternative, a variety of rocks can be purchased from rock suppliers. In these expansive yards, rocks are sorted according to size and type. You can also find flat flagstone in a variety of colors, thicknesses, and textures. Locate a rock supplier by searching your local area for "Landscape Supplies."

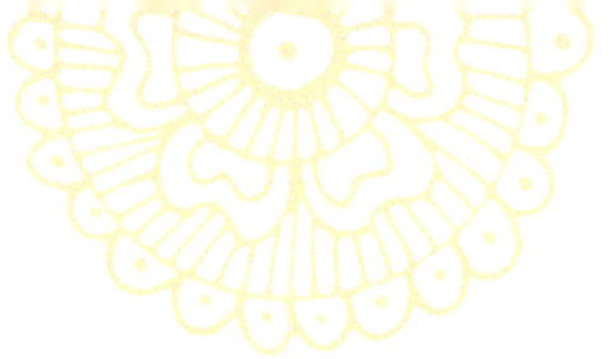

Size & Shape

Smooth and flat stones are ideal for working with ink or markers. You can paint or draw directly onto their natural surfaces. Rough and textured stones also work well if they have the desired shape. Try choosing your stones by shape: oval stones for owl or fish designs, round for mandalas, irregular shapes for other bird or animal designs. Stones have different colors that can create special effects when you paint them. For example, naturally dark or black stones are great choices for monochrome designs using white, gold, or silver ink. White, smooth stones are ideal for painting bright colors. Even rough stones with a special shape can look great after applying a few layers of paint to them.

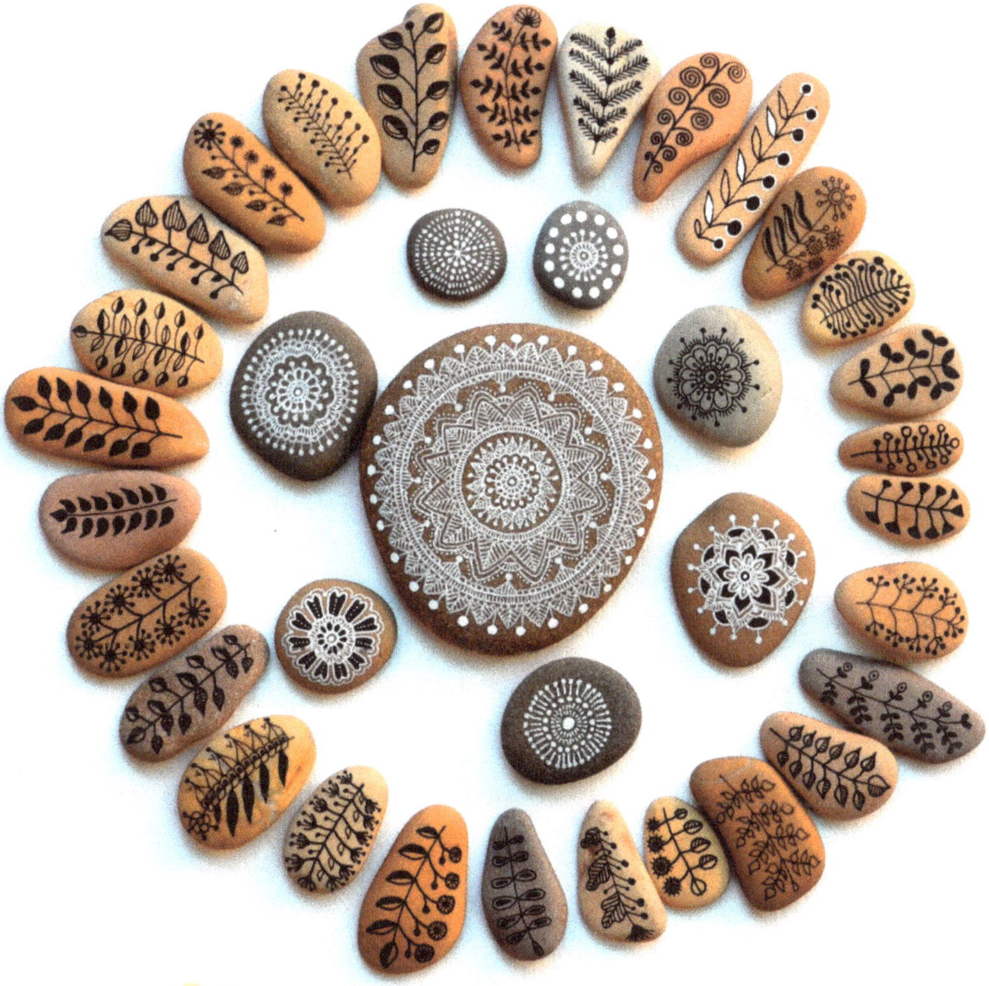

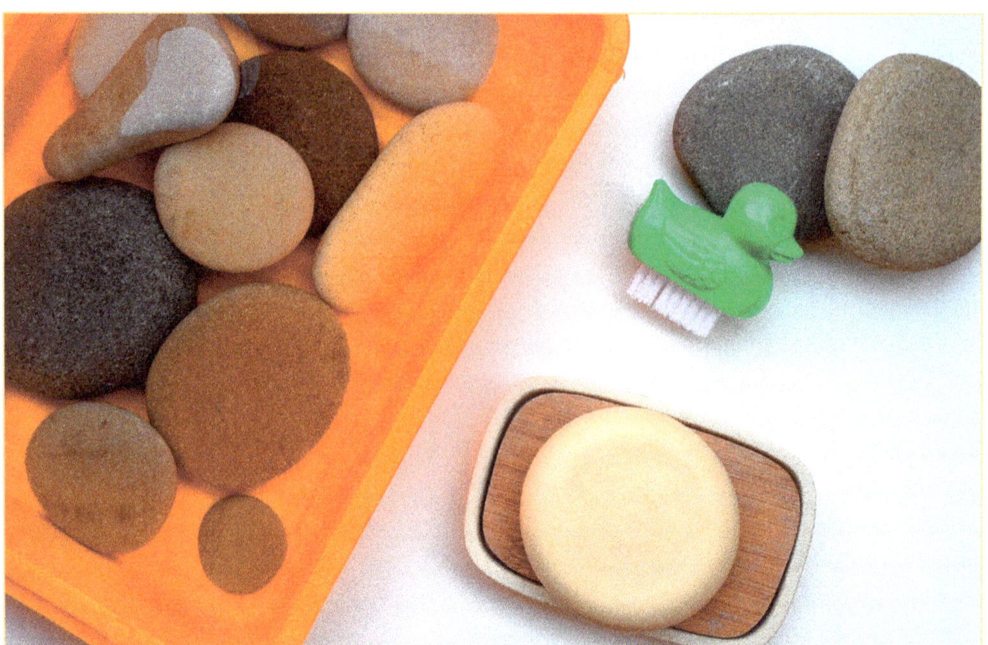

After collecting your stones, leave them in a bowl of water for a few hours to soak off any excess dirt or sand particles. Next clean them with a soft brush and mild soap. After rinsing with running tap water, leave the stones to dry for at least one day out in the sun or in a warm place inside.

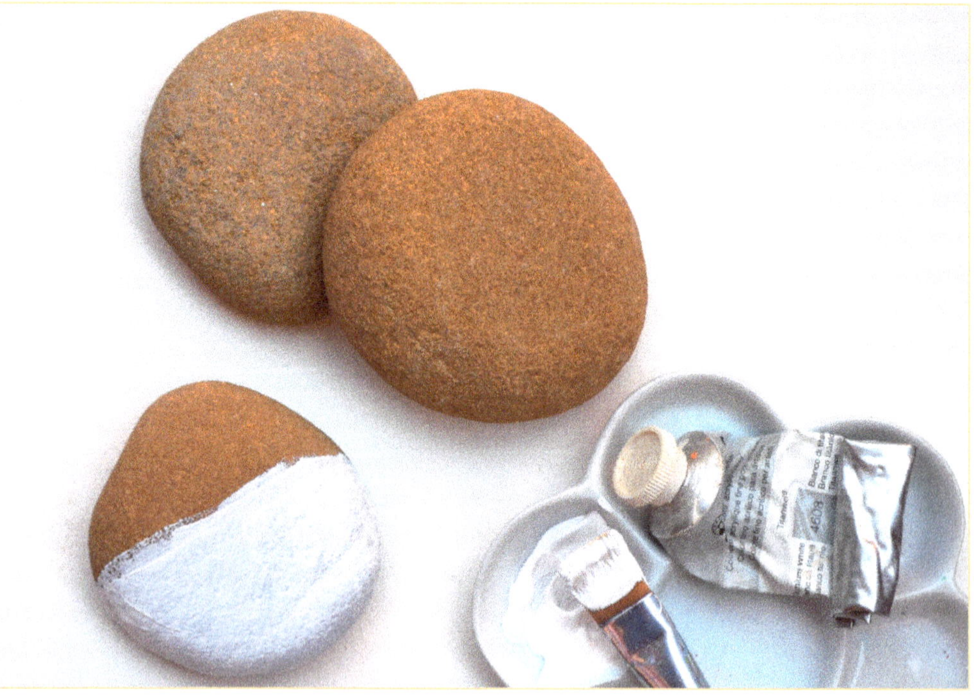

Once completely dry, your stones are ready to paint! If your rocks are rough or porous, you can make them more smooth by adding a few coats of paint. Apply one or two coats of white acrylic paint, and once the paint dries, rub the surface with very fine sandpaper to help smooth the surface for your design.

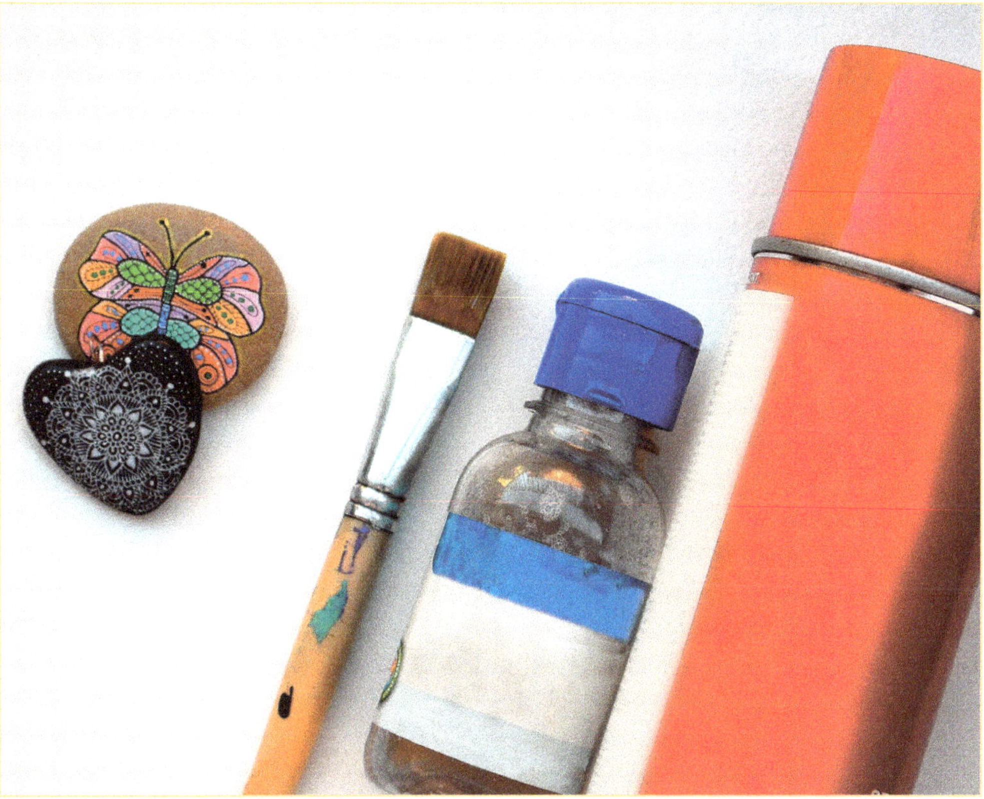

When you are finished painting your rock art, you will want to protect your work from sunshine, dust, or humidity. Use a high-quality acrylic varnish (or varnish with UV protection). Varnishes can easily be found in craft stores or art shops. Once your painted stone is completely dry, apply two or three layers of liquid varnish with a wide brush. If you are using a spray varnish, spray outdoors or in a well-ventilated area, wearing a mask. These kinds of sprays are highly flammable. After you have applied varnish, wait at least 48 hours to use your stones.

WHEN YOU COLLECT YOUR STONES, IT IS IMPORTANT TO CHOOSE THE RIGHT SIZES, SHAPES, AND TEXTURES FOR THE DESIGNS YOU WANT TO CREATE. YOU CAN COLLECT AS MANY STONES AS YOU LIKE, AND DECIDE LATER WHAT TO PAINT ON THEM, OR YOU CAN CHOOSE SPECIFIC STONES FOR SPECIFIC DESIGNS.

TIPS & TECHNIQUES

Before you begin a project, it's a good idea to practice a few basic brushstrokes and painting techniques. Don't be afraid to experiment and try a variety of painting techniques. If you make a mistake and want to start over, it's no problem; remember that acrylic colors can be washed off while they're still wet or painted over after they are dry.

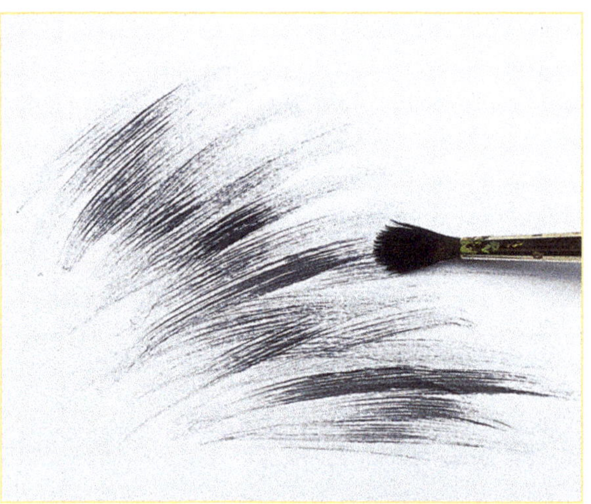

Drybrushing

Drybrushing is an easy way to create the look of grass, fur, or anything that requires soft texture. It can also be used to build up color or to add subtle shading. First load a round brush with paint and lay the bristles on paper to wick away the wetness and splay the bristles. Apply the paint using light, feathered strokes with the bristles splayed. When the paint dries, repeat as needed to build color or texture.

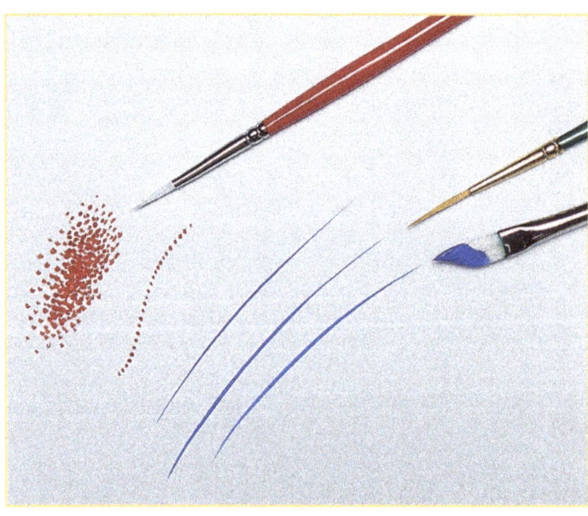

Stippling & Lining

Stippling adds color and texture while letting the underpainting show through. To stipple, dot on paint with the tip of a round brush. Use a liner brush to make clean, thin strokes; its long bristles can hold ample paint. Angled brushes also work well, especially on round surfaces. Hold the angled brush so that the chiseled edge slides lightly along the surface.

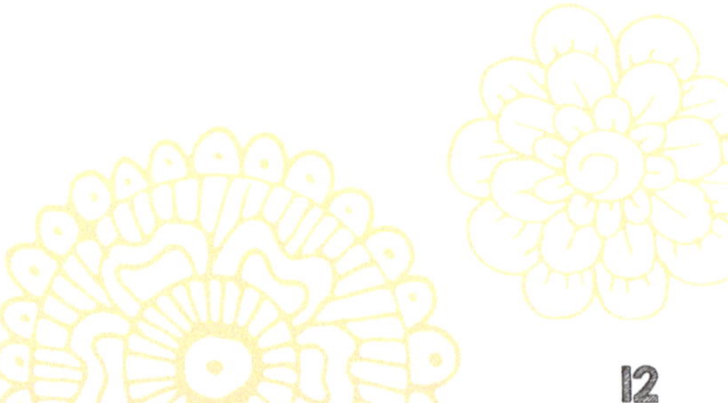

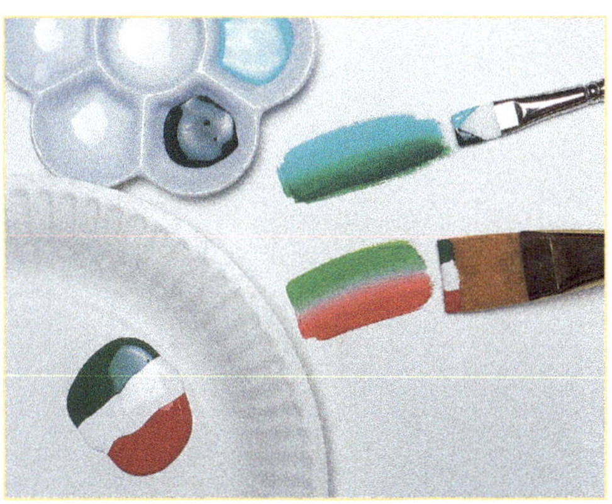

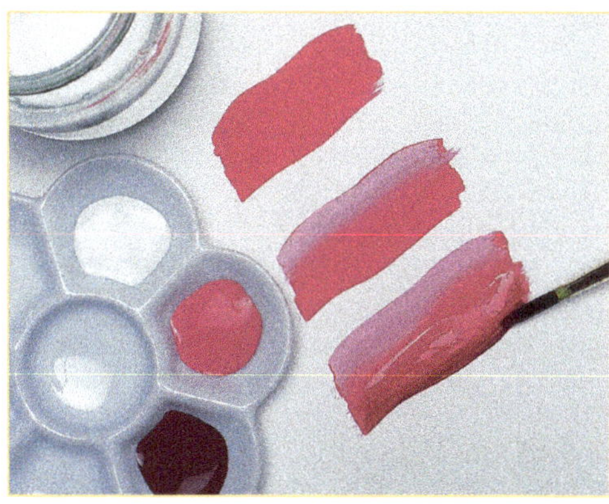

Double- & Triple-Loading

Double- and triple-loading your brushes will produce a variety of color blends and gradients. To double-load a brush, dip each side in a different color as shown above, or squeeze two colors side by side onto your palette, and dip your brush in both at once. To triple-load, simply add a third color.

Wet Layering

To highlight an edge, apply your base color and let it dry. Then dip a round brush in clean water and wet the area just below the edge to be highlighted. Choose a color lighter than the base, and highlight the dry edge, stroking it into the wet area. Dry your brush on a towel, and then use it to absorb any excess moisture.

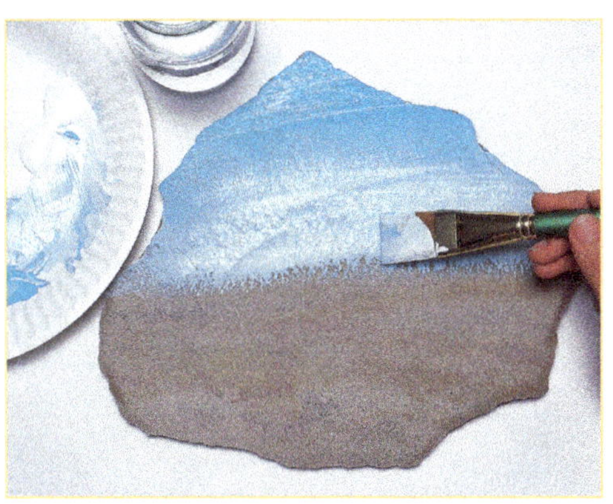

Stone Slab

A large, flat stone slab or piece of flagstone can be used for a unique canvas that can be displayed on an easel. The layered edges of the flagstone can be left unpainted for added effect. Wash the flagstone well to remove any loose layers that could easily chip off during painting.

When an otherwise perfect rock is marred by a hole or a crack, wood filler can correct the imperfection. Fill in the hole with a putty knife, and then remove the excess. If desired, sand the filler after 15 minutes. Let dry for 2 hours before painting.

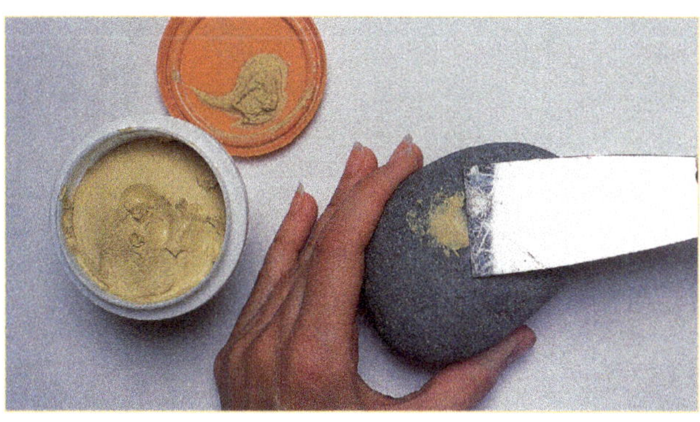

Monochromatic Designs

Bare and painted stones are perfect for monochromatic designs. To create a monochrome design on your stone's surface, work with dip pens, tiny brushes, and acrylic inks. After you sketch your design on the stone, draw over the sketch with ink or a fine-liner pen to cover all sketch lines. When you are finished creating your design, add contour lines with dip pens and acrylic ink.

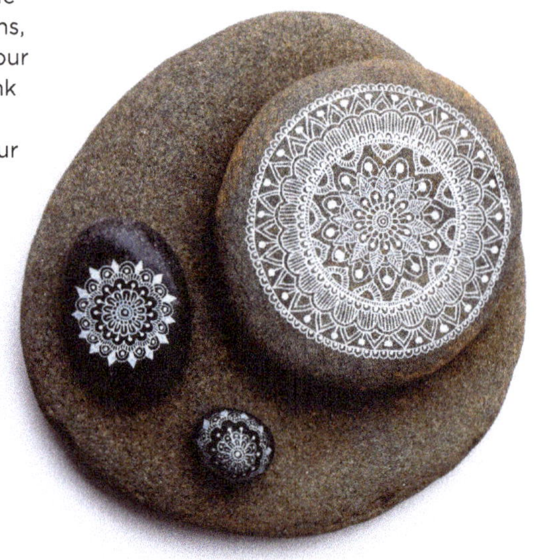

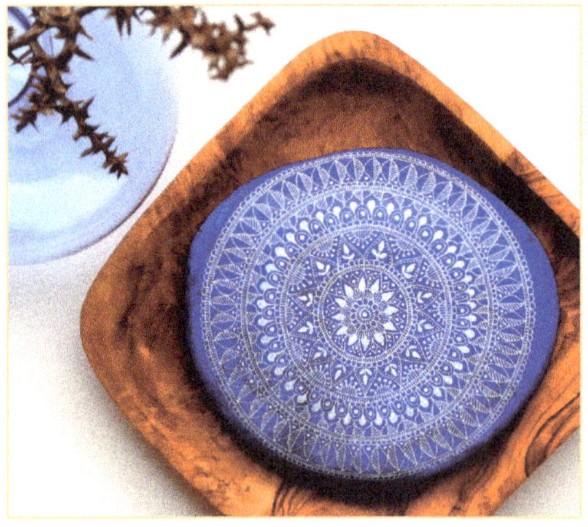

Bare Stone

This method is perfect for when you have flat, smooth-surfaced stones. Just sketch your design on stone and fill it in with your chosen colors.

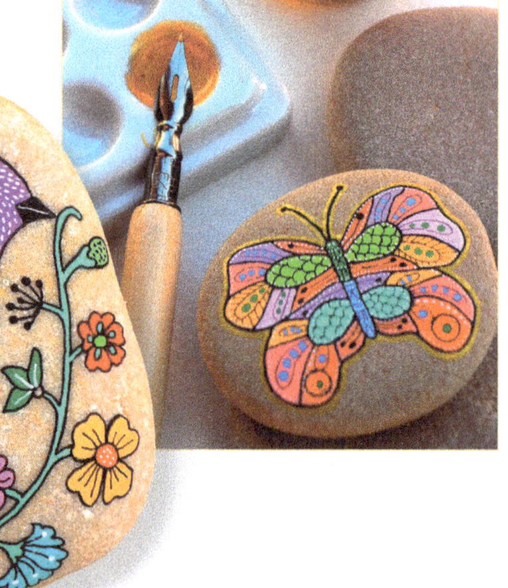

Painted Stone

Use this method if the surface of your stone is covered with acrylic paint or ink. Once the painted surface is completely dry, add your design with pencil.

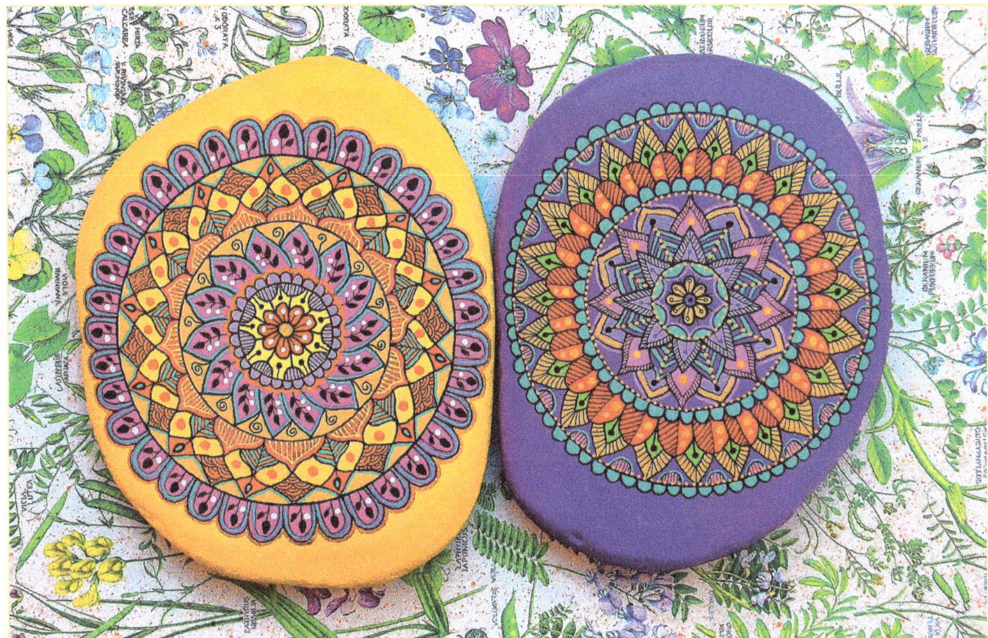

When you start to paint your design, use brushes, acrylic paint, paint pens, acrylic inks, or tiny brushes. Try to cover all areas, and stay inside sketch lines. Let the paint dry for one hour. Then, if the colors are not as bright as you wish, you can pass a second layer over them. When this layer dries, use fine-liner pens to draw outlines.

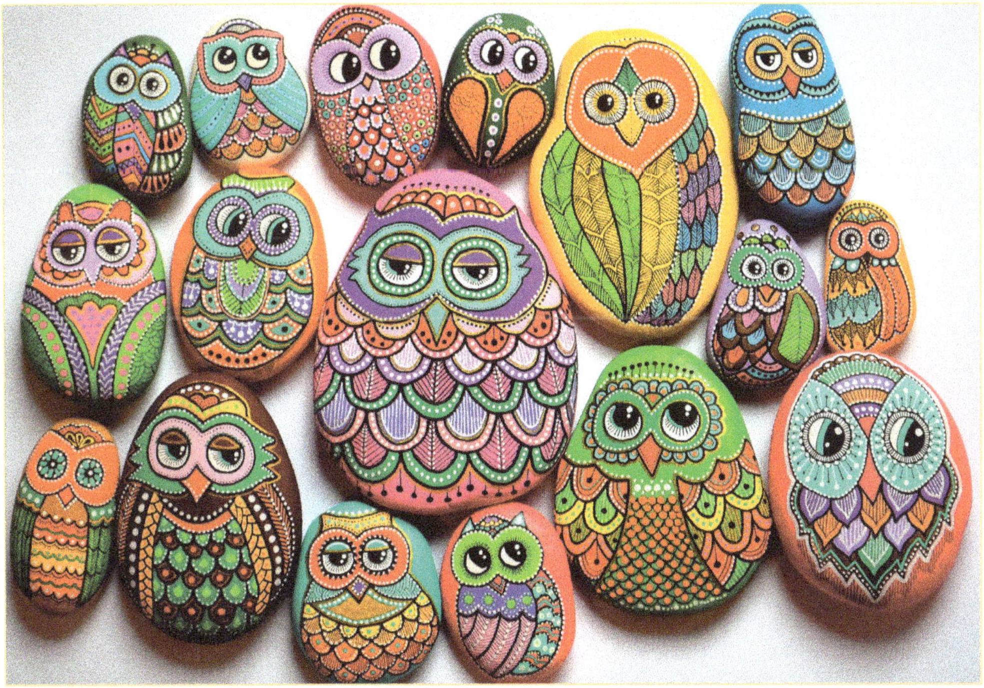

Sponging

Sponge on beautifully blended backgrounds for your favorite Zen inspirations. See page 124 for some commonly used words.

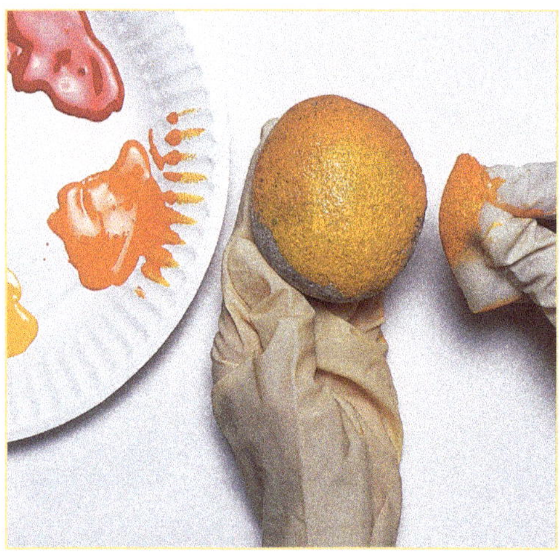

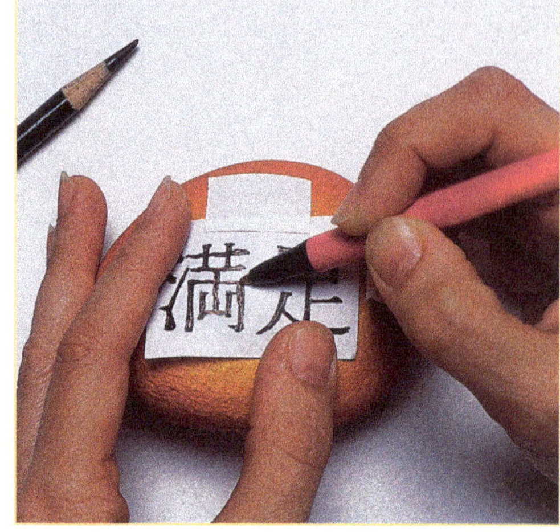

1 Dip the sponge in your lightest color, and dab the paint onto the exposed half of the rock until it's covered. Immediately sponge your medium color into the wet paint, leaving a portion of the top area untouched. Sponge your darkest color into the wet edge of your medium color and down as far as you can go.

2 After the paint dries, turn the rock over and continue sponging the darkest color onto the bottom of the rock. Let the paint dry overnight. Then transfer the chosen symbols to the center of the top of the rock (see below).

To transfer a design onto a rock, first reduce or enlarge the design to fit your rock. Color the back of the design with white pencil for dark rocks and black pencil for light rocks, so the paper acts like carbon paper. (You can use carbon paper also, but it smudges more easily.) Cut out the design and tape it down with low-tack artist's tape. Transfer the image by tracing over the lines with a ballpoint pen, using light-to-medium pressure.

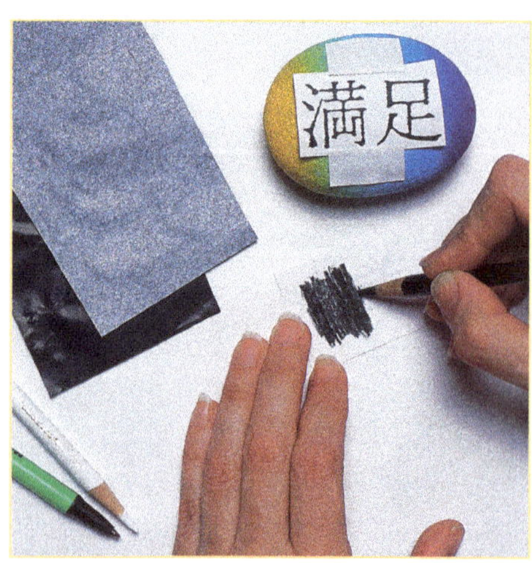

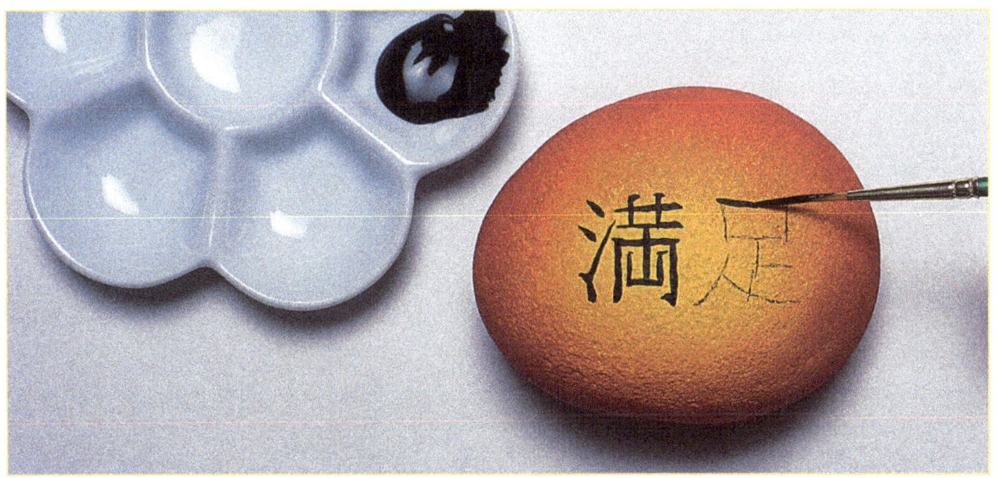

3 Next paint the symbols using a liner brush. Try to always stroke toward the thin end of a line, lifting the brush up and away as you finish. If your strokes are skipping over the rock, dilute the paint more—being careful not to thin it too much or the paint will be runny and transparent—and stroke more slowly.

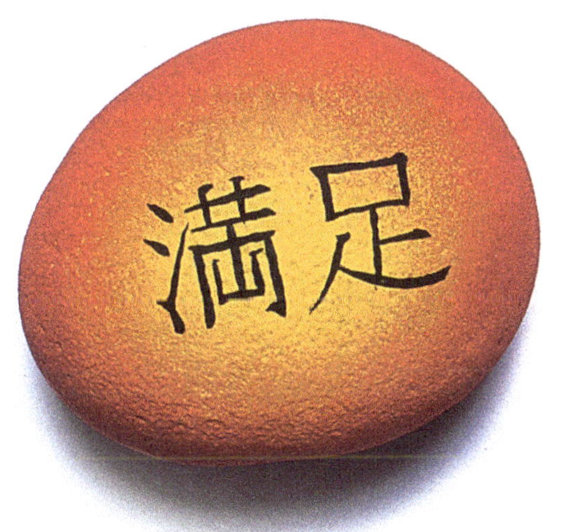

4 When you're done painting, examine the rock to see if you can find any small mistakes. It's always easier to touch up errors when the paint is dry. Once you're satisfied with your results, seal the rock with clear matte acrylic spray.

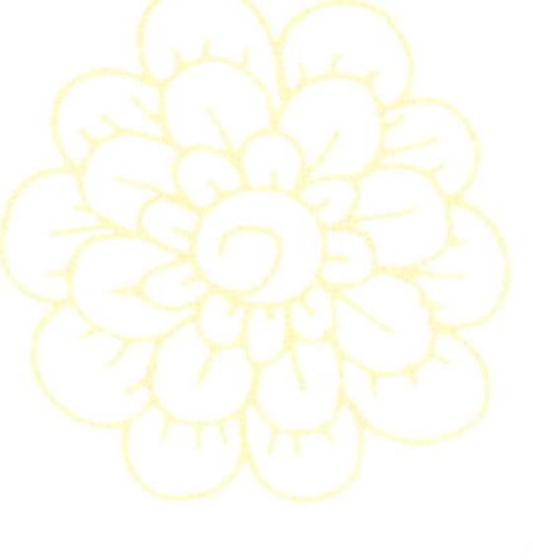

Rock Lettering

A rock paperweight that you have hand-lettered with your favorite inspirational saying makes a thoughtful gift or a useful affirmation for yourself. To master lettering techniques on a rounded three-dimensional surface, you'll want to choose smooth, flat rocks with no pits or ridges.

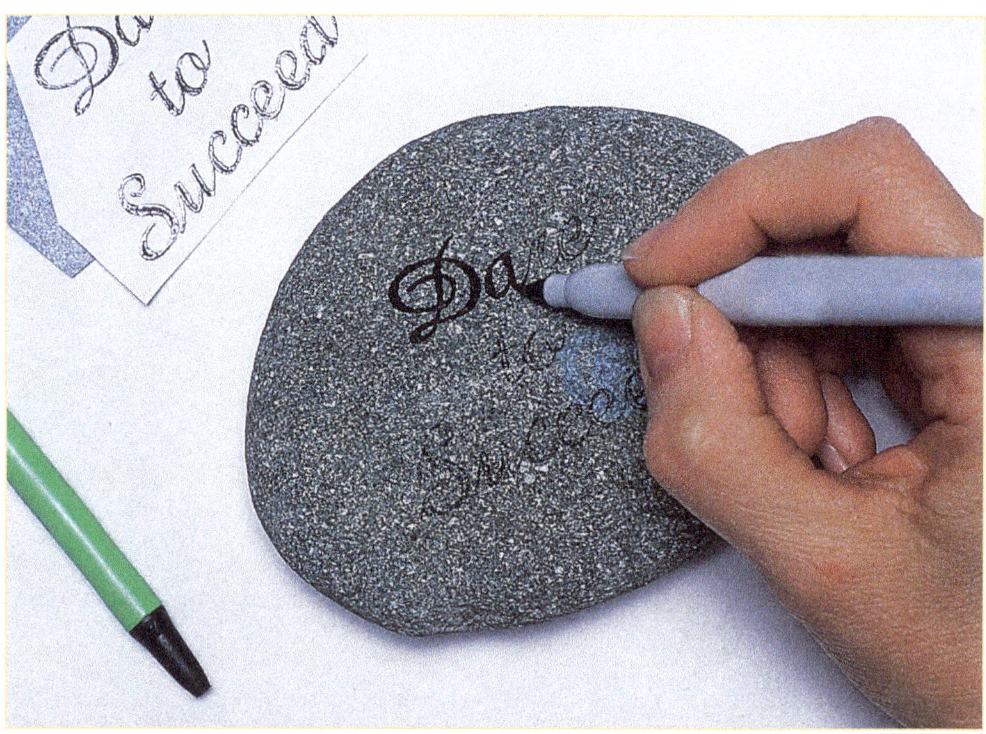

Permanent Marker When lettering on a bare rock, use an extra-fine permanent marker for better control. Use a light touch and keep the maker moving; the ink may bleed if you press in one place for too long.

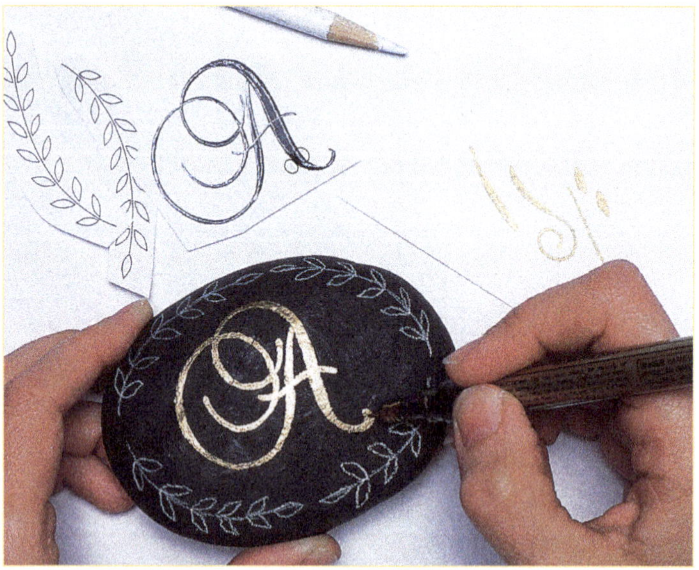

Paint Marker To letter on a painted rock with paint markers, first apply your base color with a wide, flat brush. Once dry, transfer your design with a white pencil. Then use a metallic paint marker to paint the center initial and the surrounding leaf sprays; keep the marker moving and use a light touch for best results. When the metallic color is dry, touch up any mistakes with your background color.

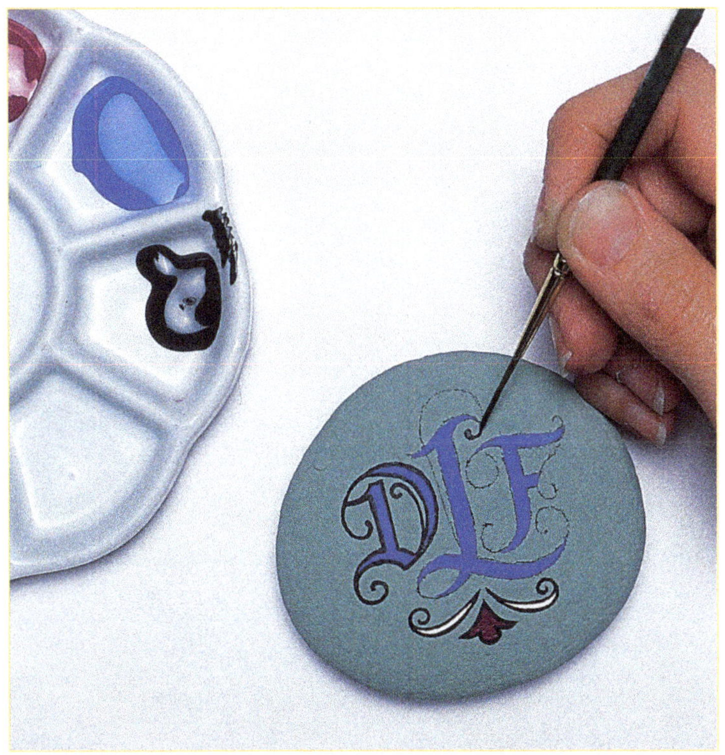

Paintbrush Transfer your design onto the rock with colored pencil (it is least likely to smudge on the paint). Then use a liner brush to fill in the wide portions of the letters and the flourish with color. Outline the design with black, keeping the brush tip tapered and clear of buildup. Create the swirls in parts, always pulling the brush toward you.

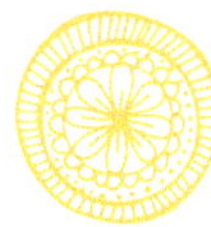

A glossy clear coat will enliven and enhance color enormously. Enrich and protect your rock creations at the same time with a permanent, waterproof, clear acrylic spray finish. A light coating is all that is needed. For serious water- and weatherproofing, spray several light coats. (Consult the specific directions for the brand you choose.)

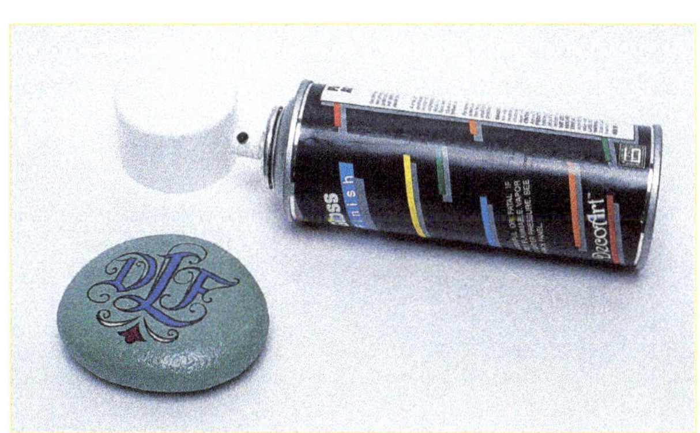

PRACTICE HERE

Use these practice pages to work out your ideas, patterns, and designs.

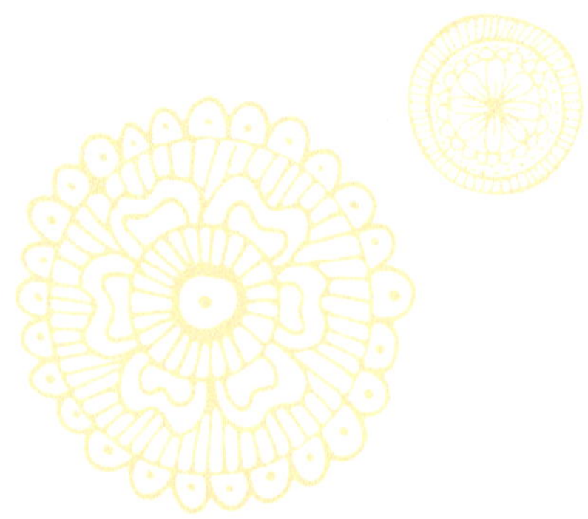

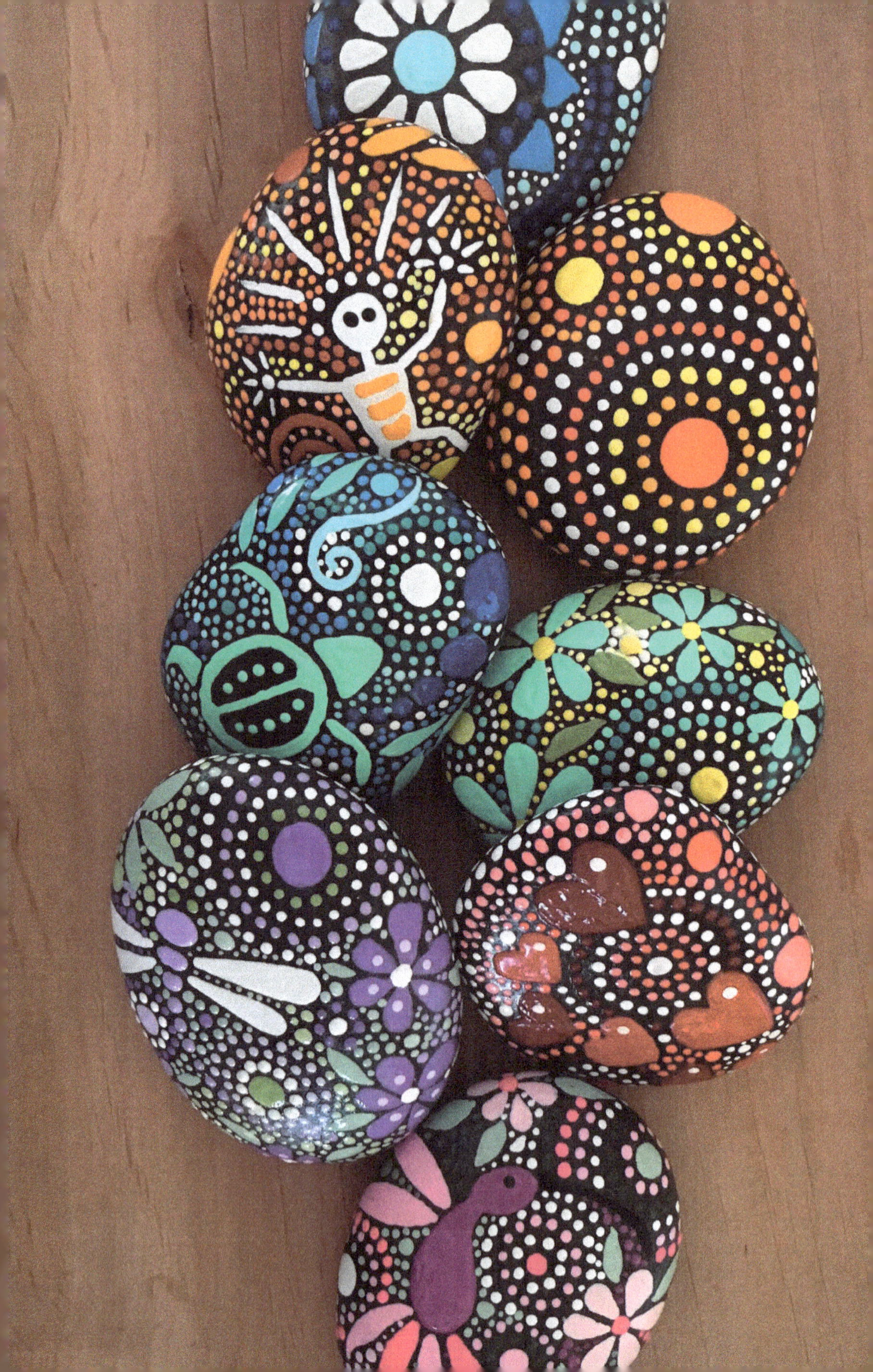

PART II: COLORFUL PATTERNS

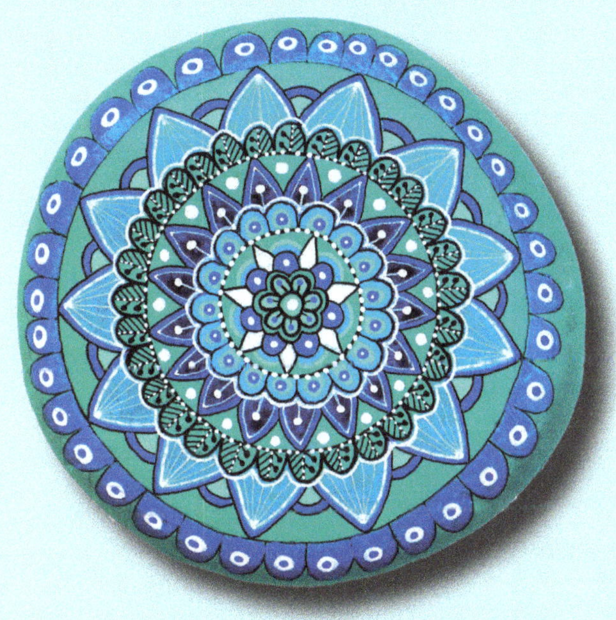

SUNSET

Mandala dot rock painting is a meditative practice. The size and irregular shape of this natural canvas, along with the need to focus on the size, color, and placement of each dot of paint causes the mind and body to slow down and focus on the small world you are creating.

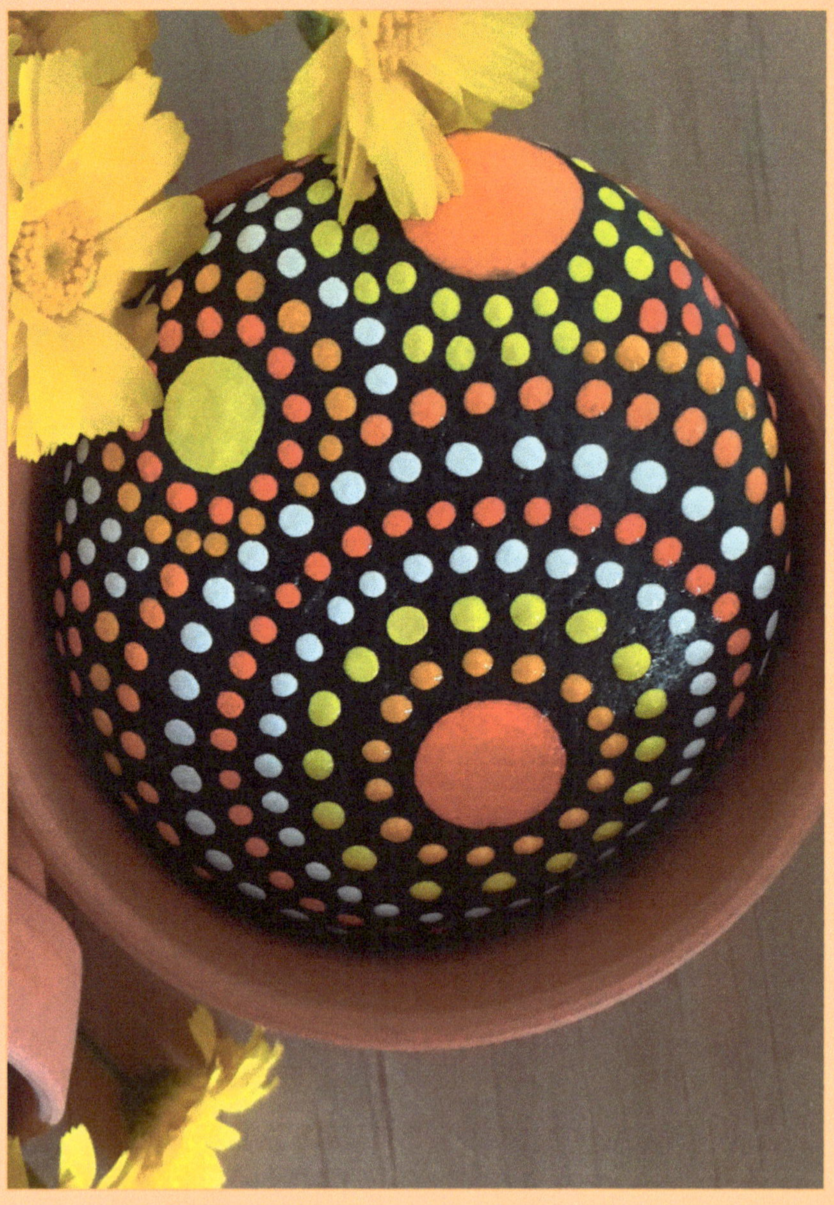

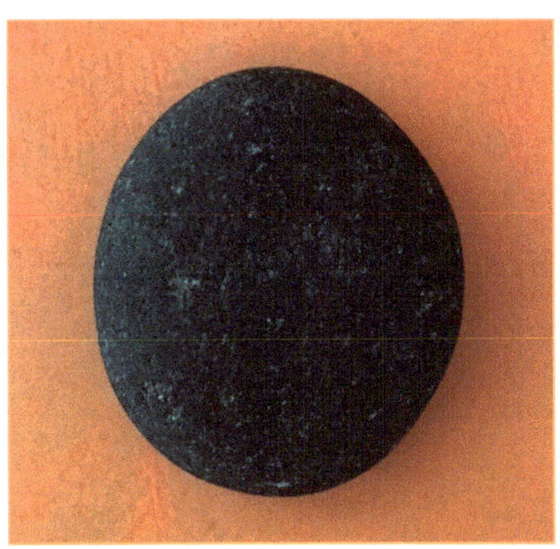

1 Choose a flat, smooth rock with a shape you like. The rock's shape, size, and texture will determine your mandala design. Wash the rock well to remove any dirt from the surface and let it dry completely.

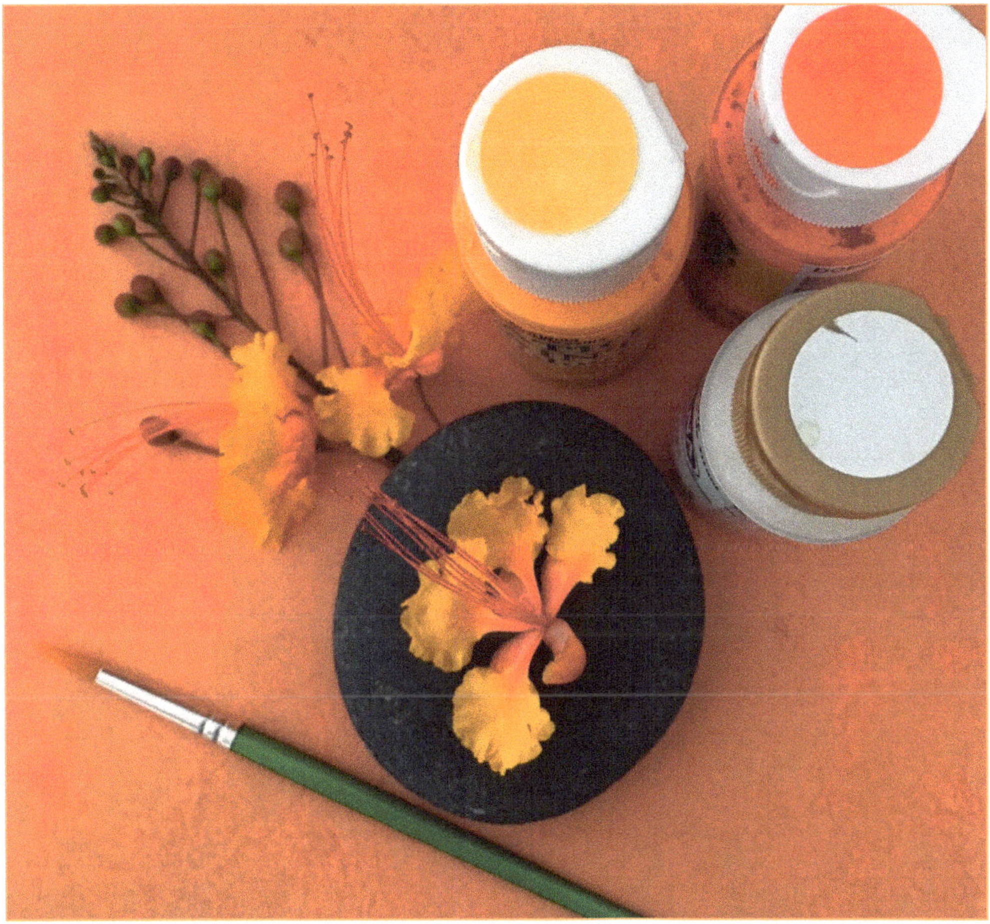

2 Choose a color scheme and inspirational concept (field of desert flowers, wedding bouquet, sunset sky, or hummingbird's breast) before you begin. Because the canvas is so small, choosing three or four colors, with white and black as balancing colors, keeps the design focused.

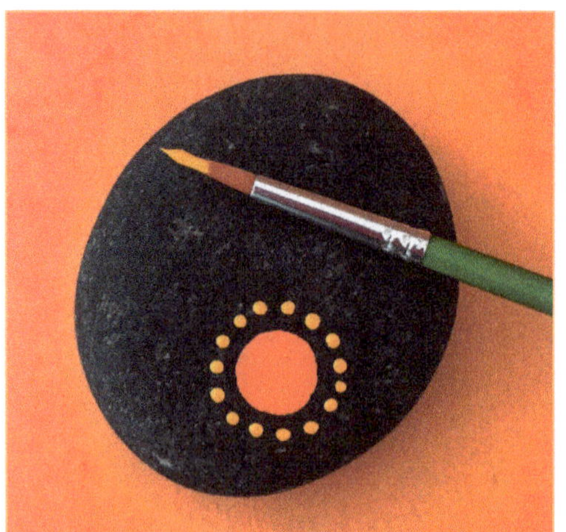

3 Let the rock tell you where to begin and how to proceed. Unlike a traditional square or rectangular canvas, rocks are rarely a perfect circle or shape, and the surface may have slight dips and grooves in it. Use those imperfections to inspire your design. The rock's shape and surface can help you determine the size of your first circle and guide your other ring colors and sizes.

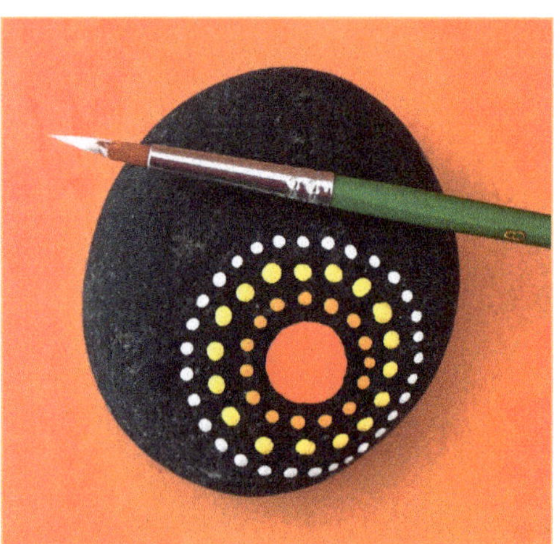

4 When choosing to use a dot pattern to create your mandala, take your time with each dot. To create a uniform-like pattern, the dots of each ring should be a similar size and distance from the previous ring.

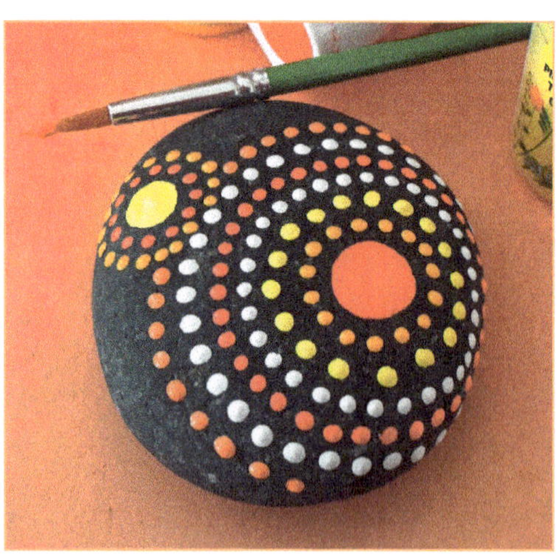

5 Varying the size and colors of the dot rings you create, will provide texture and unique design elements to your mandala. Don't overthink this process. Let the rock and your own instincts guide you. Let sections of the paint dry completely before handling the rock to access other sections. Most acrylic paint takes 10 minutes to dry.

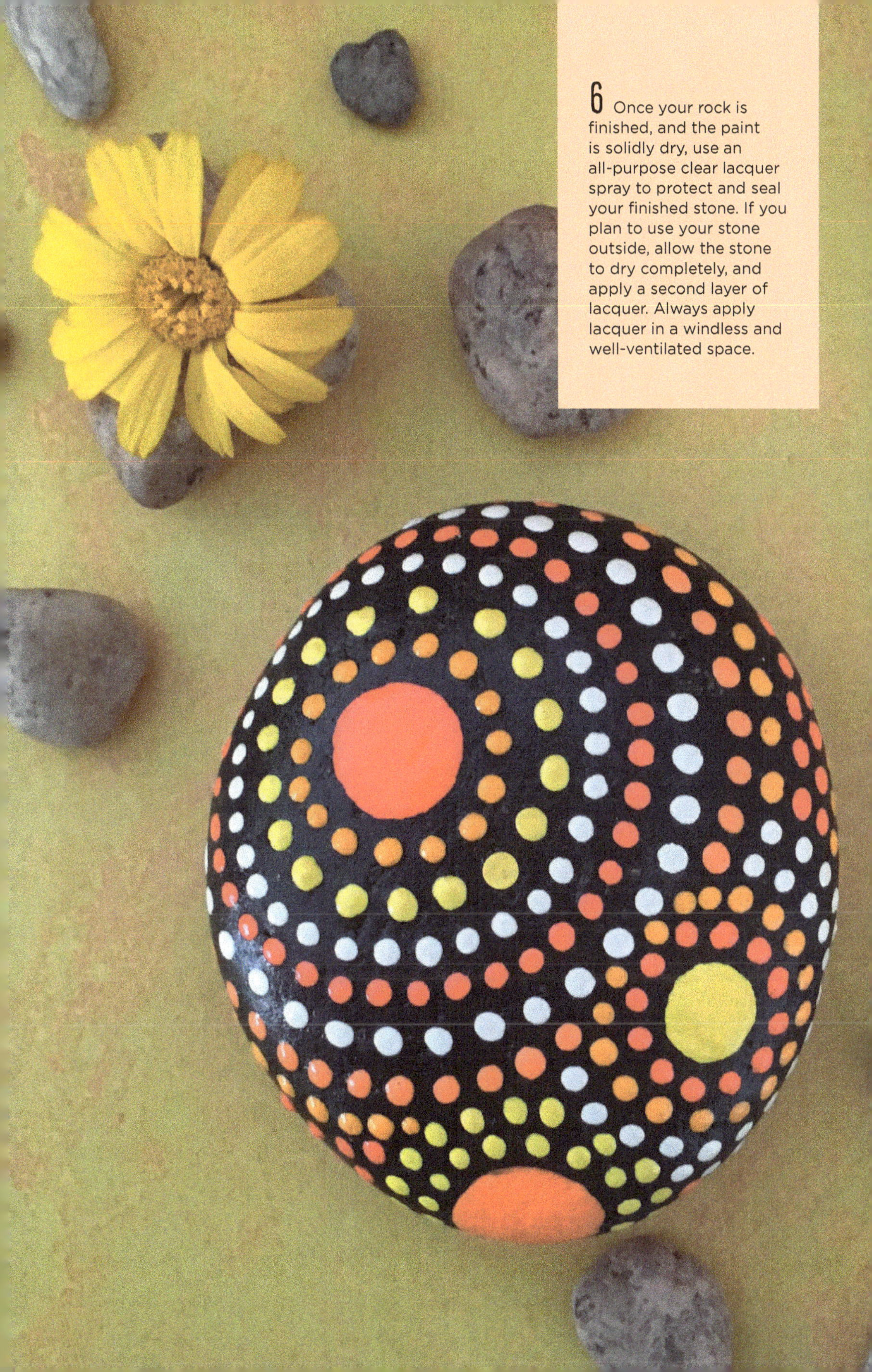

6 Once your rock is finished, and the paint is solidly dry, use an all-purpose clear lacquer spray to protect and seal your finished stone. If you plan to use your stone outside, allow the stone to dry completely, and apply a second layer of lacquer. Always apply lacquer in a windless and well-ventilated space.

BLUE MANDALA

Your mandala stone can be used as a paperweight, bookend, or as a decorative object in your home or garden. Try turning your stone into wall art by attaching it to a wood panel and framing it. You can also simply use your stone for personal meditation. The choice is up to you!

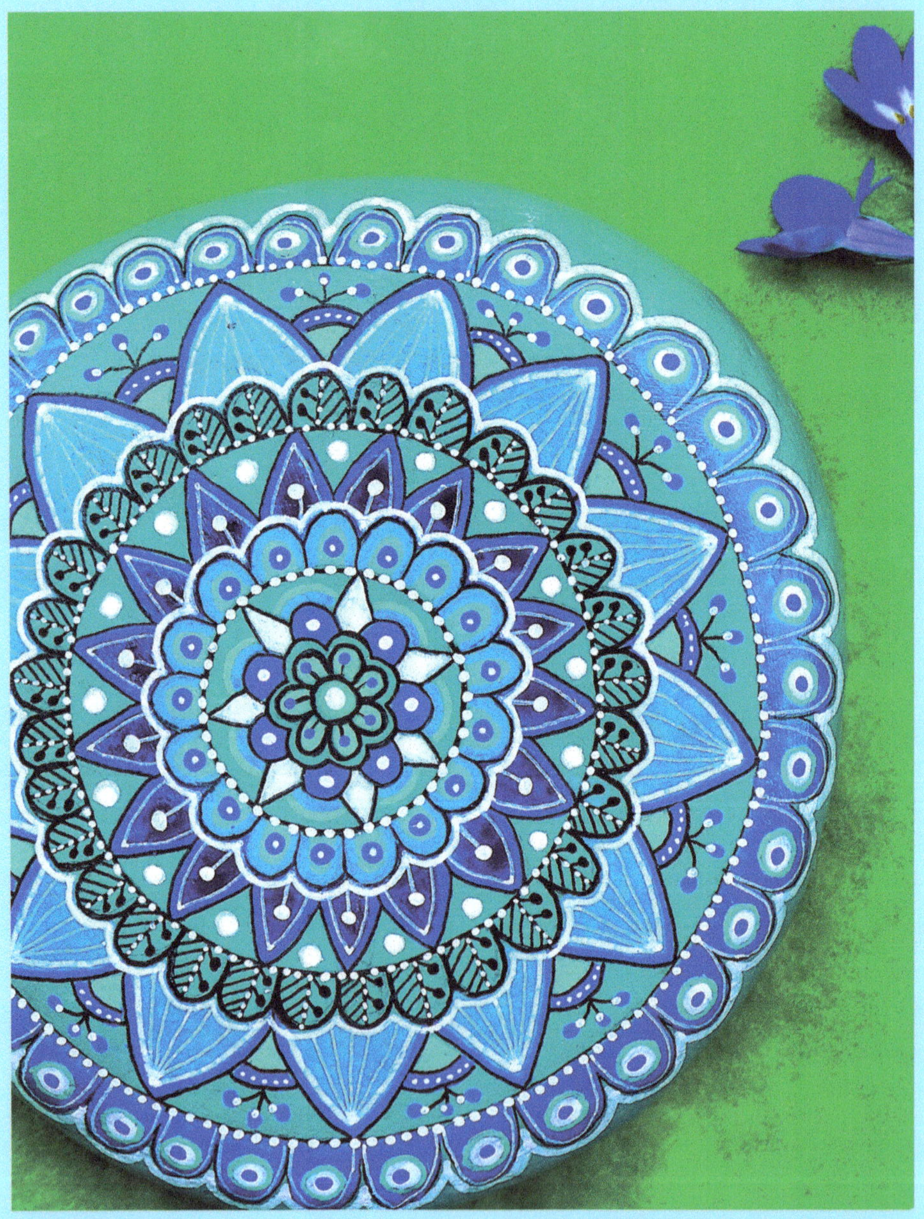

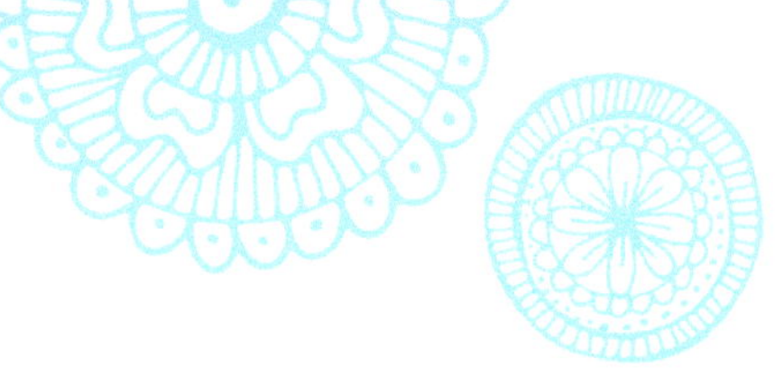

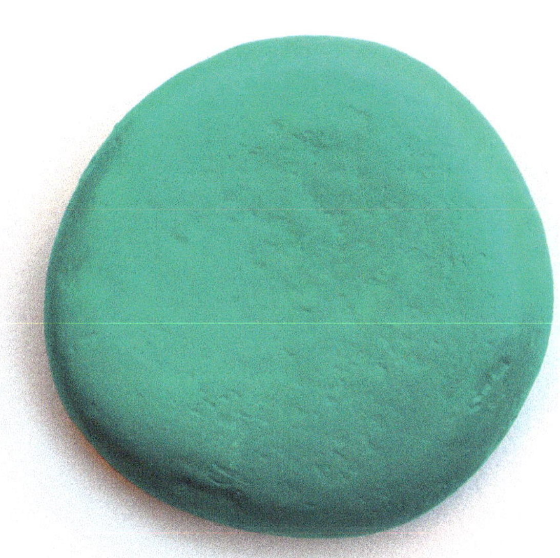

1 Paint the surface of your stone with turquoise acrylic paint and a large brush. If your stone's surface is porous, fill in the porous parts with paint by applying soft pressure to your brush. Wait until the paint is completely dry to continue.

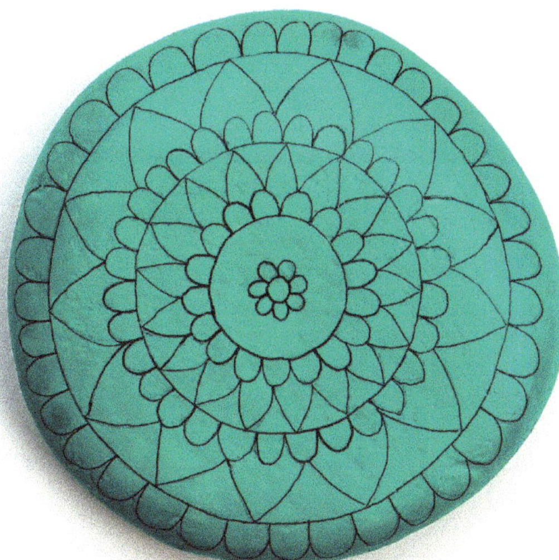

2 When the paint is dry, sketch your design on the stone with a pencil. Begin with a small circle in the center; then draw three concentric circles with spaces between them. Fill in your mandala design with rows of semi-ovals, triangles, and leaf-like patterns around the circles. If your pencil lines are difficult to see, pass over them with a thin black liner pen.

3 Add color tones to your design with acrylic ink. Use different hues: light blue, cobalt, and ultramarine. You can pass a second layer of inks if you want brighter colors. Once dry, add some contour lines to the painted parts of your mandala design using paint pens. These lines will define the different hues of the color and add a stylish look to your mandala design.

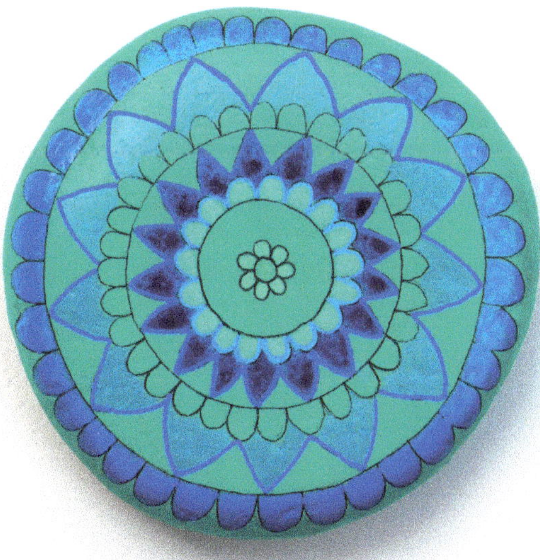

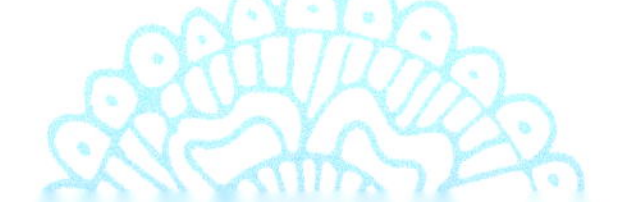

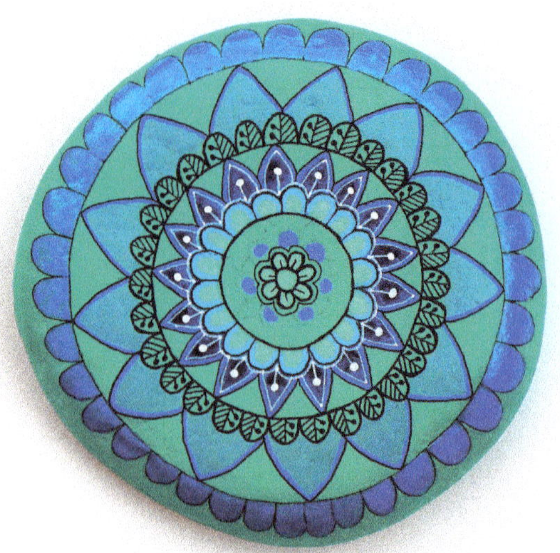

4 Add triangle and leaf-like rows to the center part of your design. Pass black contour lines over your design. Fill some parts in with thin, parallel lines (black dots and lines). Pass another contour line around the rows with white ink and a thin dip pen. Use white dots and lines to fill triangles and other design elements.

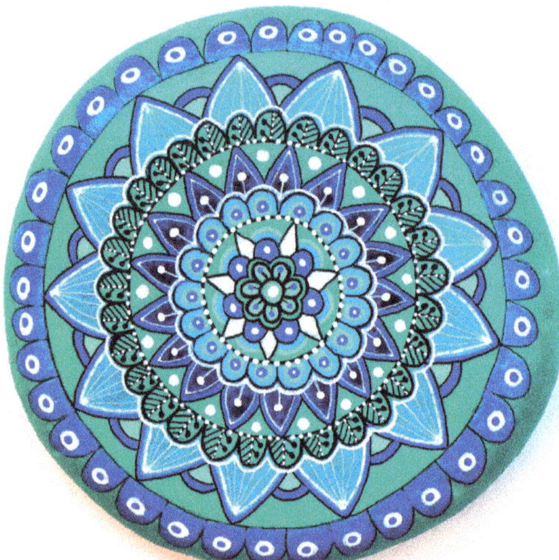

5 Add more details to your mandala design in this phase. Draw white lines inside of big triangles. Use white and blue dots in different empty spaces of your design. Put small white dots over the main circle lines of your design. Add a white contour to the inside of each semi-oval on the outer design.

6 To finish adding details to your mandala design, draw a bold white contour to the outside of semi-ovals as a border. Add plant-like motifs to empty spaces between the big triangles. Use acrylic varnish to seal and protect your painting.

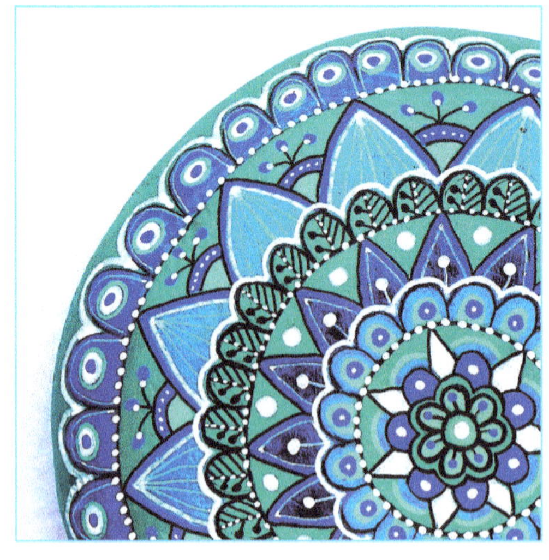

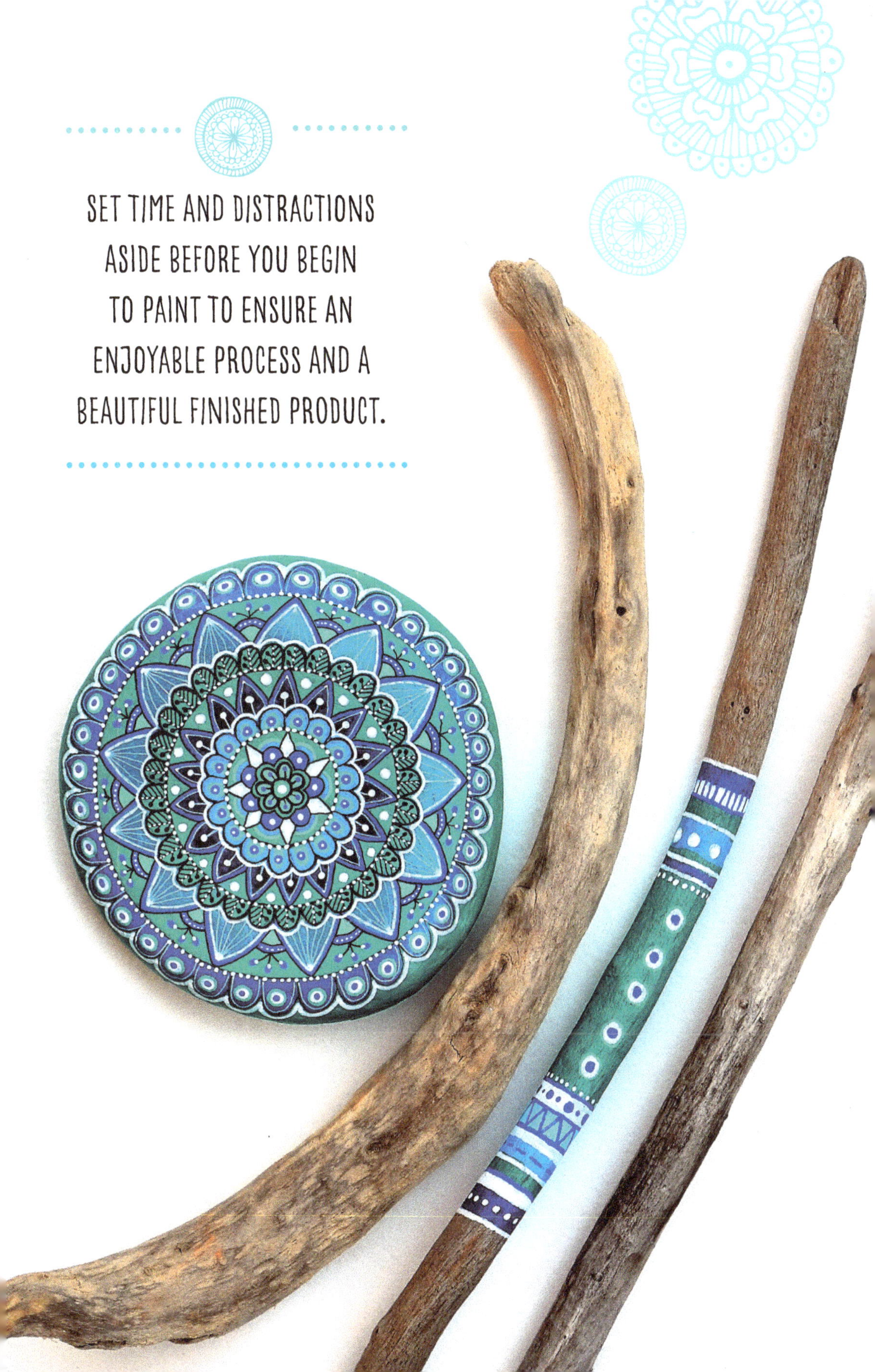

SET TIME AND DISTRACTIONS ASIDE BEFORE YOU BEGIN TO PAINT TO ENSURE AN ENJOYABLE PROCESS AND A BEAUTIFUL FINISHED PRODUCT.

COLORFUL MANDALA

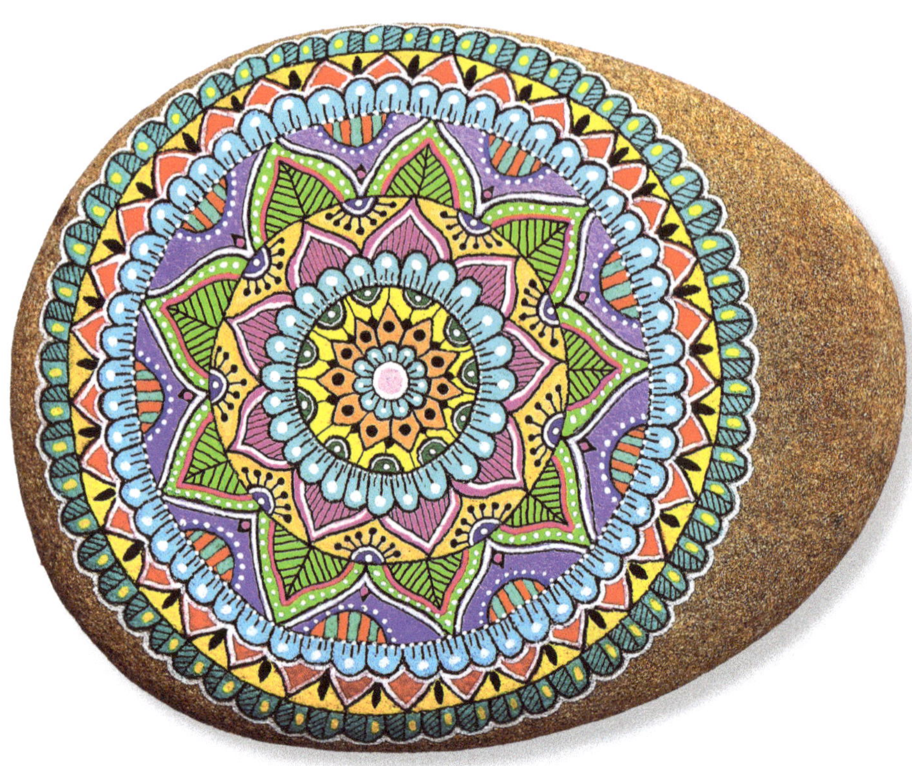

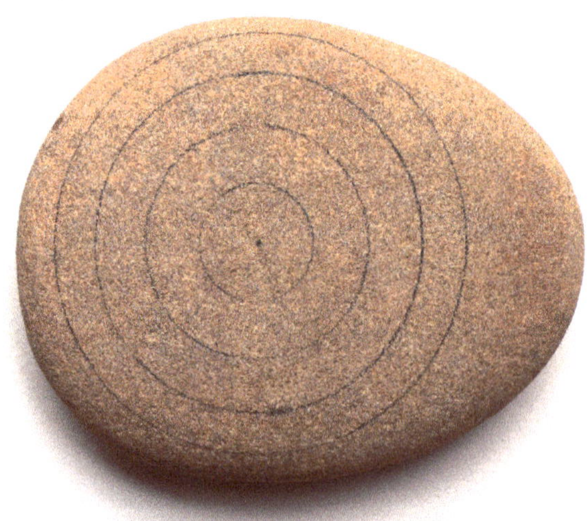

1 Look for a round, flat stone with a smooth surface. Mark your center point on the stone to begin your mandala. Use an H2 pencil to draw four concentric circles around your center point. Make sure to leave enough space between the circle lines. You can use a compass for the circles, or you can draw them freehand.

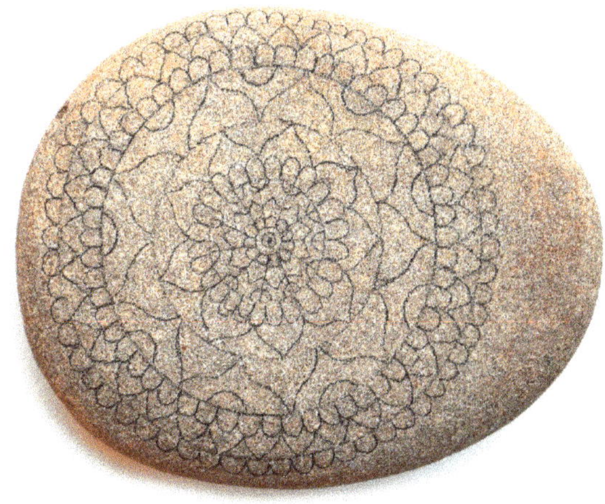

2 Add all the details of your mandala design, drawing rows of half circles, leaf-like shapes, semi-ovals, and triangles around the circle lines.

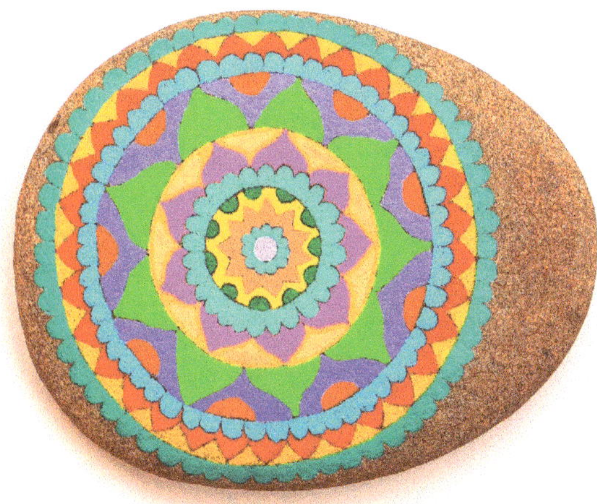

3 Start to fill your design with paint. You can use acrylic paint and acrylic inks as well. Use very thin round brushes to work easily in the small spaces. Choose bright, bold colors to give contrast to your design.

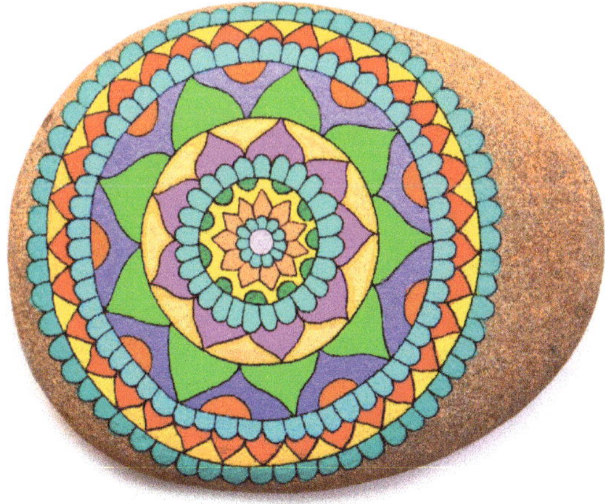

4 Using a fine-tip black liner pen, draw contour lines throughout your design for a clean and defined look.

5 Now you are ready to add the details to your stone, as described in detail on the opposite page. Start from the center so that pen lines will dry as you move on to the next details.

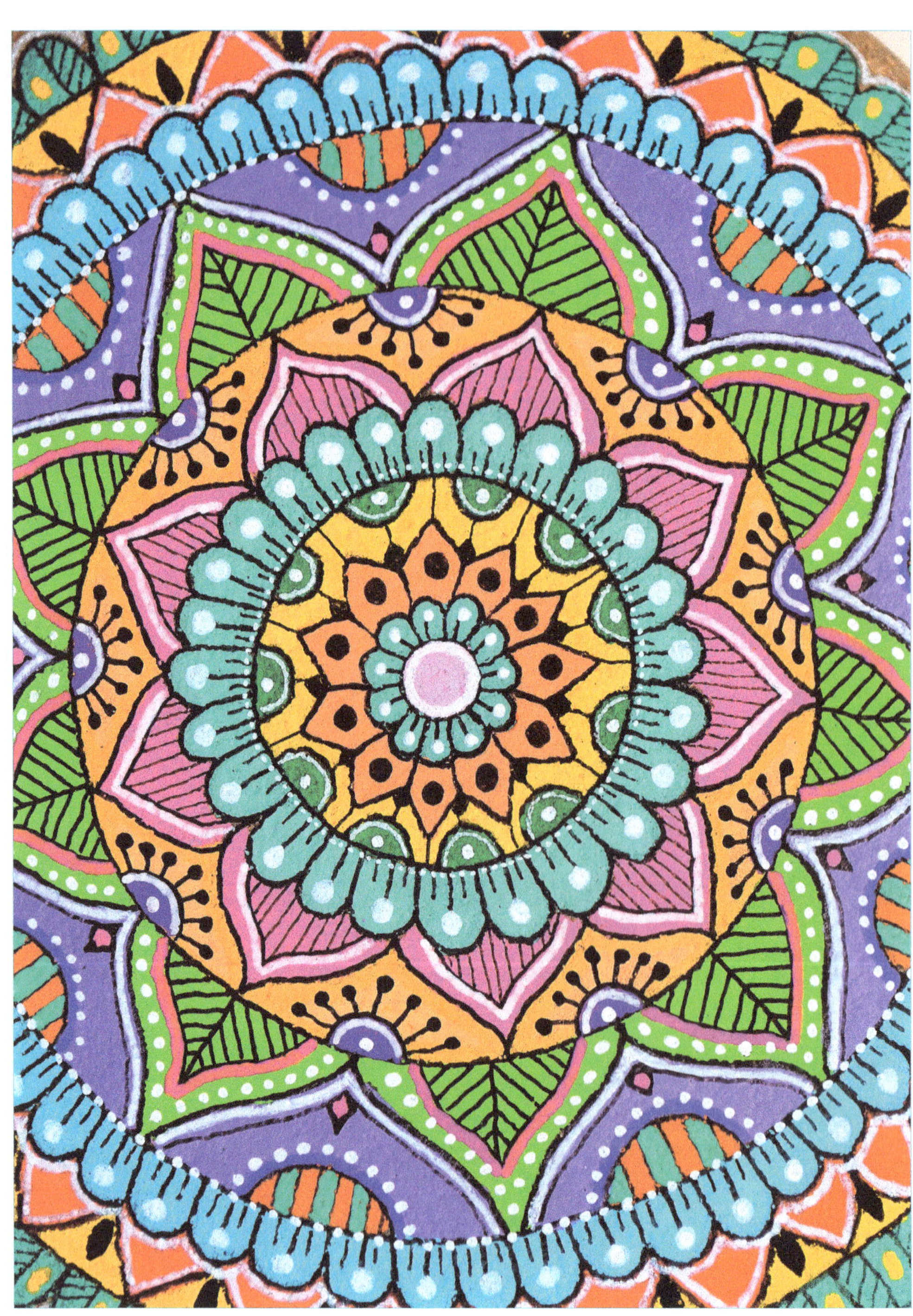

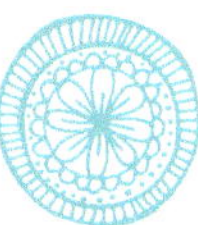

- Add white dots and black lines to row 1 and black dots to row 2.
- In row 3, draw some small black triangles between big triangles.
- In row 4, draw semicircles above the black triangles, and draw a white contour inside them; then add white dots.
- Draw thin lines inside the semiovals on row 5, and then add dots to the longer lines.
- Make smaller triangles inside the leaf-like triangles in row 6, and pass a white contour over them. Draw thin, vertical, parallel lines inside the smaller triangles.
- To fill the space between the leaf-like triangles, add some lines with dots to the semicircle motifs in row 8. Also add white contour lines and white dots inside the semicircles.
- Draw smaller triangles inside the big triangles in row 10. Use white dots in the spaces between the two triangles. Divide into smaller triangles with a thin vertical line, and fill each part with diagonal, parallel lines, as shown in row 9.
- Pass a contour through the smaller triangle with a colored paint pen, and a white contour around the bigger triangle. Add another black triangle between the big triangles, and add dots around them.
- Add parallel vertical lines to the semicircles in row 12, and paint over some of these empty spaces with another color.
- Add a contour line to each semicircle in row 11 with a colored paint pen and put some white dots over it.
- Draw thin black lines inside the semiovals in row 13, and add white dots to the longer lines.
- Pass a white contour line inside the red triangles in row 14, and add small black leaf motifs between the triangles.
- In row 15, divide the semiovals in two with a thin, vertical line, and draw diagonal parallel lines inside one half. Put a yellow dot in the other half.
- Finally, draw a white, bold contour line over the tops of the semiovals.

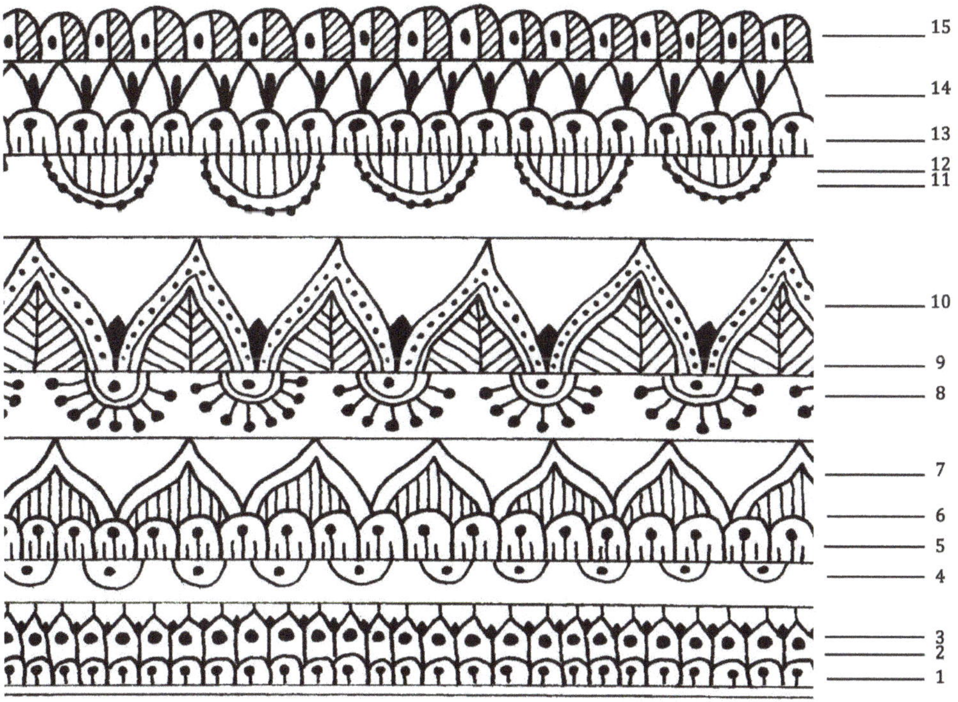

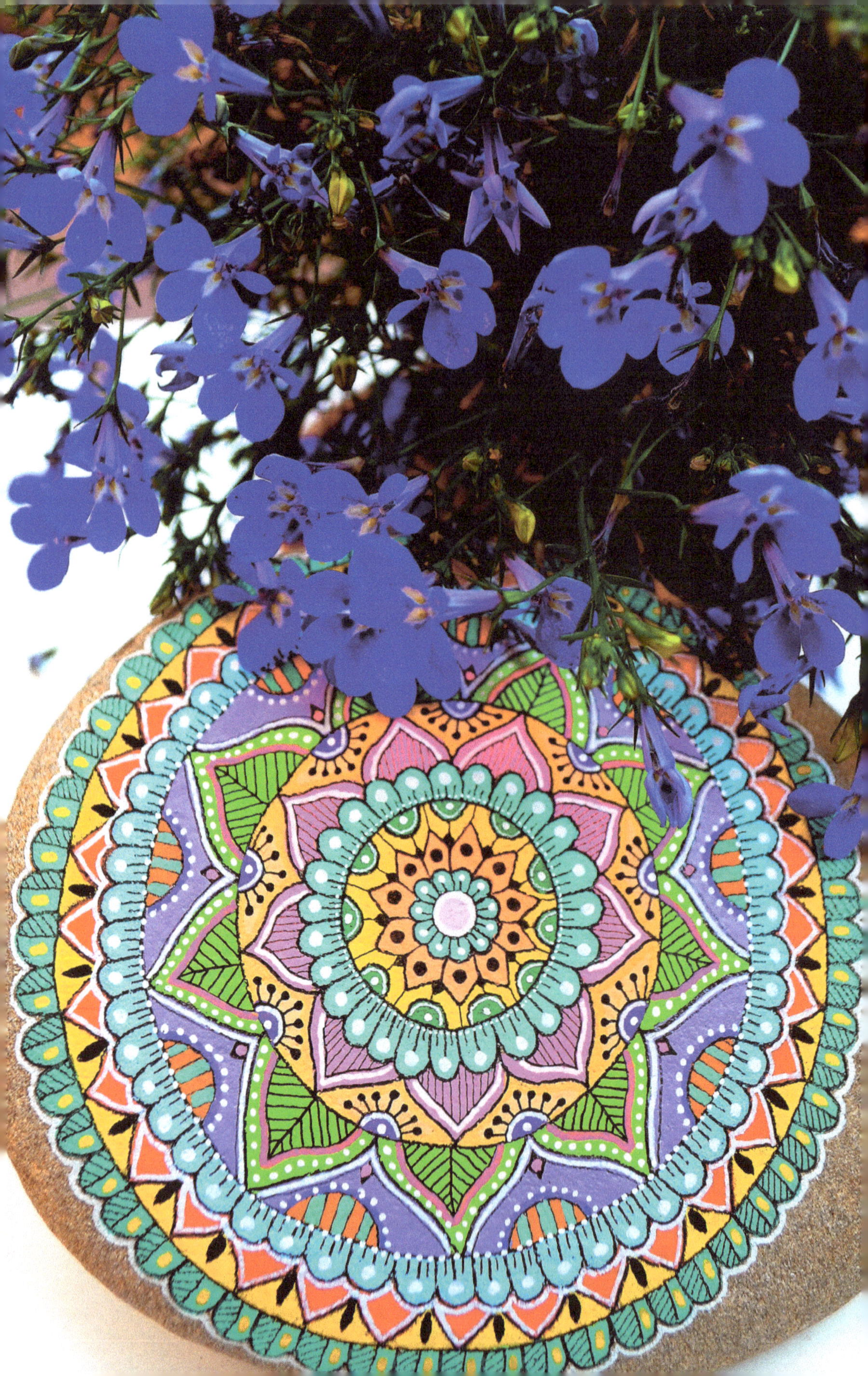

PRACTICE HERE

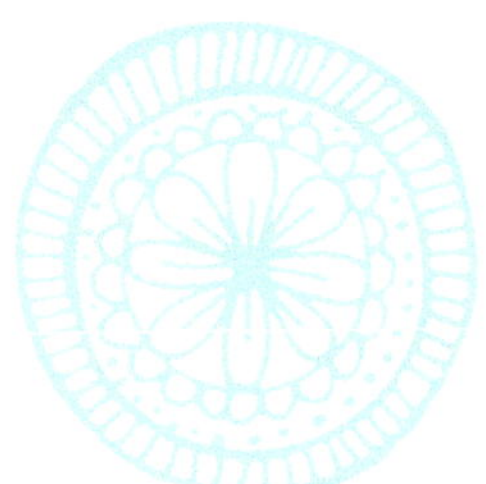

LINES & DOTS

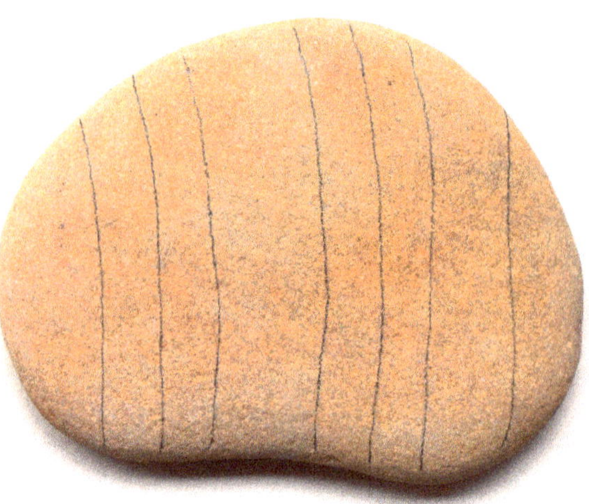

1 Wash your stone well with water and let it dry. When the stone is completely dry, use a pencil to draw some vertical parallel lines directly on the natural surface of the stone.

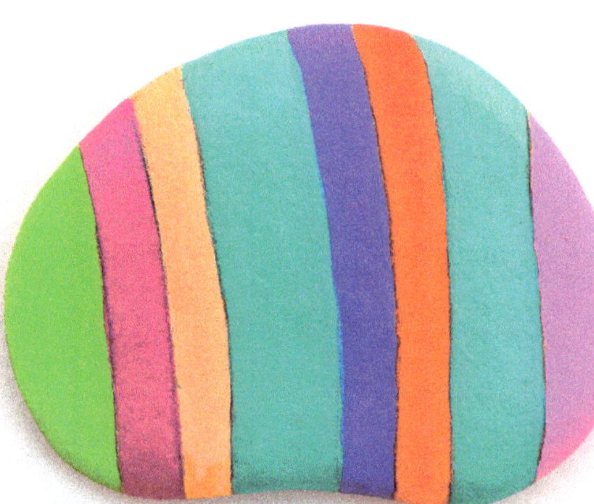

2 Use acrylic paints or inks and a round brush to paint the space between the parallel lines with different colors.

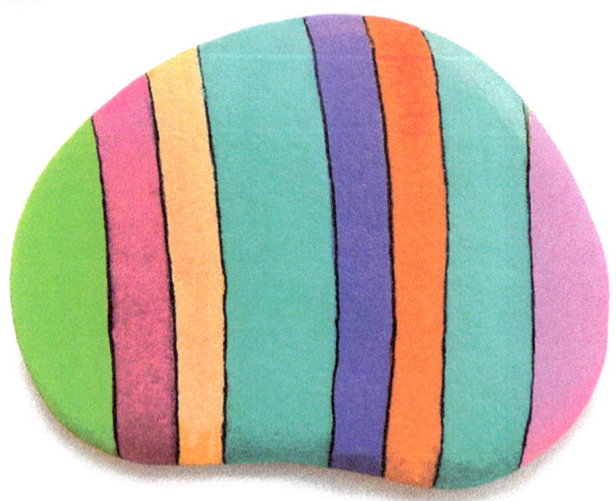

3 After your paint dries completely, draw contour lines with a black fine-liner pen between your colored spaces.

4 Next add details to your pattern. For every line, use a black fine-liner pen to add rows of semicircles or ovals. Fill in the semicircles and ovals with different colors to create a contrast with the background. Use fine-point paint pens to add color to small spaces.

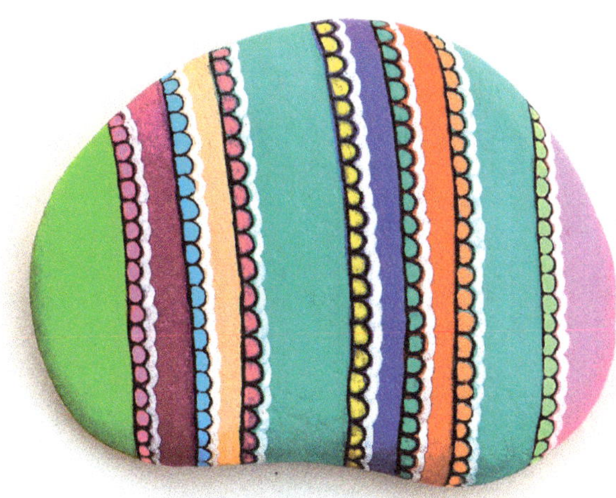

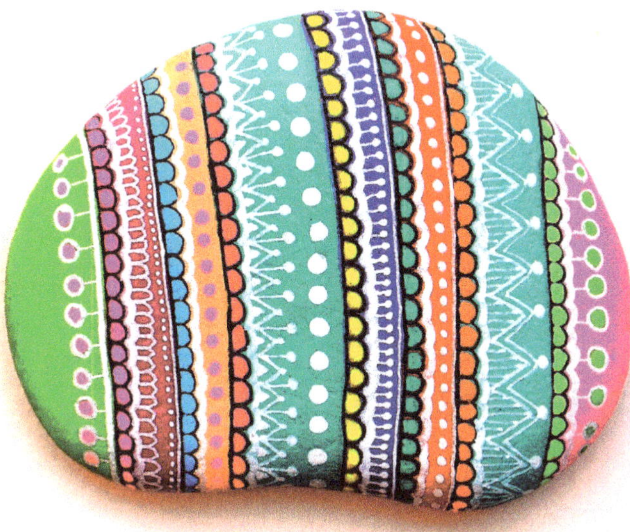

5 Now you can add detail to your design. Use white ink and a dip pen to add contours around each row, fill spaces with dots, add rows of triangles, or create lines. Add dots with contrast colors and contain them with white contour lines.

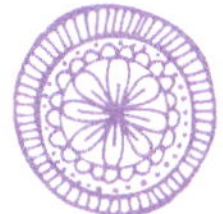

When the paint is completely dry, use an acrylic varnish to seal and protect it. Use your stone as a paperweight, bookend, or as a decorative piece in your garden. You can also turn your stone into wall art by attaching it to a wood panel and adding a frame.

PRETTY GARDEN

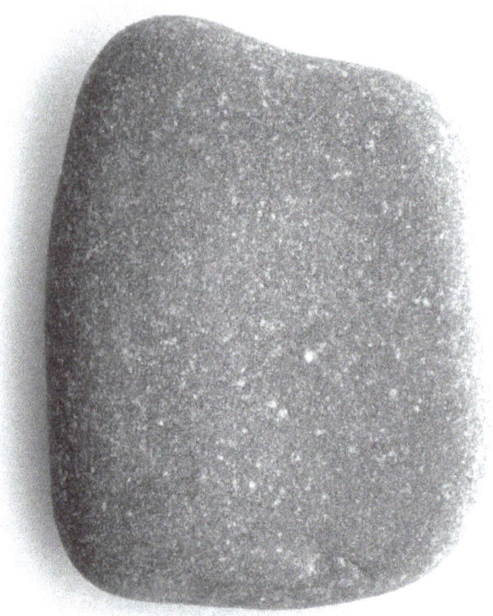

1 Find a flat, smooth stone. Wash the stone well, and let it dry. The shape of the stone isn't important when painting patterns.

2 Use a pencil to draw your pattern directly onto the natural surface of the stone. Create your pattern with semicircle rows, leaf-like motifs, flower parts, circles, or triangle rows.

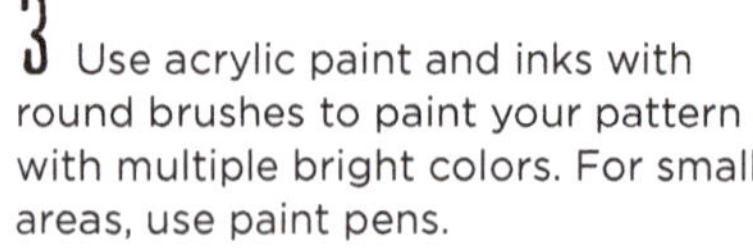

3 Use acrylic paint and inks with round brushes to paint your pattern with multiple bright colors. For small areas, use paint pens.

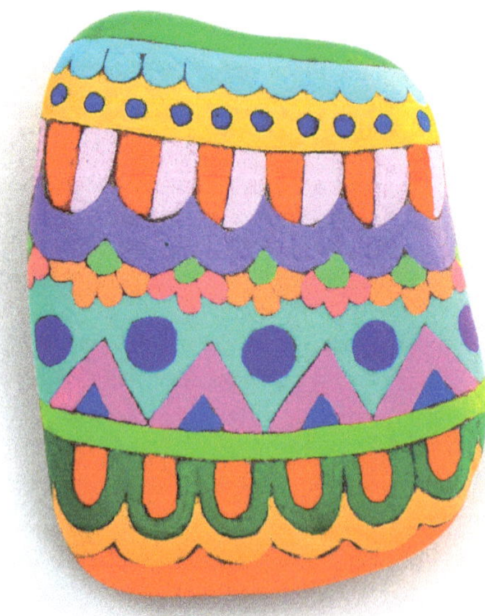

4 When the paint is dry, use a black, fine-liner pen to add contour lines to your pattern.

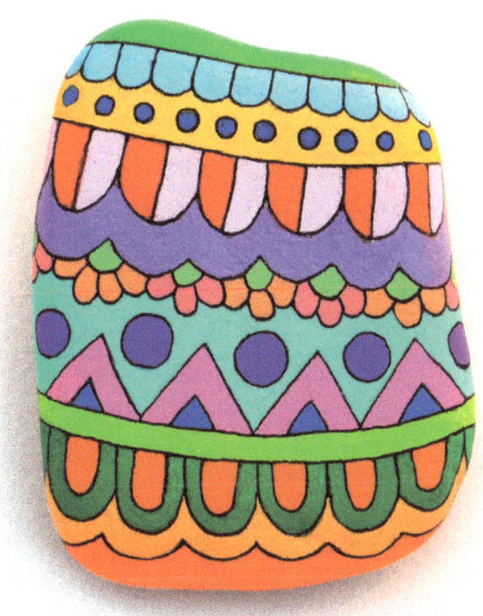

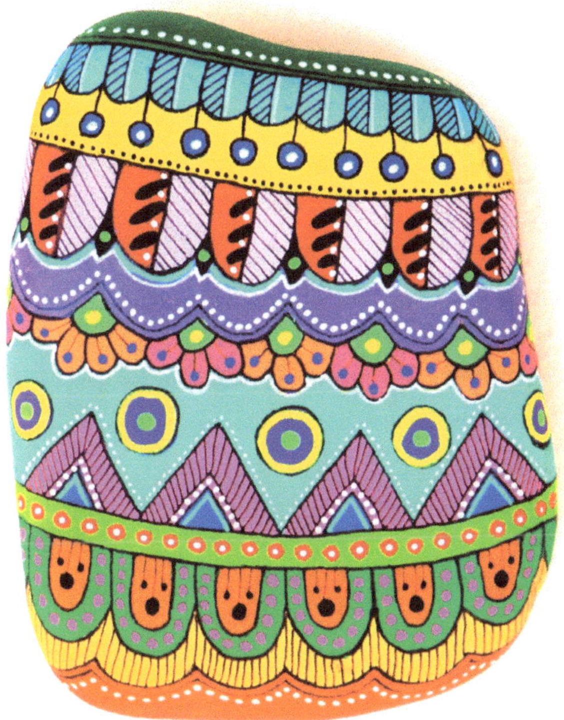

5 Now it's time to add details. Once your contour lines are dry, you can add thin, parallel lines inside leaf-like rows, or in semi-circles to divide them in half. Add little black leaves, parallel lines to triangle rows, contour rows with contrast colors, or add small black or white dots between rows. Let dry and use an acrylic varnish to seal and protect it.

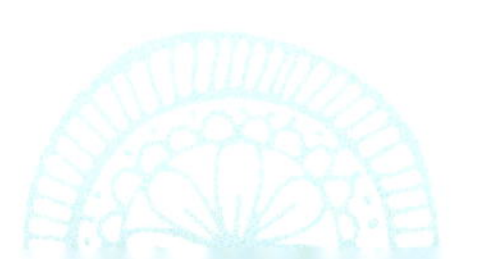

HEARTS

Using patterns is a great way to decorate and adorn a rock. Using similar shapes and colors in a repeating manner can create beautiful art on any canvas. This method is particularly nice on natural stones.

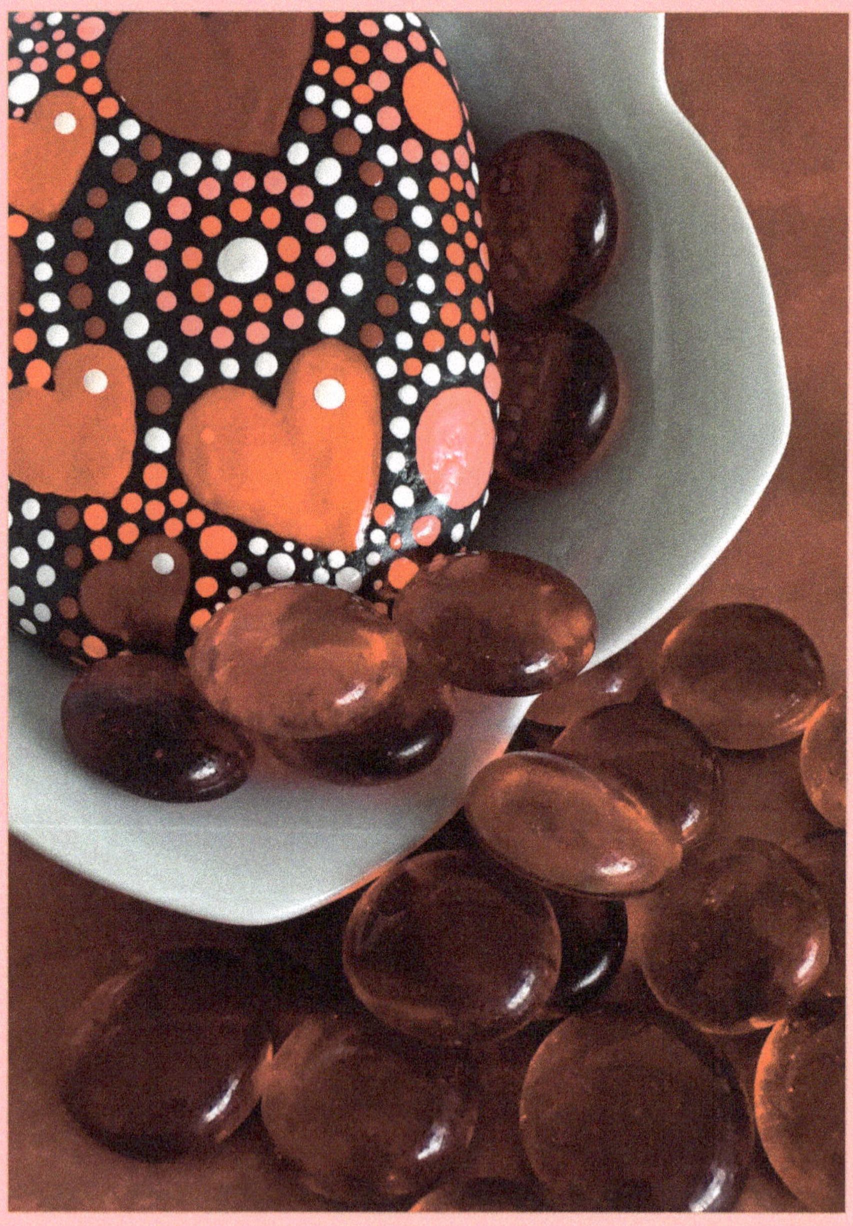

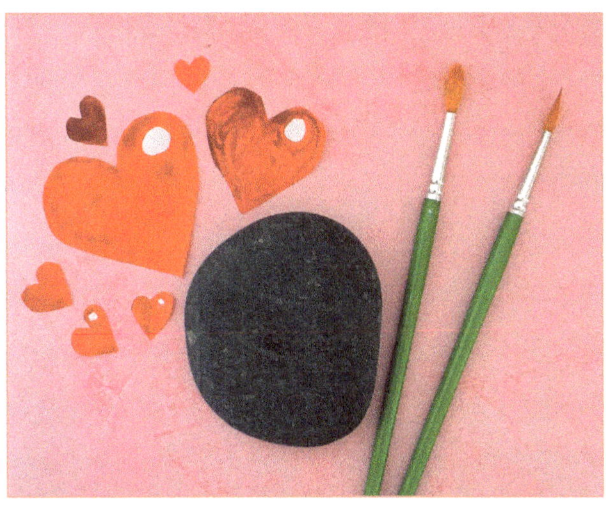

1 Choose a flat, smooth rock with a pleasing shape. Wash the rock well to remove any dirt from the surface. Let it dry completely. Determine a color scheme and pattern.

2 Find a starting point for your pattern. Let the rock's shape, size, texture, and color guide your design choices.

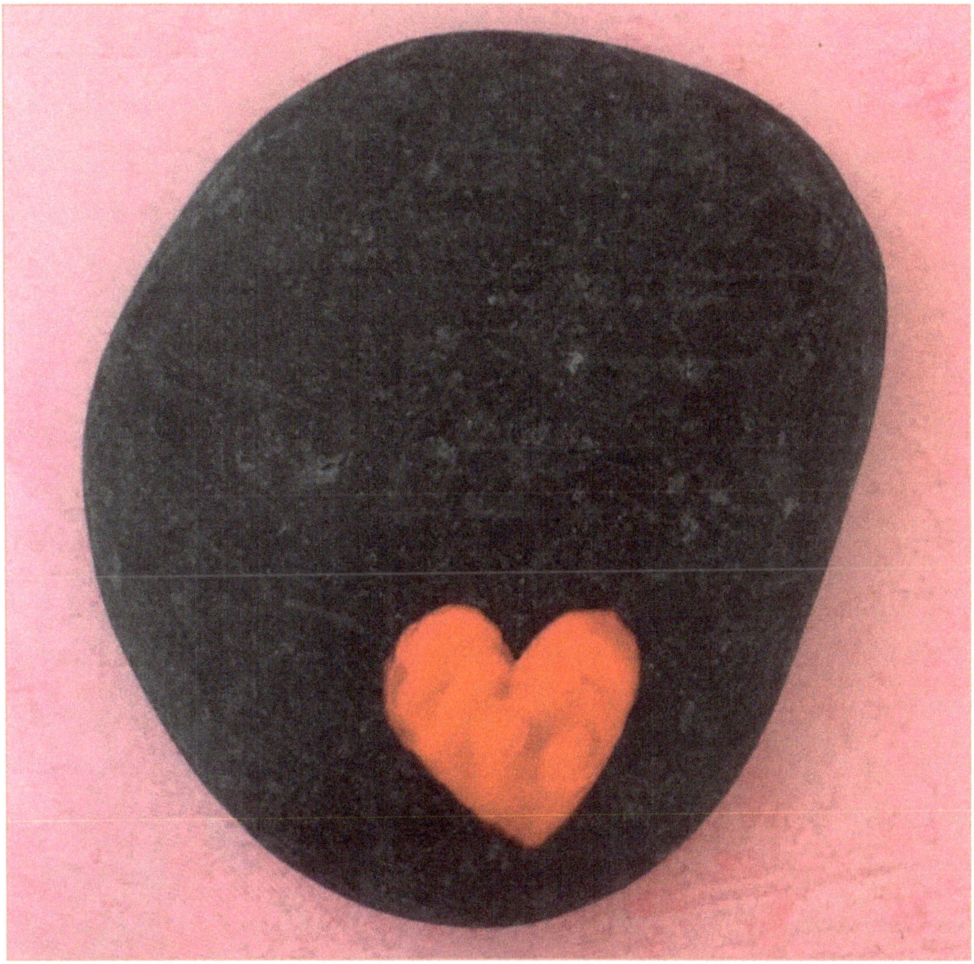

3 Next, using the rock's shape and size as a guide, place a pattern of hearts on the rock. Use different shades of red to add interest to the pattern. A dot or square on one side of each heart can simulate a glint of light bouncing off the surface.

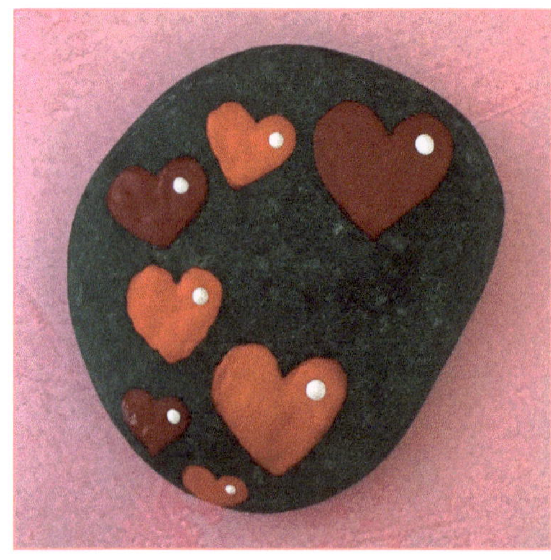

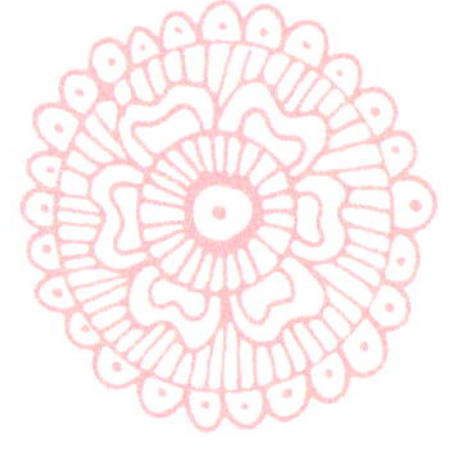

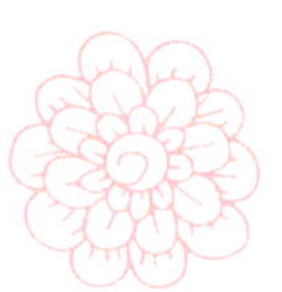

4 As you work your way across the surface of the rock, let each section dry completely before moving on to the next section. Most acrylic paint takes up to 10 minutes to dry. Once your main pattern is complete, fill in the negative spaces with dot art.

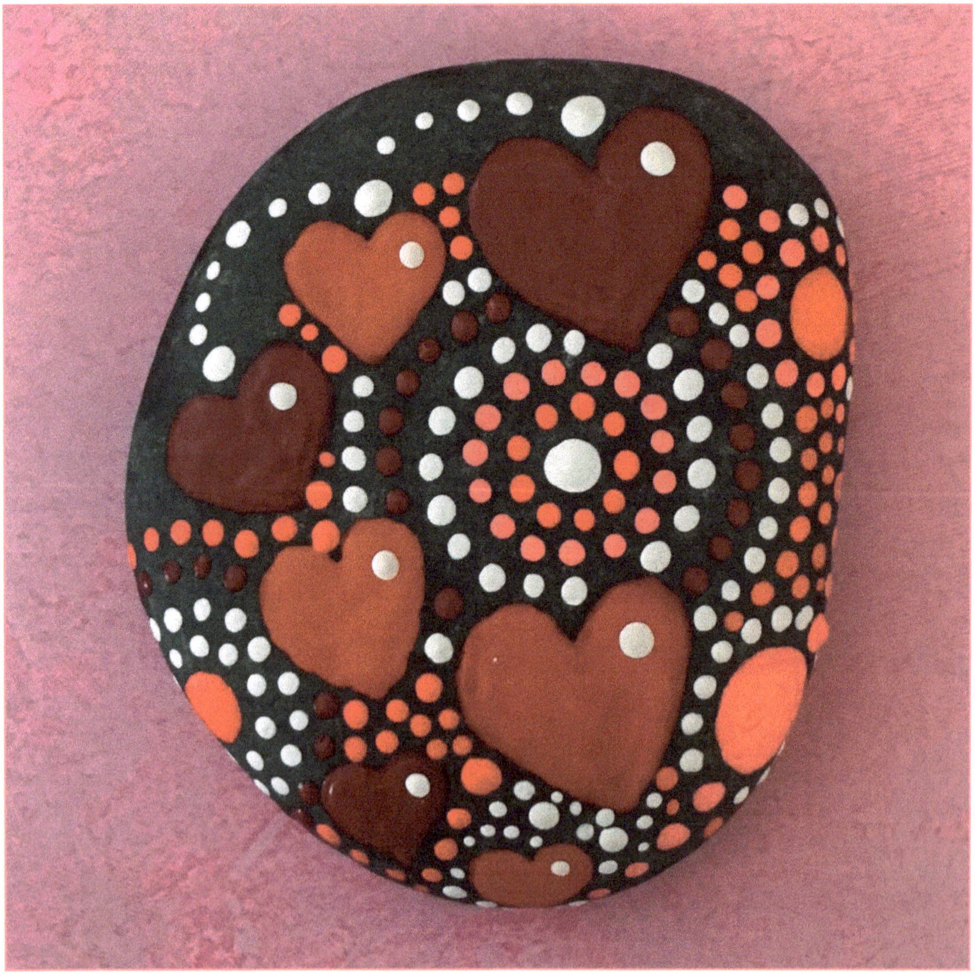

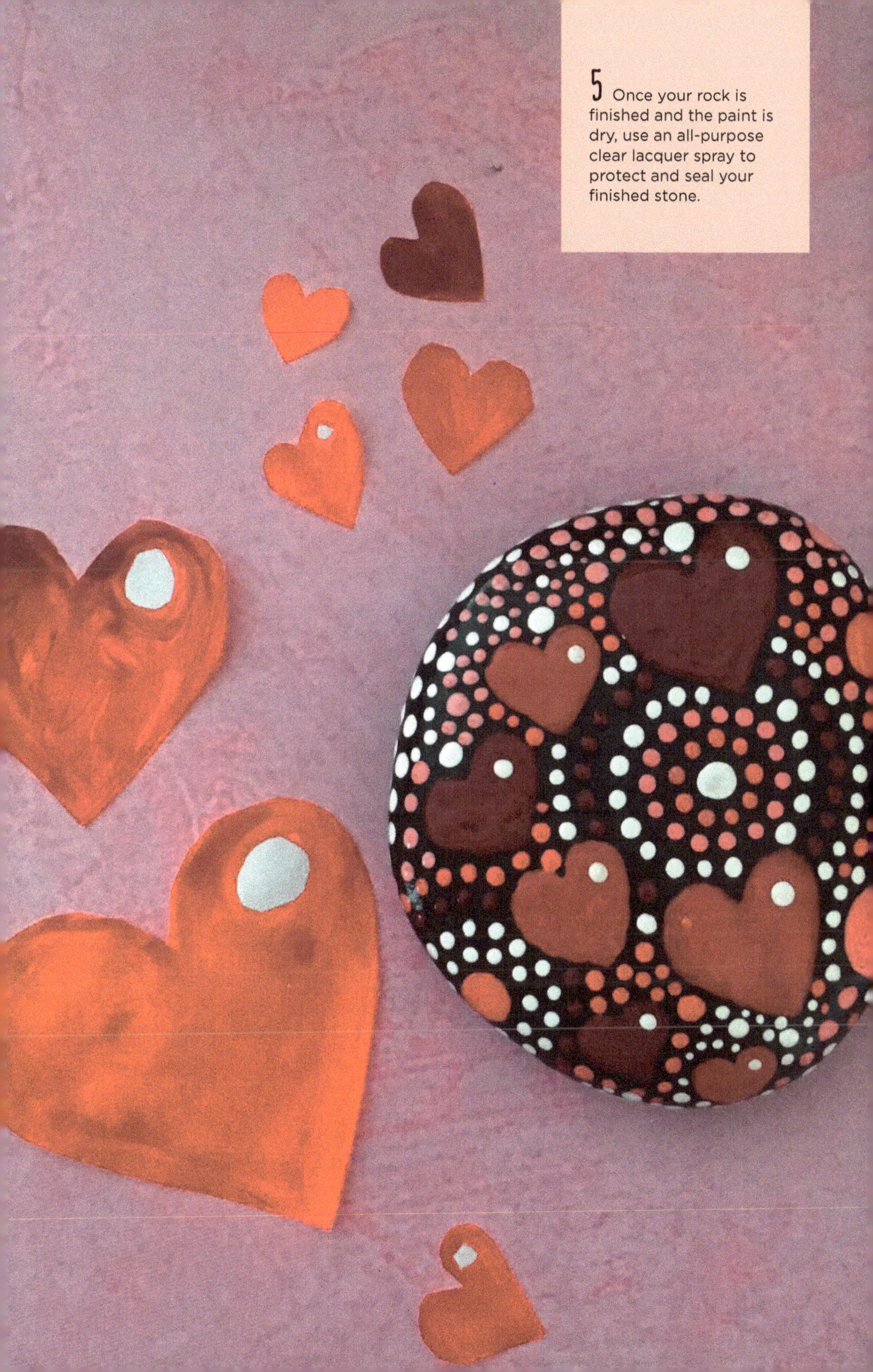

5 Once your rock is finished and the paint is dry, use an all-purpose clear lacquer spray to protect and seal your finished stone.

FLOWERS

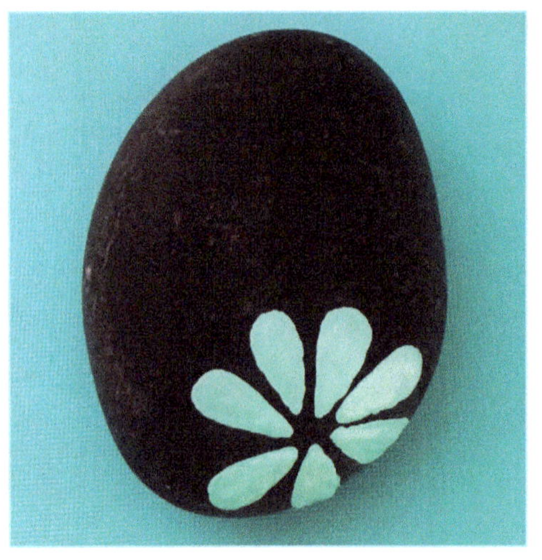

1 Find a starting point for your pattern using the size, surface texture, and shape of the rock to guide your design. Next begin to place a pattern of flowers on the rock.

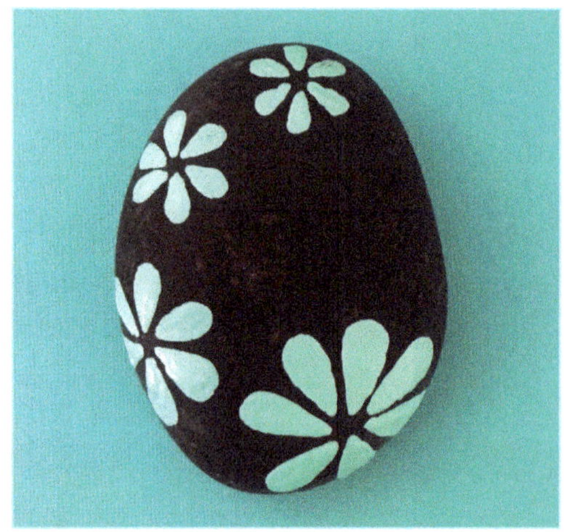

2 Color your rock using varied shades of blue and yellow—or stay with the same blue and yellow. Use different shades of blue, yellow and green to accent the design. Remember to let sections of the paint dry completely before handling the rock to access other sections.

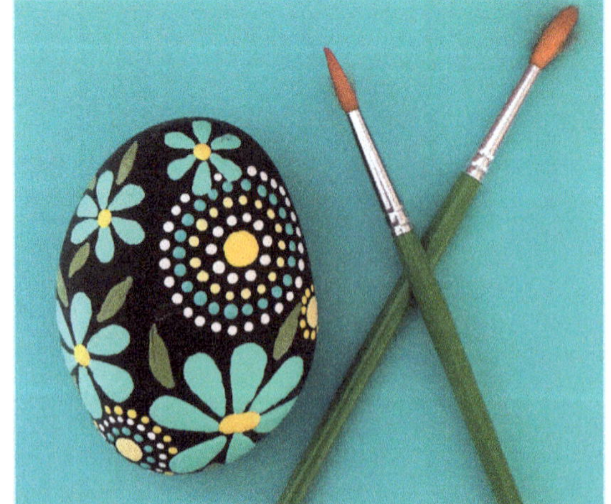

3 Once your pattern-themed images are complete, you can leave them on their own or fill in the negative spaces with dot art.

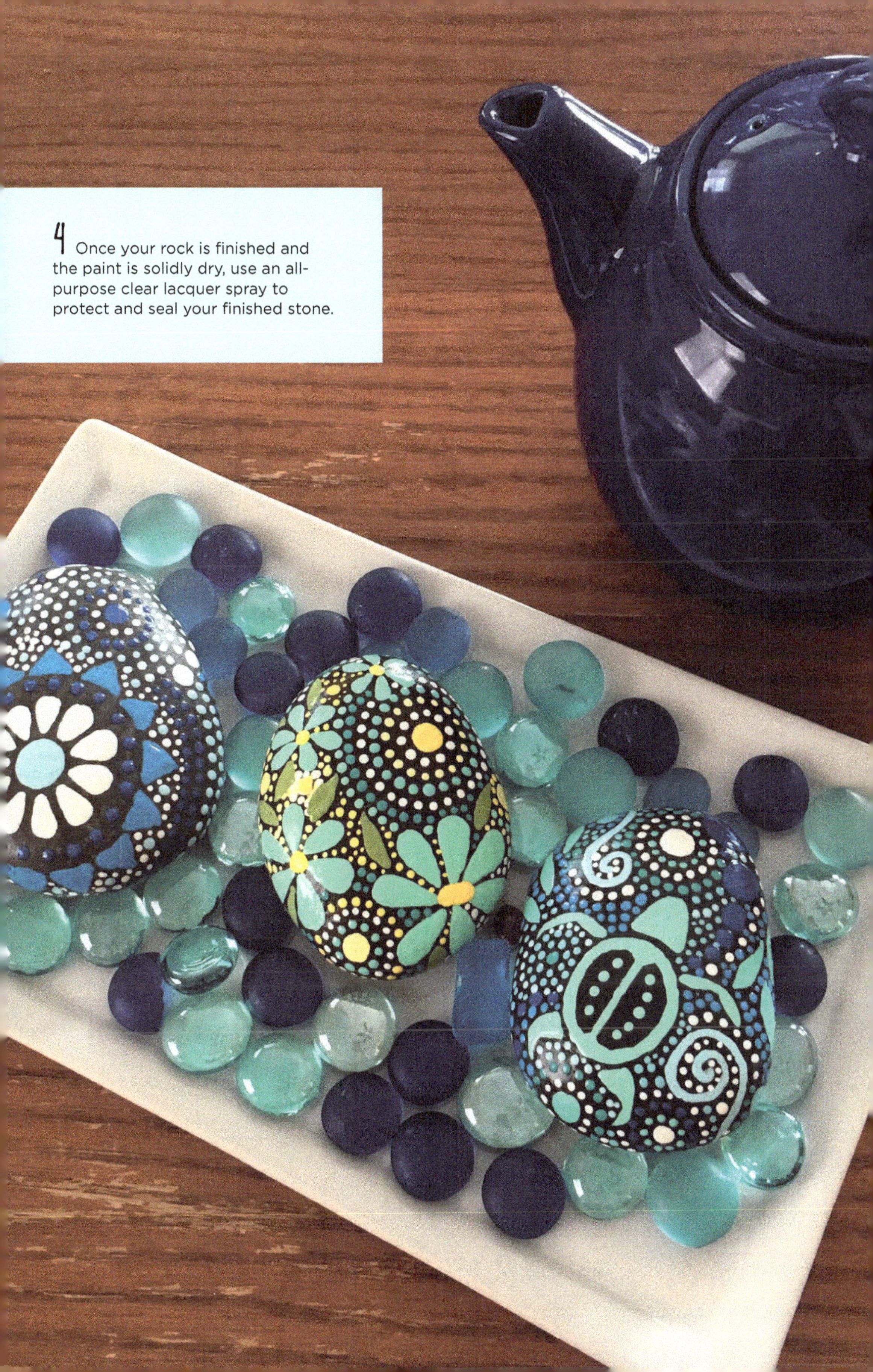

4 Once your rock is finished and the paint is solidly dry, use an all-purpose clear lacquer spray to protect and seal your finished stone.

PETROGLYPH

Petroglyphs are Native American and indigenous Australian carvings that make wonderful sources of inspiration for your designs. Adding other elements like dot art, mandalas, and natural accents will enhance the design.

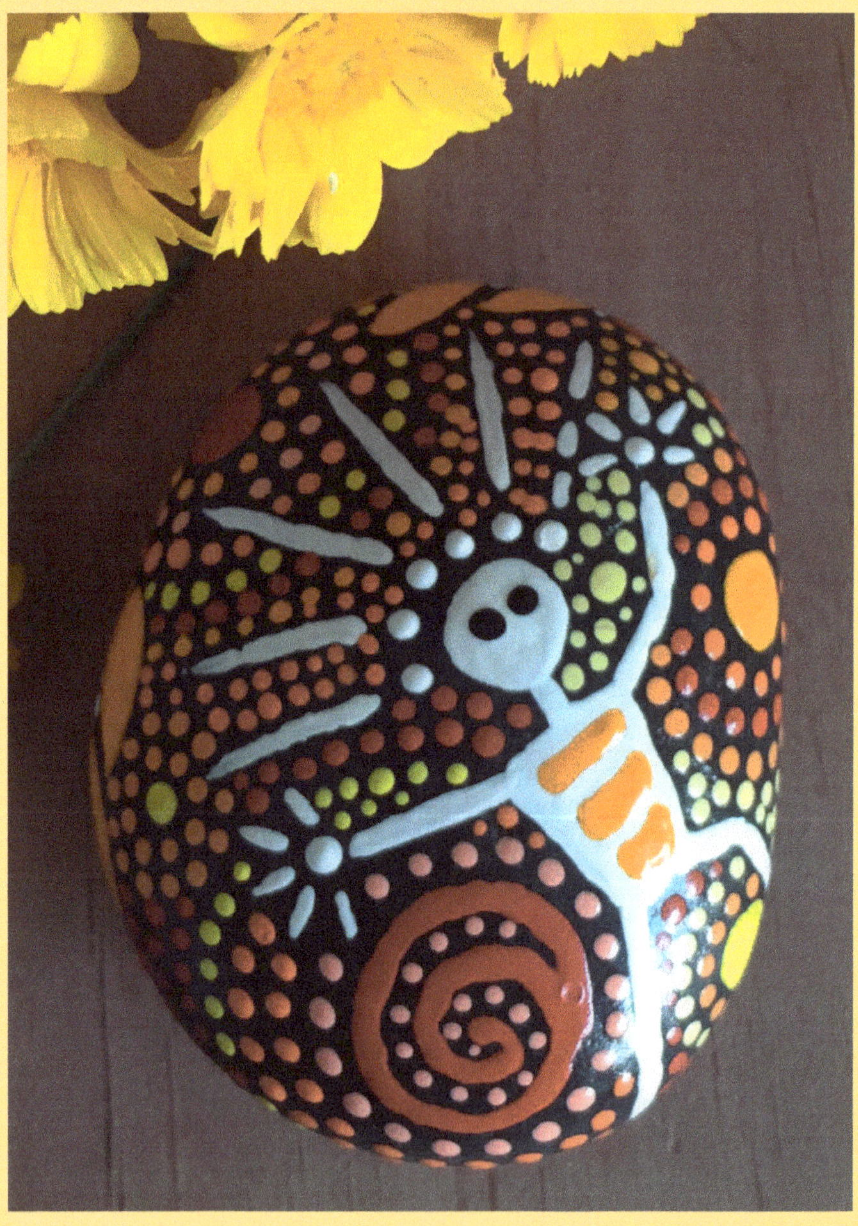

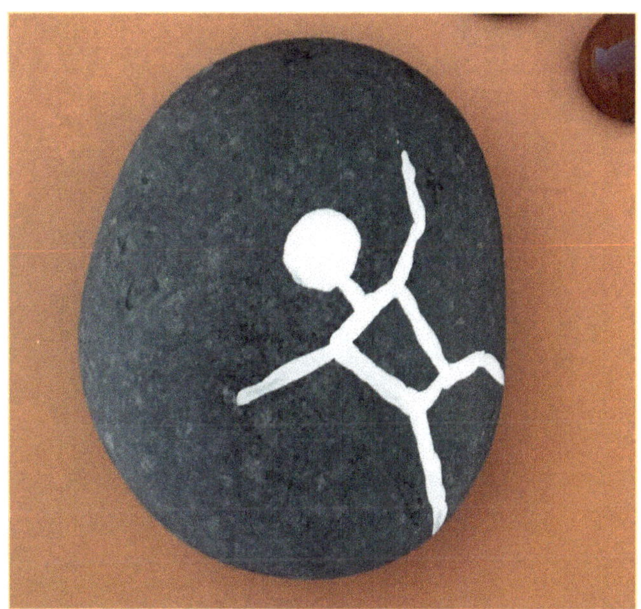

1 Use a natural palette of burnt oranges and dark yellows. Find a starting point for your petroglyph using the size, surface texture, and shape of the rock. Using ancient designs as a guide, set the dancing figure at a slight angle to help communicate movement and energy.*

2 Your figure can be as elaborate or as simple as you want. You can accent the headdress, garment, hands, feet, and facial features.

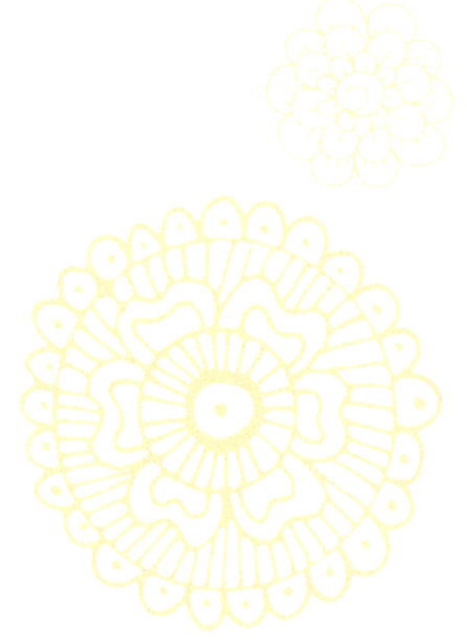

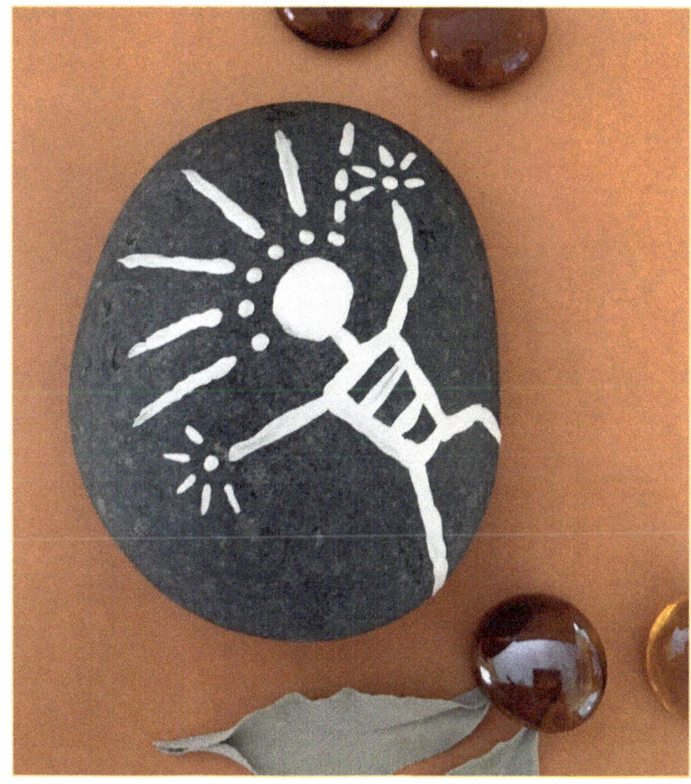

*This petroglyph design was referenced from *A Field Guide to Rock Art Symbols of the Greater Southwest*, Johnson Printing Company © 1992 by Alex Patterson.

3 Once your petroglyph is set, you can complete your rock design using other petroglyph symbols such as sun designs, spirals, or handprints. Natural elements such as flowers and leaves are also nice additions.

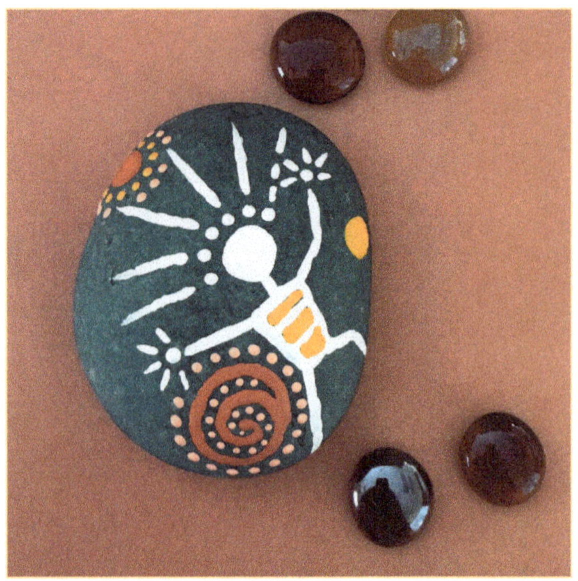

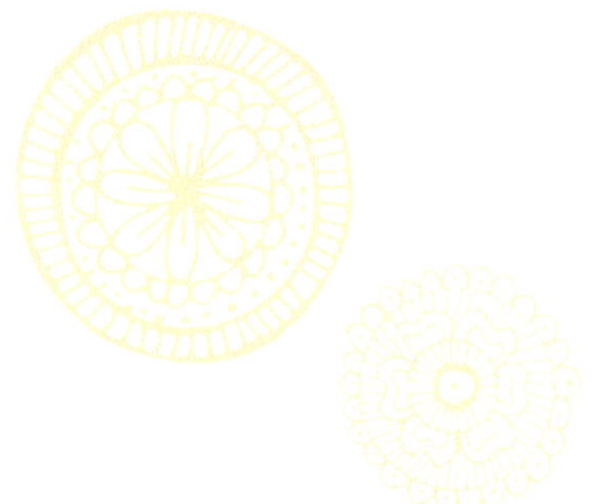

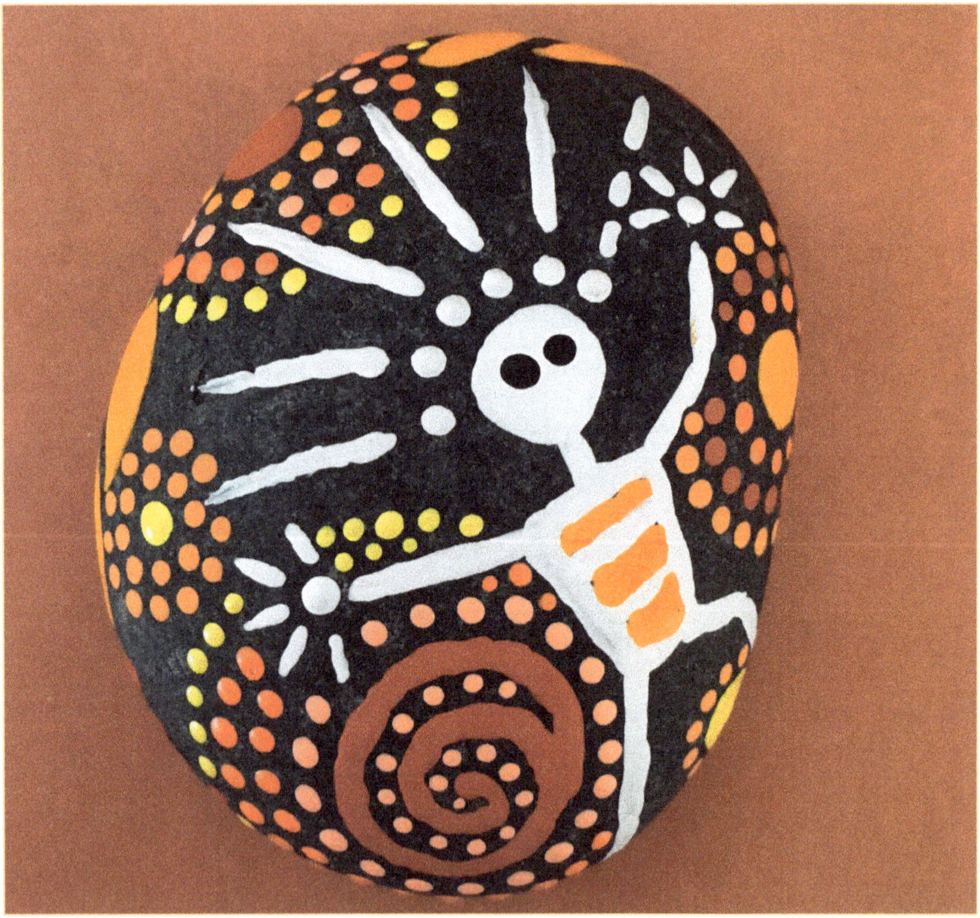

4 Be very careful to let sections of the paint dry completely before handling the rock to access other sections. It is easy to smudge and ruin finished sections if you skip this step.

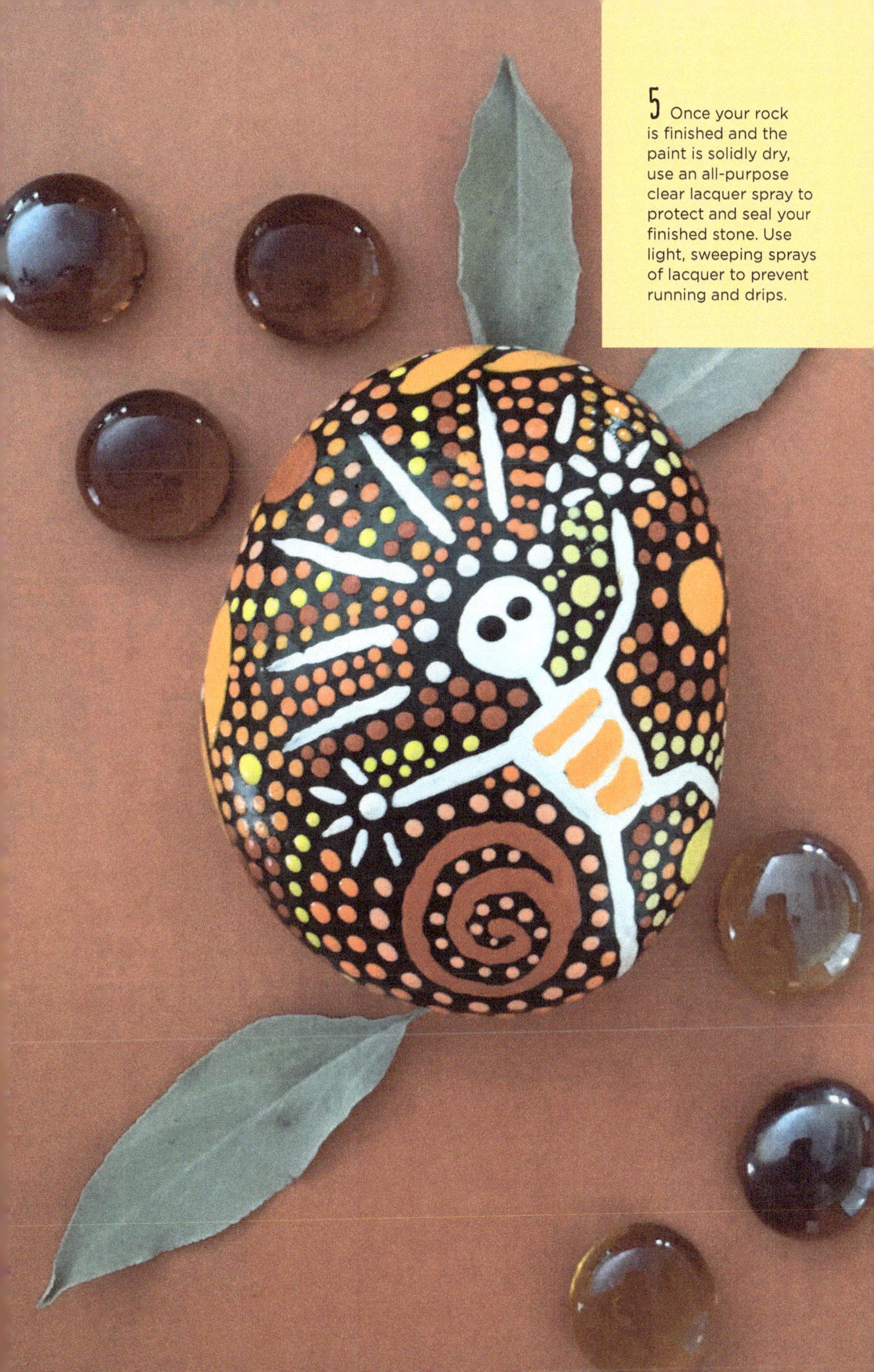

5 Once your rock is finished and the paint is solidly dry, use an all-purpose clear lacquer spray to protect and seal your finished stone. Use light, sweeping sprays of lacquer to prevent running and drips.

PRACTICE HERE

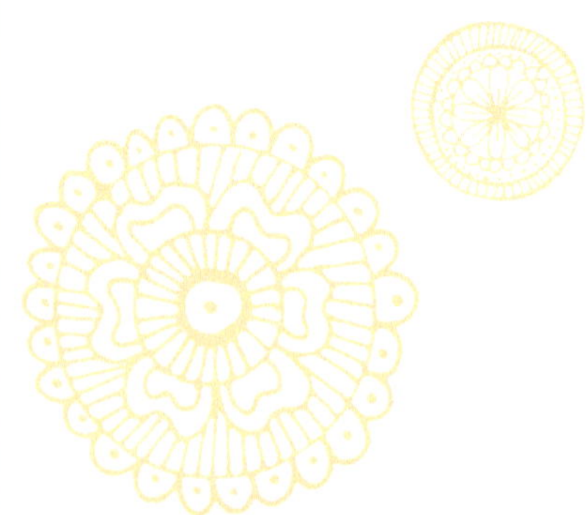

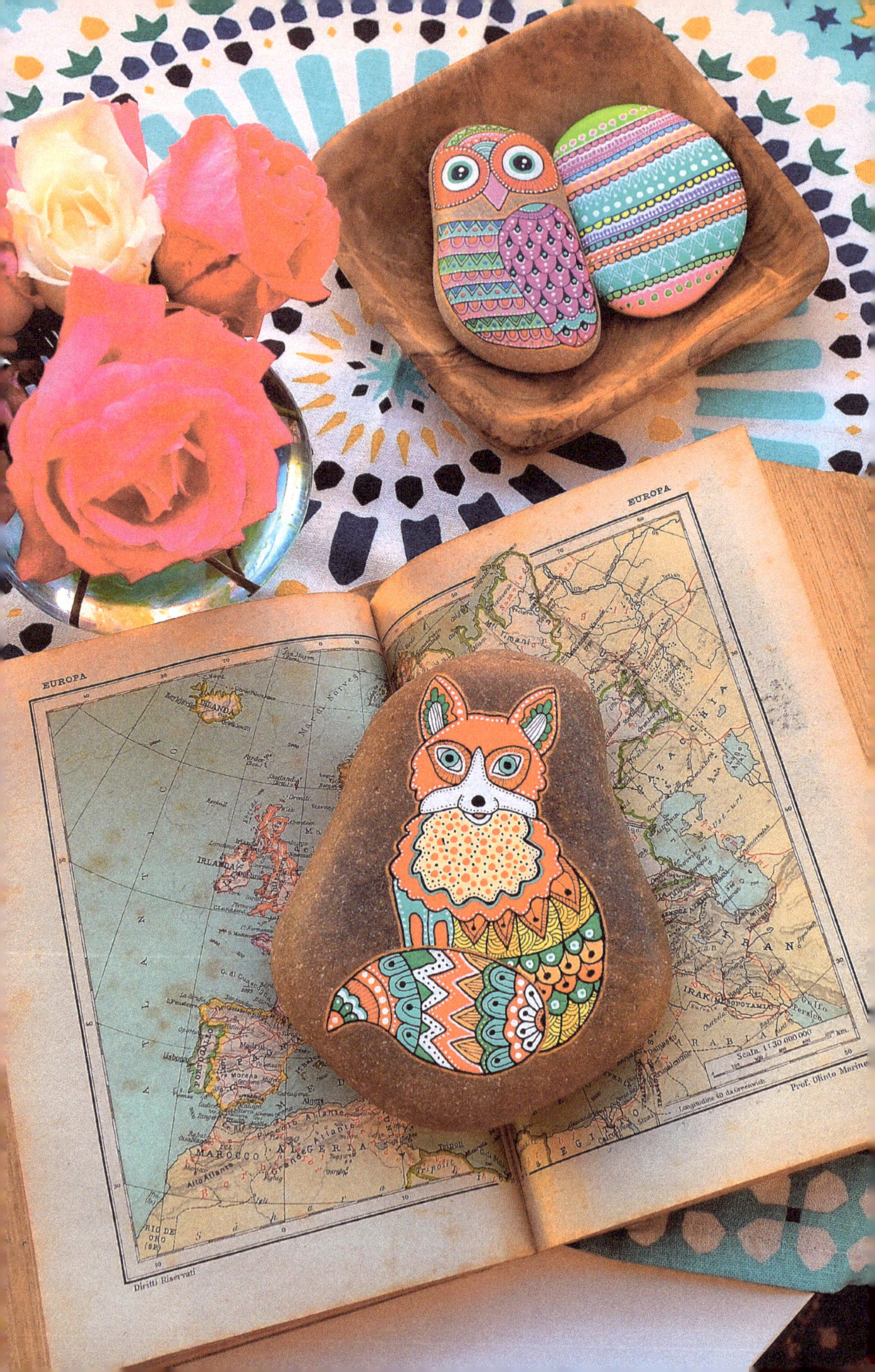
EUROPA
EUROPA
ISLANDA
IRLANDA
MAROCCO
ALGERIA
IRAN
Scala 1:30.000.000
Diritti Riservati

PART III: ANIMALS

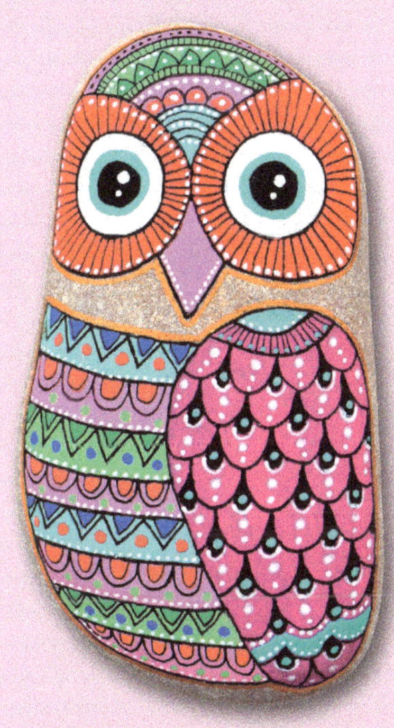

DRAGONFLY

The dragonfly seems like a creature from another world. It symbolizes change and flexibility. This creature is the perfect inspirational symbol for decorating your rock. It is an ideal keepsake for someone in need or in the midst of change.

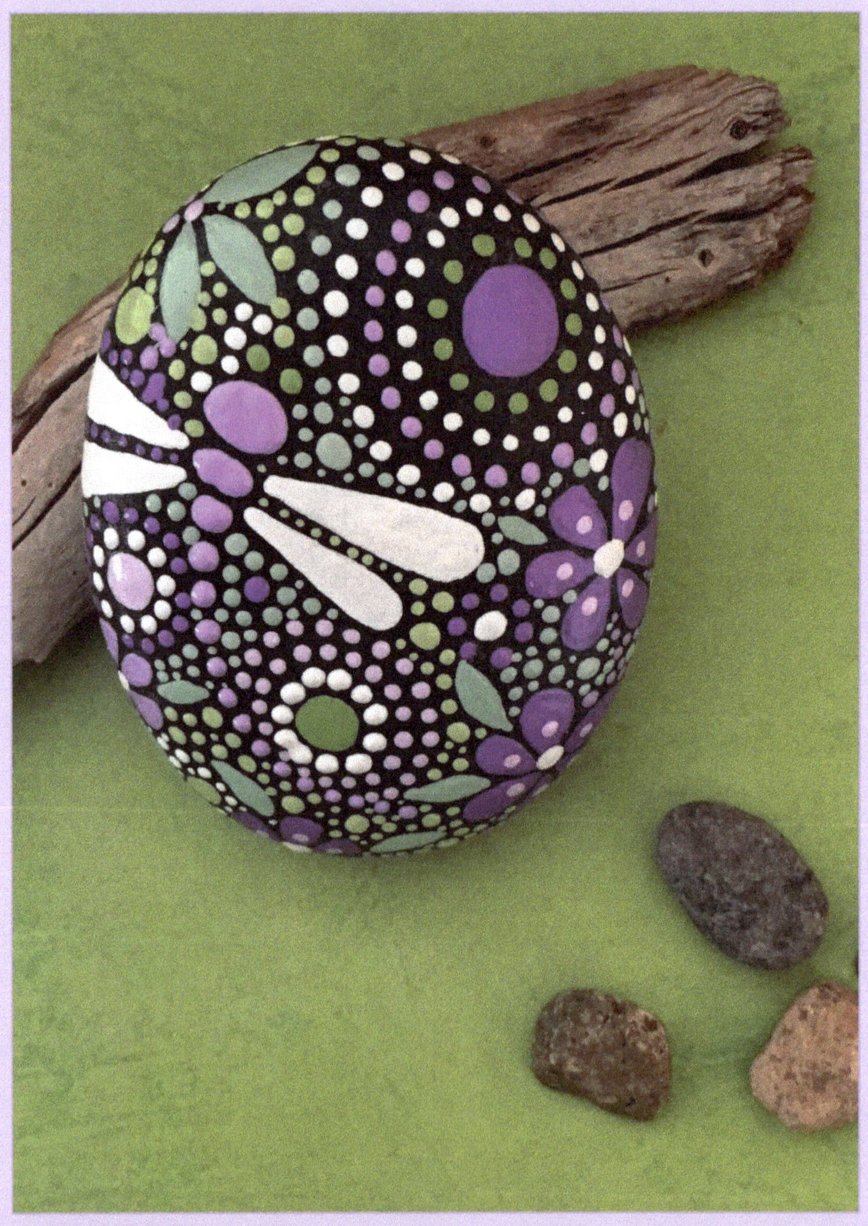

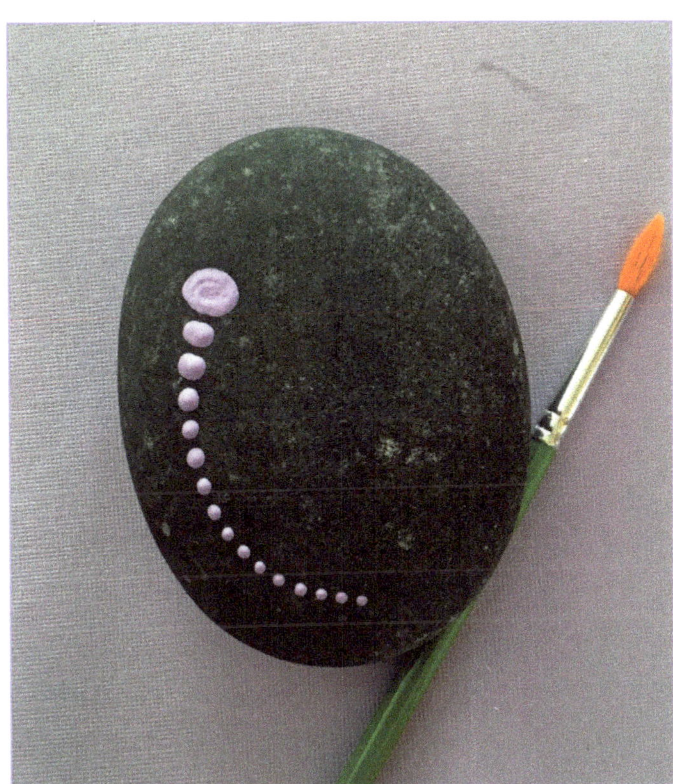

1 Separate the dragonfly into circular parts: the largest part is the head, with smaller circles for the body and tail. In nature, dragonflies come in a variety of beautiful color combinations. Surrounding your dragonfly with flowers and mandala images will help you choose your dragonfly's colors.

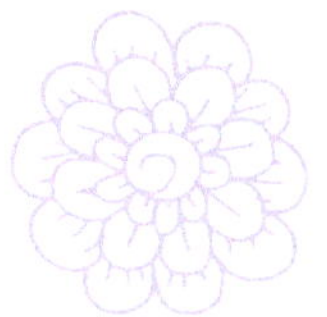

2 Next add wings near the body and two small circles for eyes. You can vary colors to make certain parts of the dragonfly stand out, or keep the body, wings, and eyes the same to create a more minimalistic design.

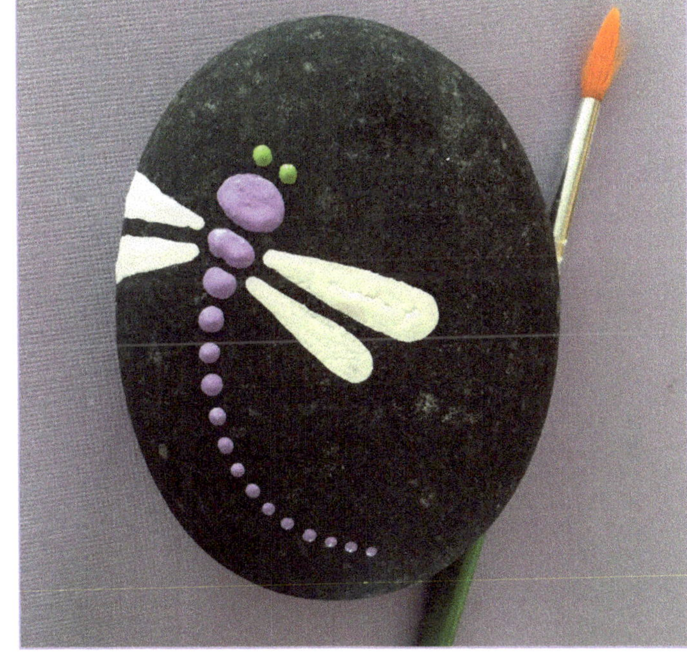

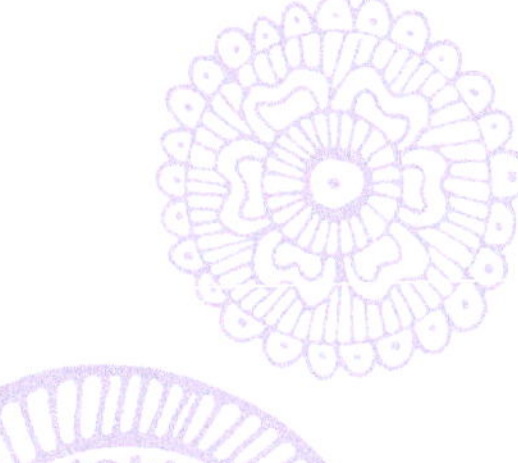

3 Surround the dragonfly with flowers, mandalas, and other natural elements. The position of your dragonfly on the rock will help you decide where to place other decorative elements. Remember to let sections of paint dry completely before handling the rock to access other sections.

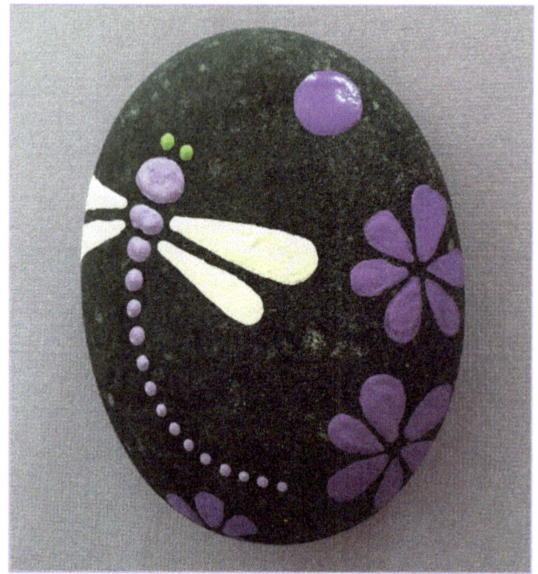

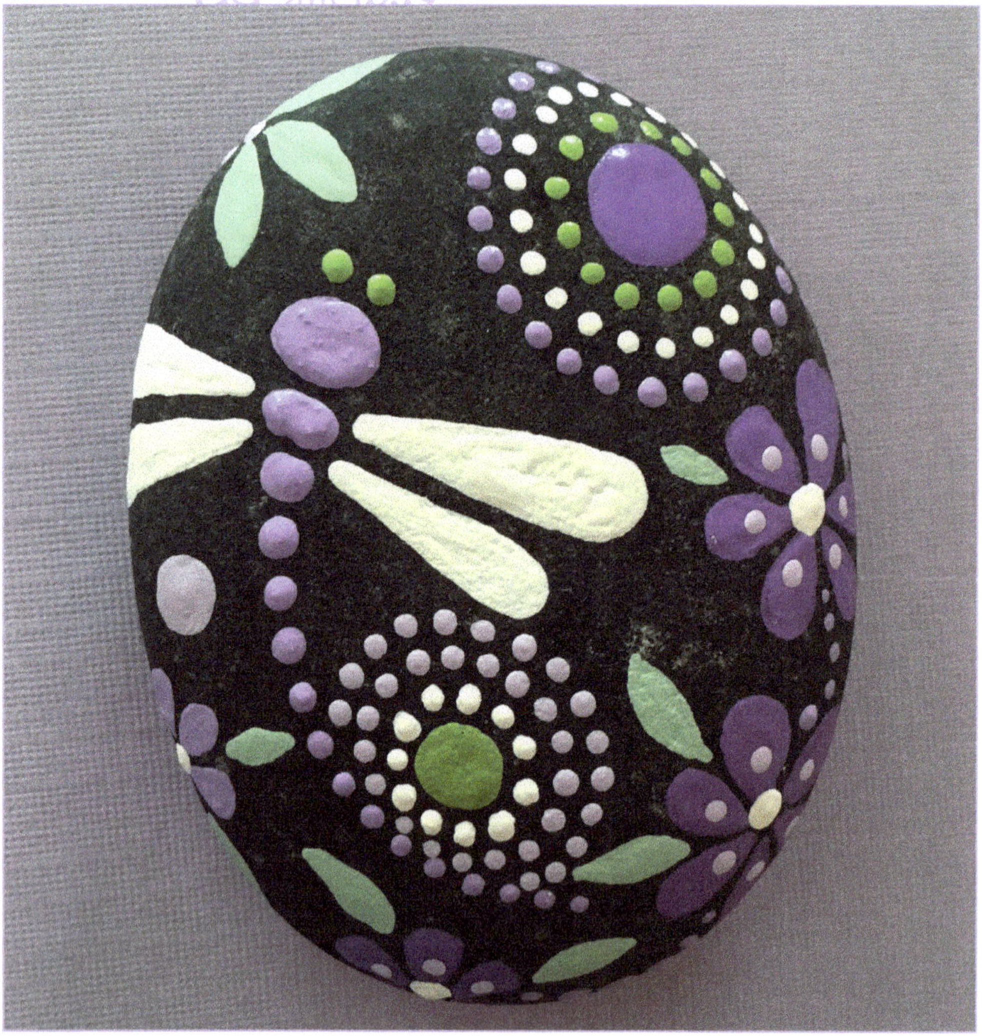

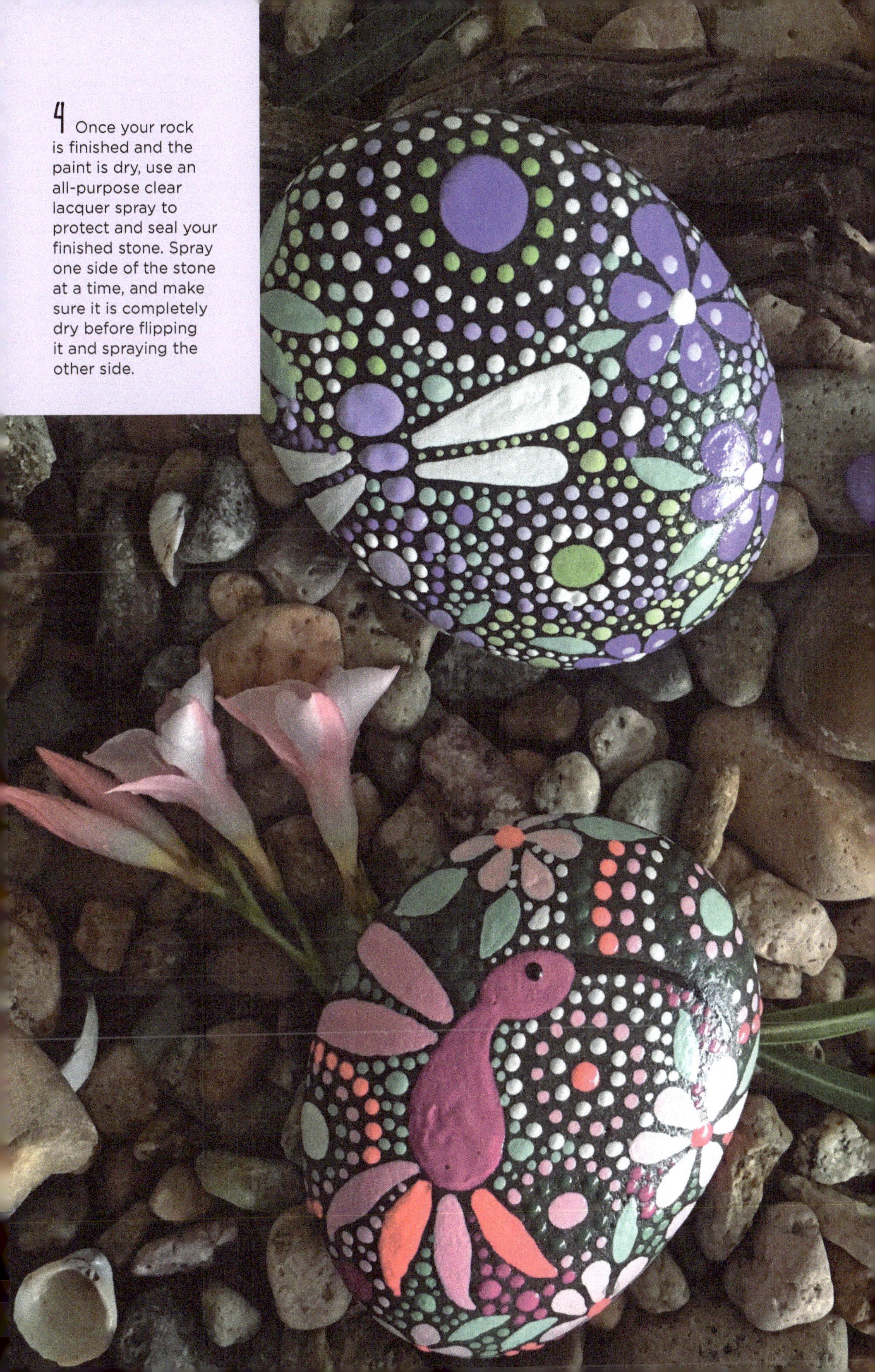

4 Once your rock is finished and the paint is dry, use an all-purpose clear lacquer spray to protect and seal your finished stone. Spray one side of the stone at a time, and make sure it is completely dry before flipping it and spraying the other side.

HUMMINGBIRD

Hummingbirds are one of my favorite creatures. Happily darting about the garden, they are flying jewels of joy. Their varied colors make hummingbirds the perfect subject for rock art.

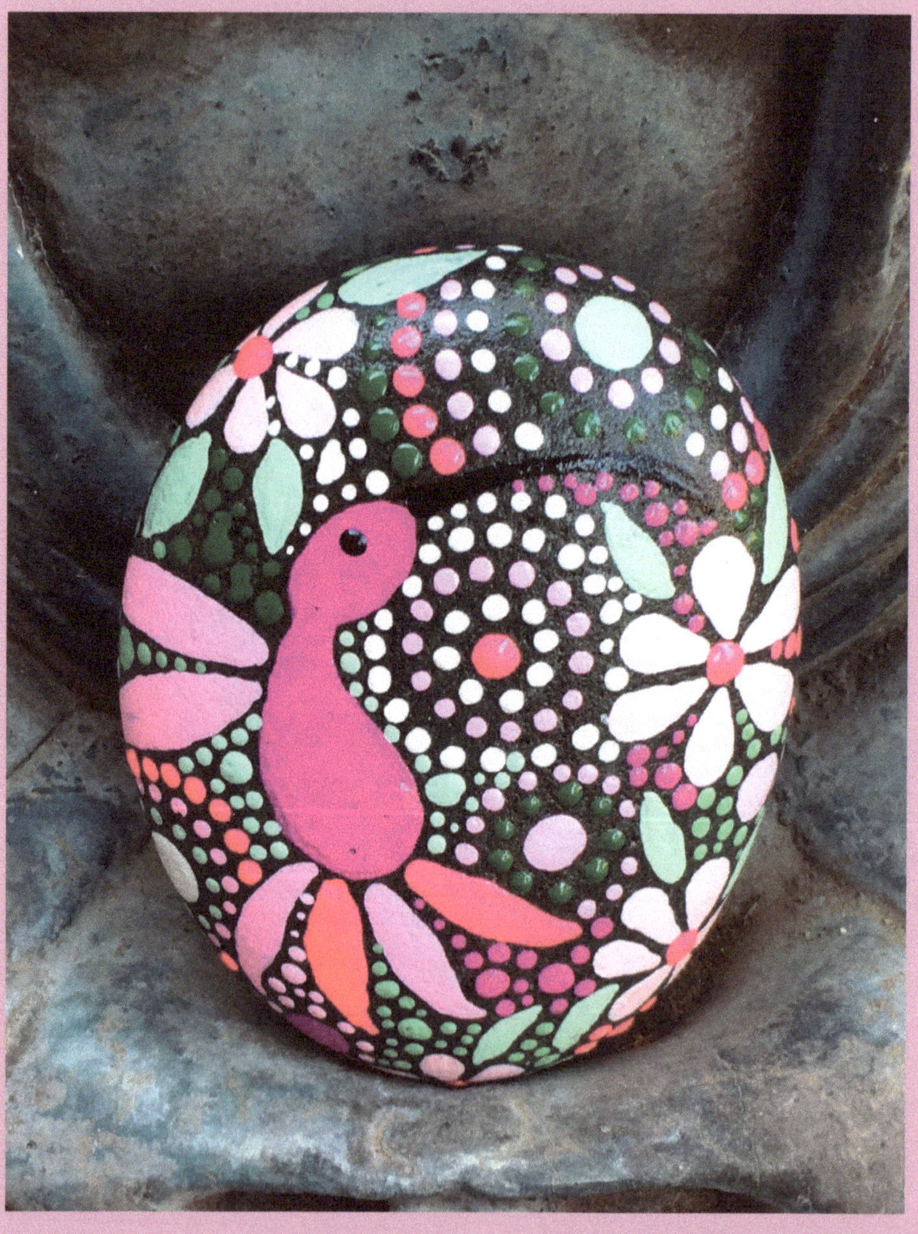

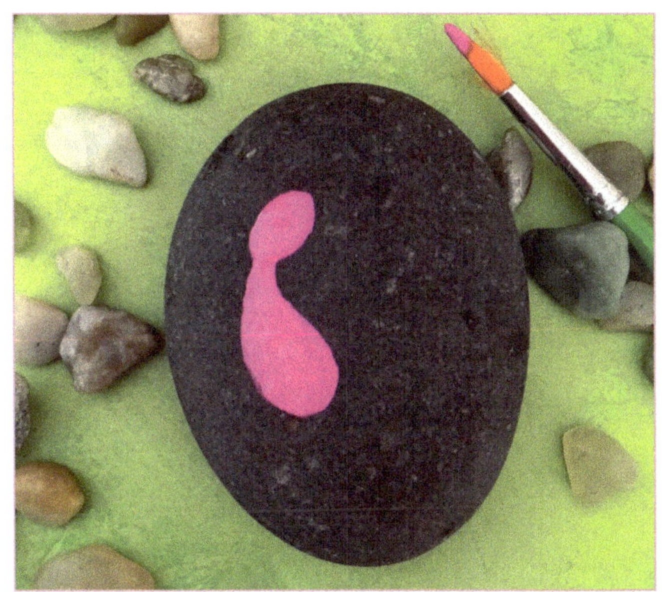

1 Start by placing the hummingbird's head and body. Leave room around your hummingbird for accents to the scene. It doesn't matter which color palette you choose; however, use similar colors for the body and head to help distinguish the outline of the hummingbird, and then use a variety of different but similar hues for the wings and tail feathers.

2 Next add wings to the back of the body and tail feathers to the bottom of the body.

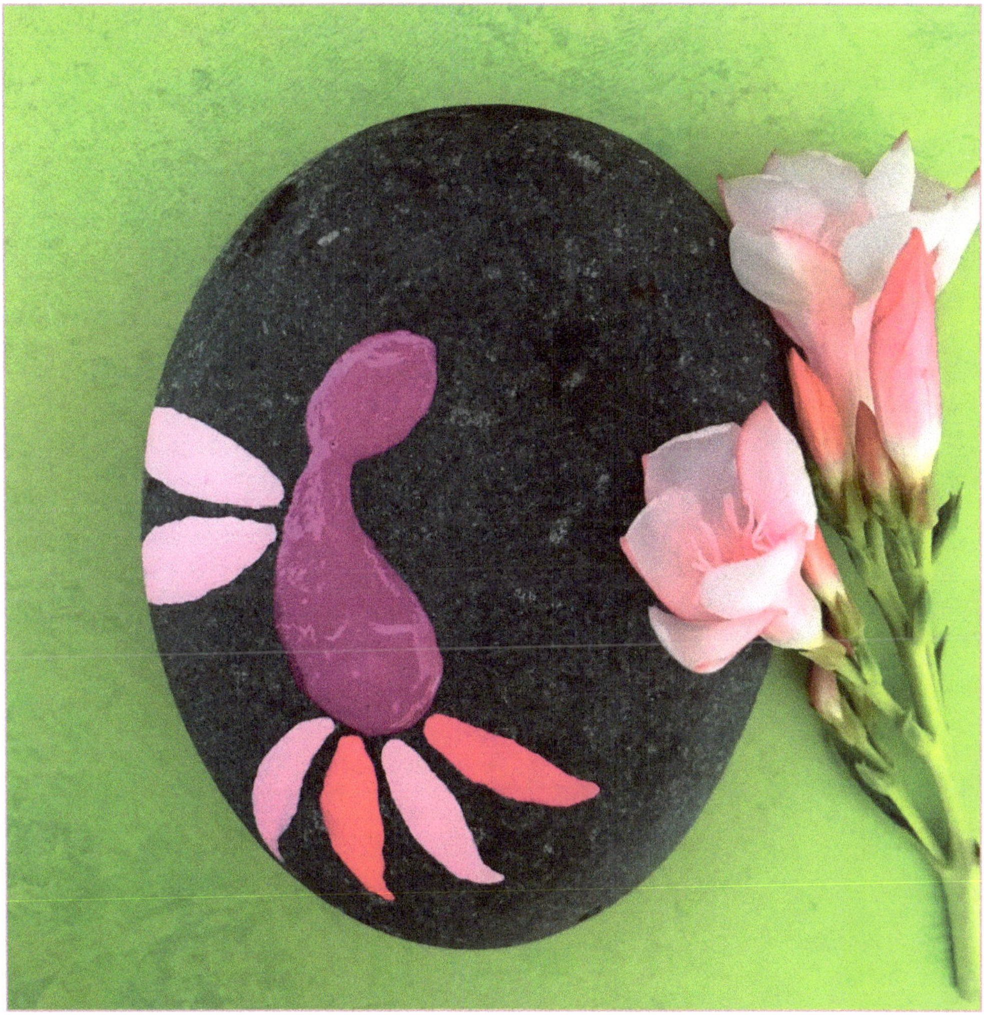

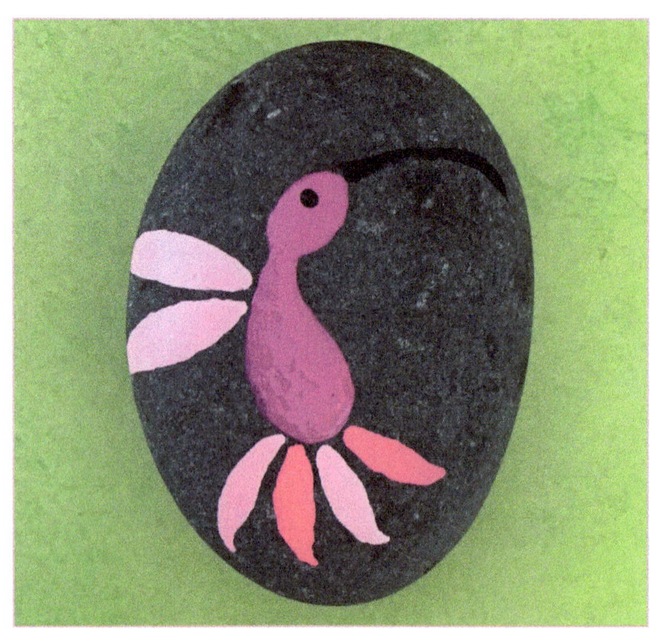

3 When the paint on the hummingbird's head is completely dry, and you are satisfied with the color tones, use black paint to place the eye of the hummingbird on the head and a long beak extending from the head.

4 Next create the hummingbird's garden using flowers, mandalas, sun images, and other natural elements. Remember to let each section of paint dry completely before handling the rock to access other sections.

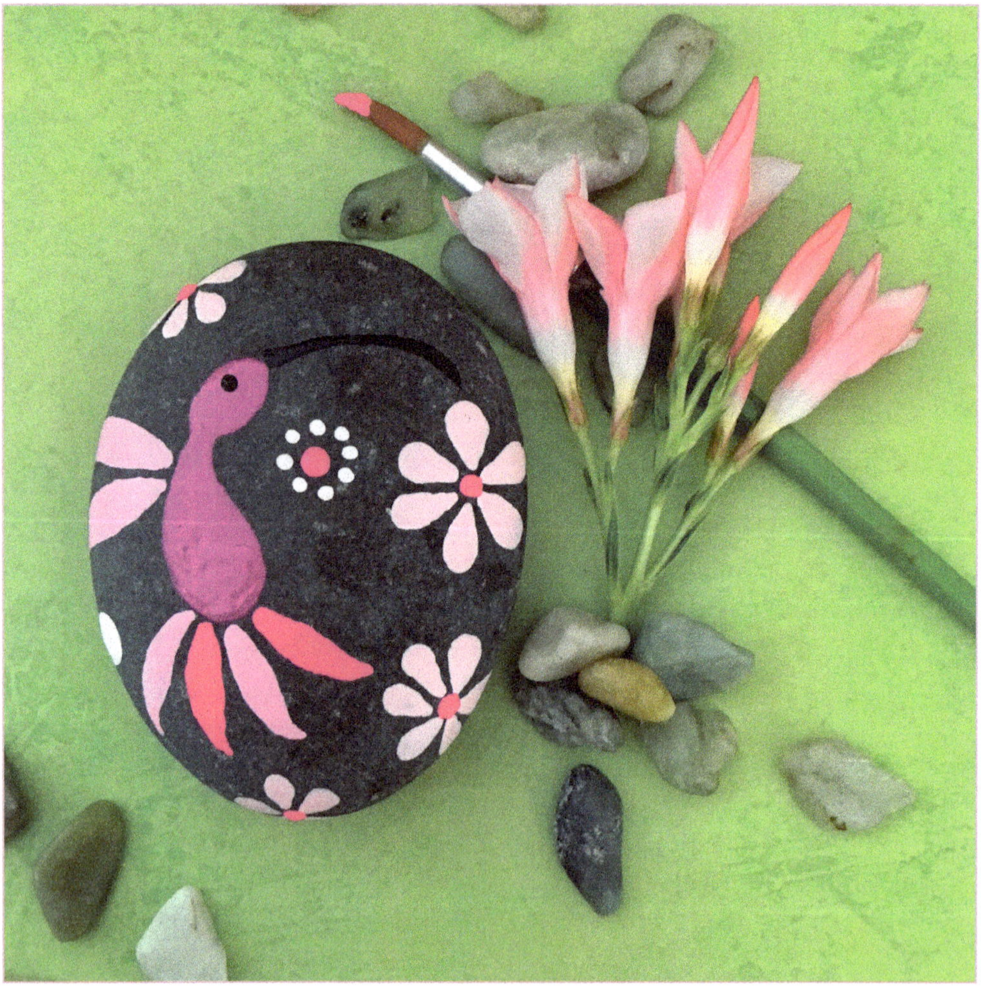

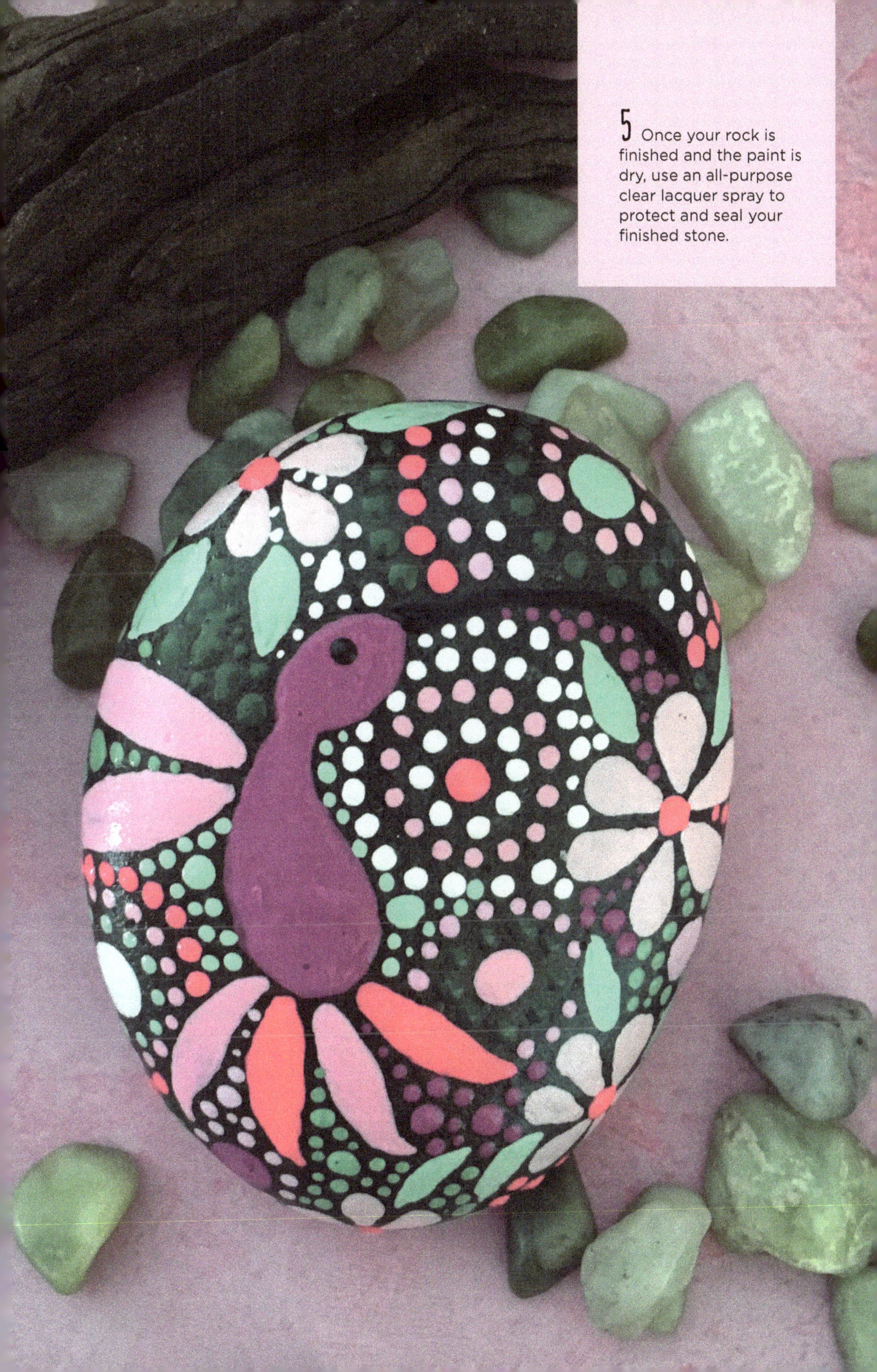

5 Once your rock is finished and the paint is dry, use an all-purpose clear lacquer spray to protect and seal your finished stone.

TURTLE

Painting on rocks is as old as mankind. Petroglyphs are great sources of inspiration for your rock designs. This sea turtle was inspired by a miniature version of a petroglyph.

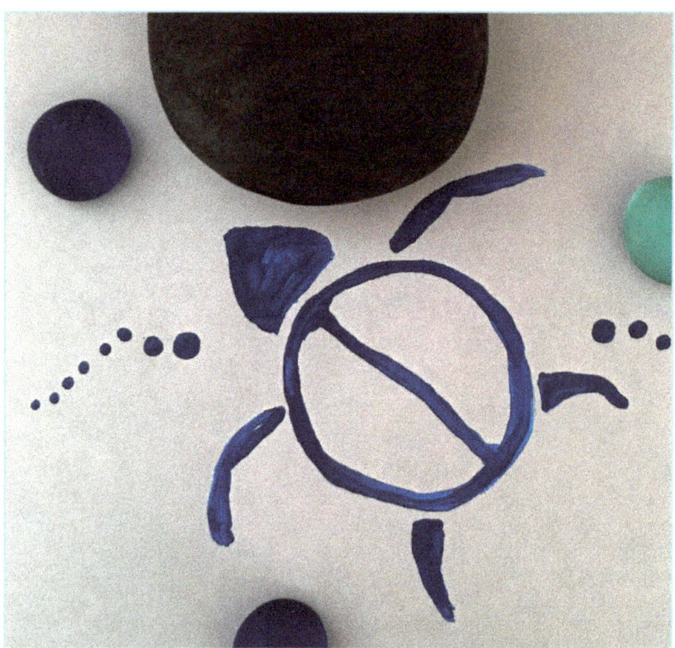

1 Determine a color scheme. This sea turtle petroglyph will use blue ocean tones. Practice your design on page 67 until you arrive at the shape and contours you like.

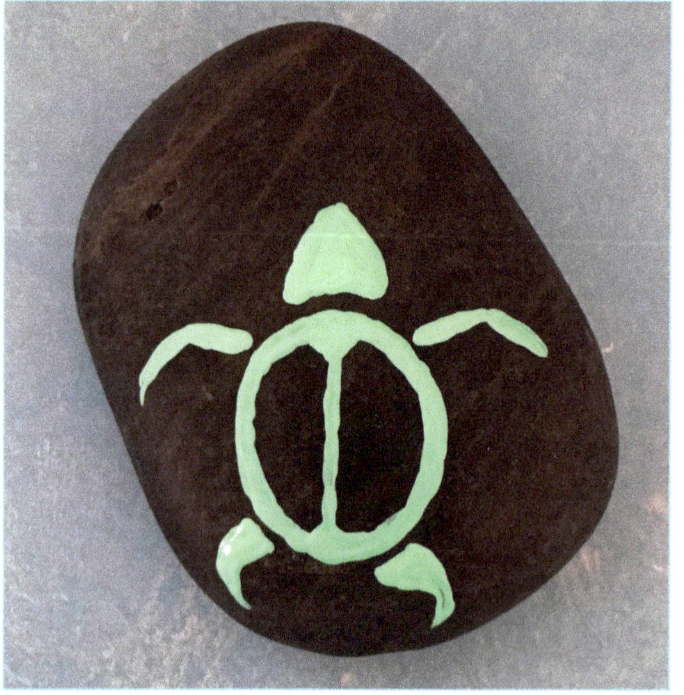

2 Find a starting point for your petroglyph using the size, surface texture, and shape of the rock to guide your design. Your sea turtle design can be simple or more detailed. You can add dots, stripes, or other geometric designs to the turtle's back, or let the color of the stone determine the turtle's color.

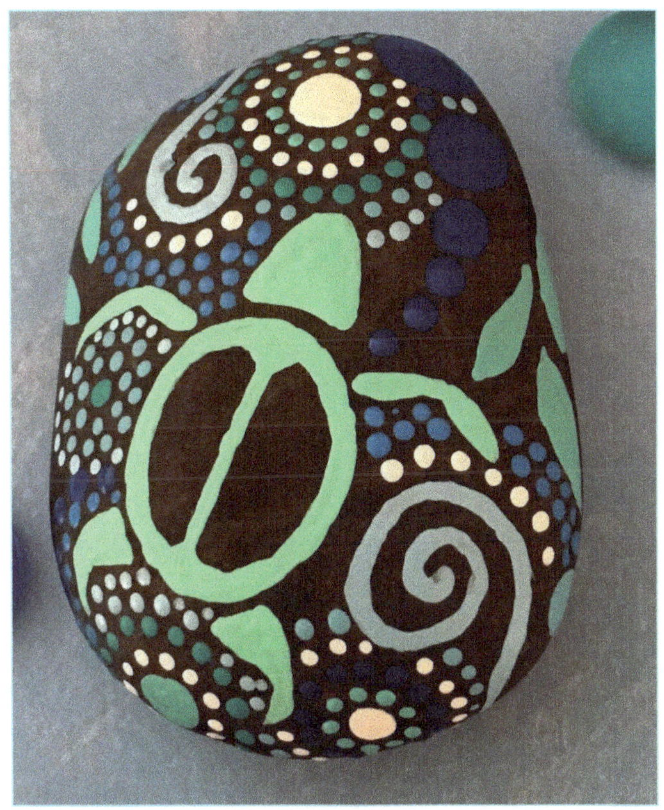

3 Once your sea turtle petroglyph is set, you can complete your rock design using other petroglyph symbols such as sun designs, spirals, fish, or dots. Natural elements such as swirls of water or kelp are also nice additions.

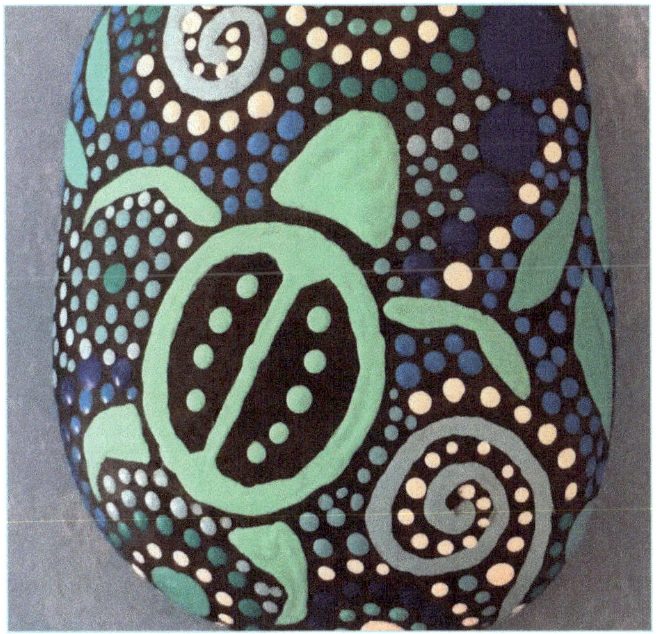

4 Be very careful to let each section of the paint dry completely before handling the rock to access other sections. Most acrylic paint takes up to 10 minutes to dry enough for handling.

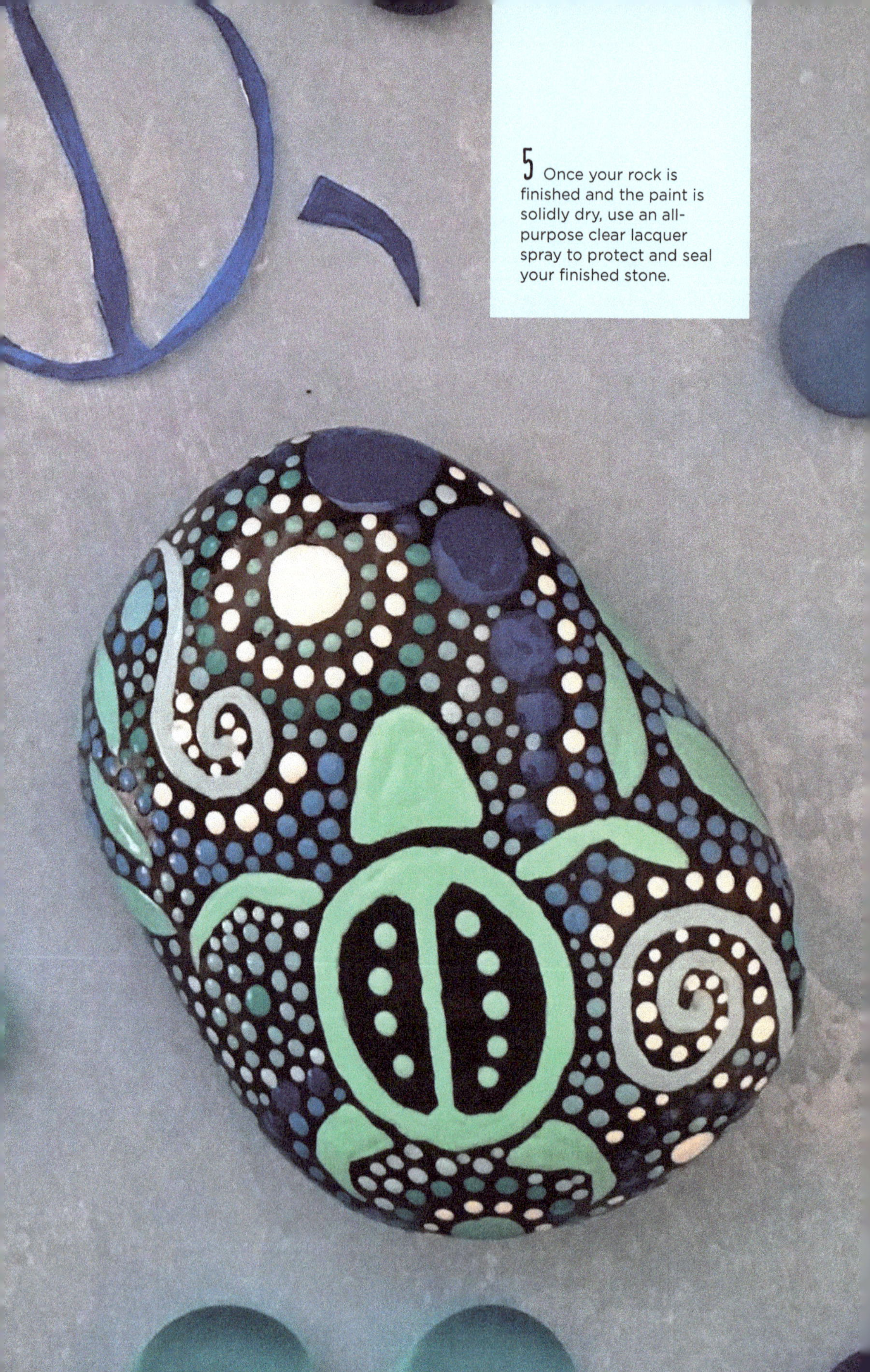

5 Once your rock is finished and the paint is solidly dry, use an all-purpose clear lacquer spray to protect and seal your finished stone.

PRACTICE HERE

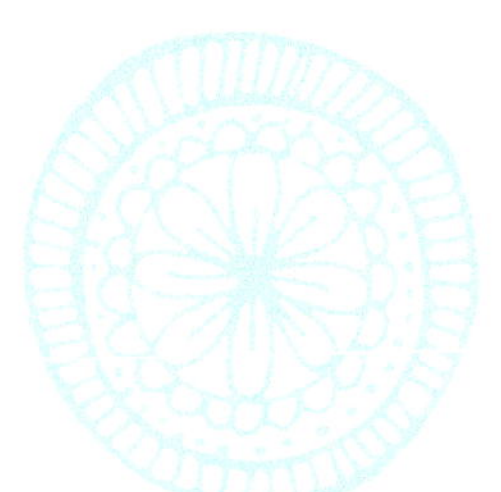

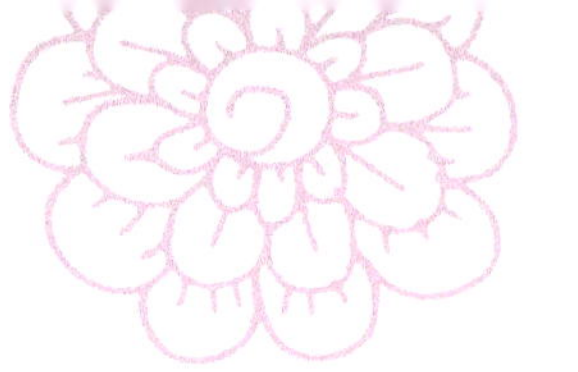

OWL

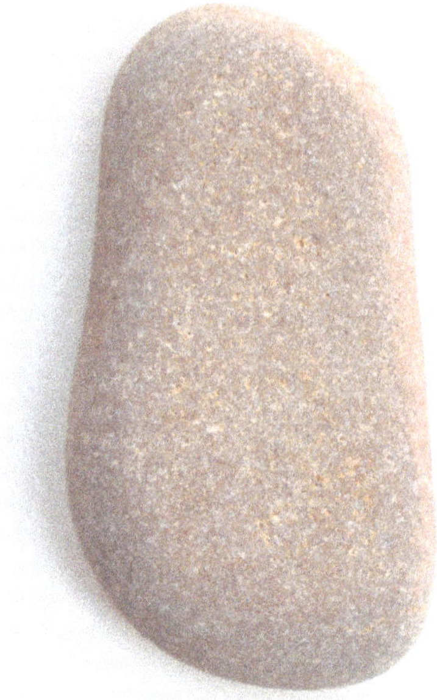

1 For this project, you will need an oval-shaped stone. A stone with a smooth surface is best because you can work directly on the natural surface of your stone.

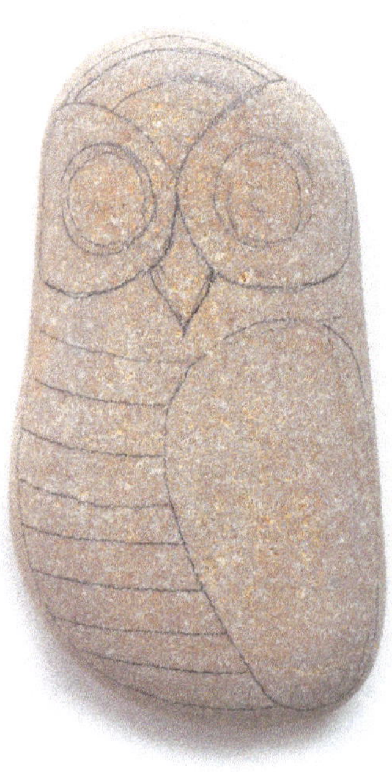

2 Start to sketch an owl on your stone with a hard-tip pencil to create clean pencil lines. Use a soft art eraser if you want to correct your design. Make a rough sketch for now; you can add details after you fill in the larger parts with color.

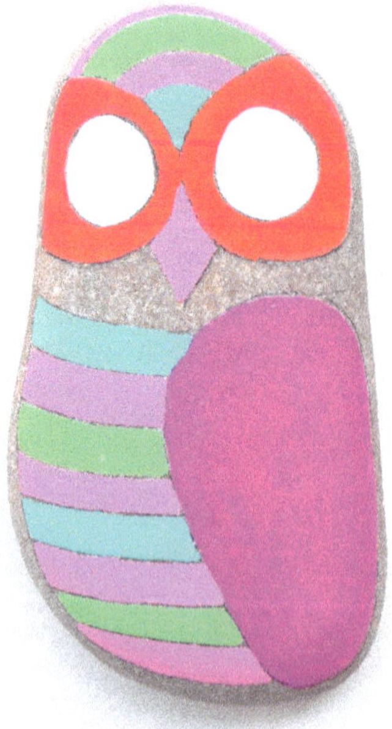

3 Begin to fill your design with acrylic paint or inks. Use thin, round brushes to work in small spaces. Choose bright, bold colors to give a contrast to your design.

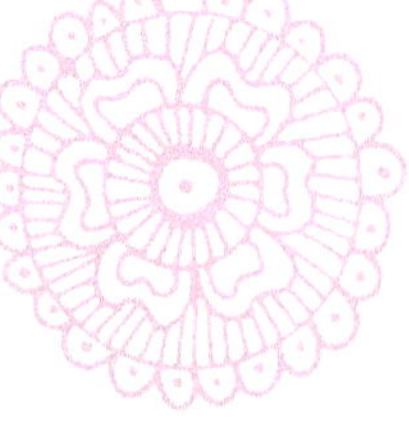

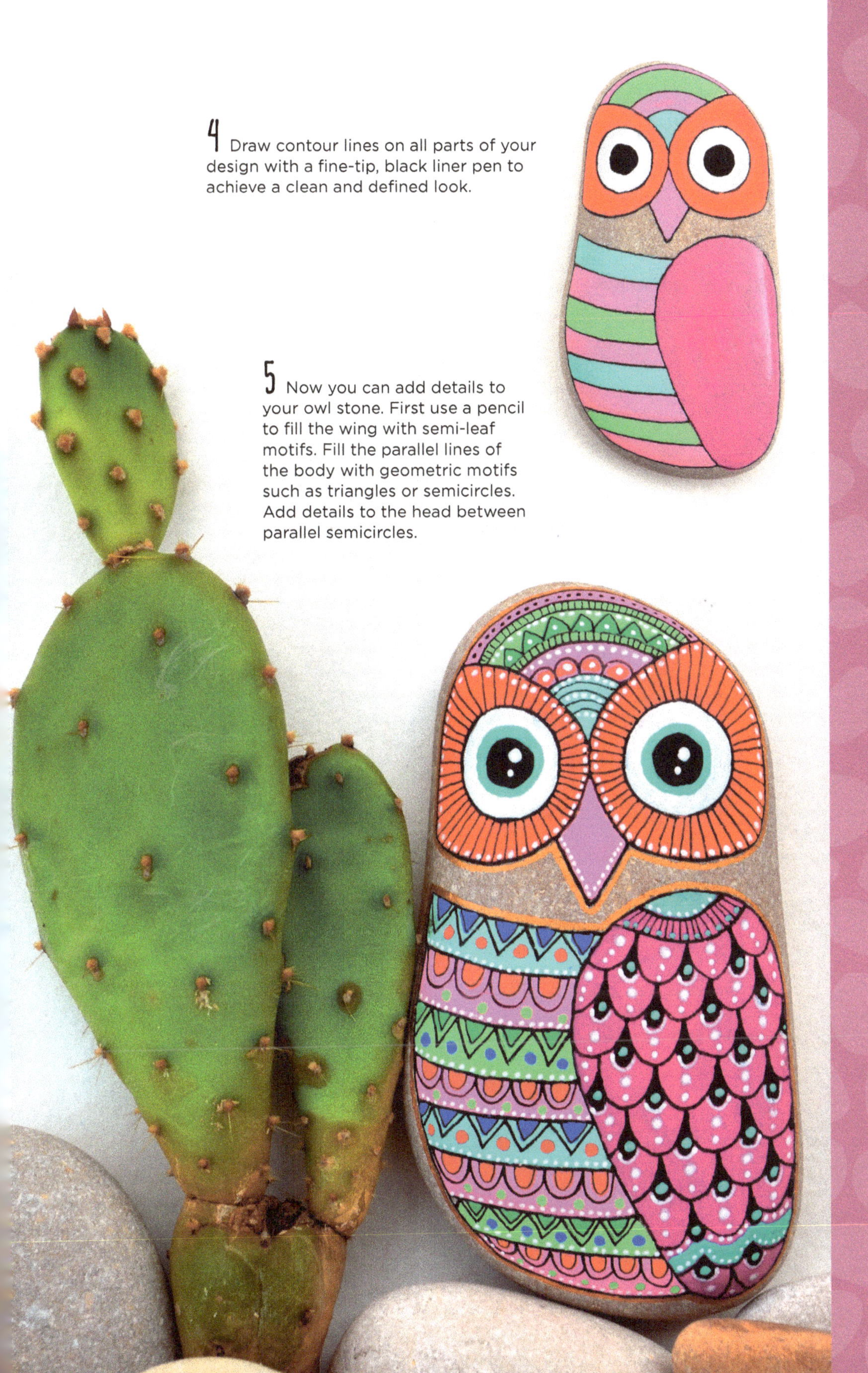

4 Draw contour lines on all parts of your design with a fine-tip, black liner pen to achieve a clean and defined look.

5 Now you can add details to your owl stone. First use a pencil to fill the wing with semi-leaf motifs. Fill the parallel lines of the body with geometric motifs such as triangles or semicircles. Add details to the head between parallel semicircles.

FOX

Animal stones are a perfect choice for a children's room. They are playful, colorful, and the possibilities are endless. This mischievous fox would make the perfect companion for a playroom!

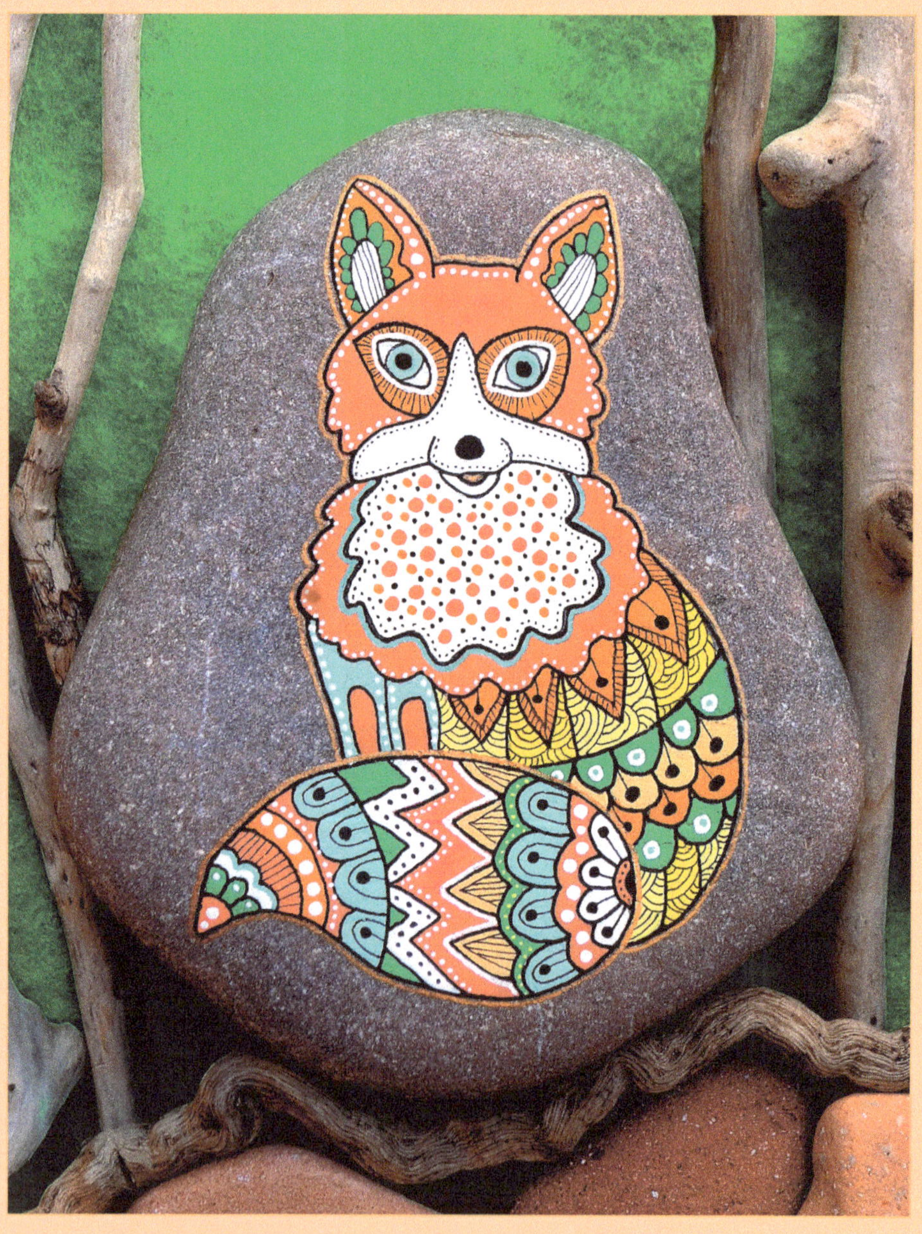

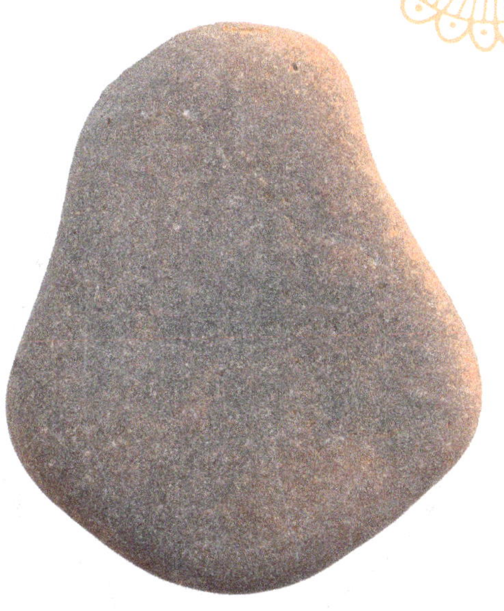

1 Find a stone that fits the shape of a fox design. The shape of this stone lends itself well to the design of a sitting fox.

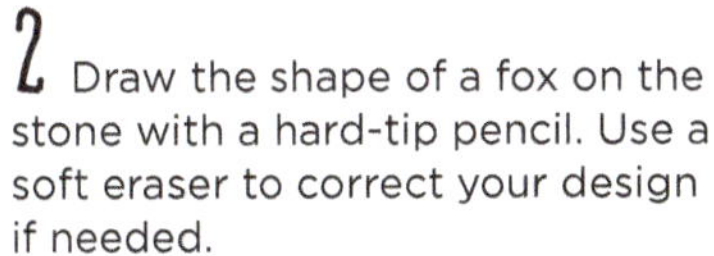

2 Draw the shape of a fox on the stone with a hard-tip pencil. Use a soft eraser to correct your design if needed.

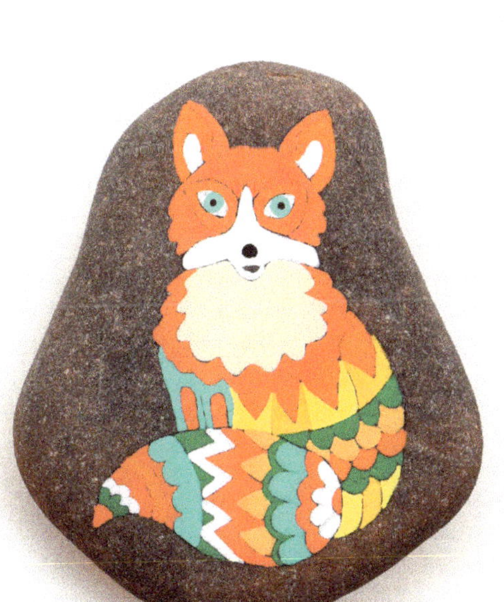

3 Use a thin, round brush to fill the small spaces of your design with color. Bright and bold colors will add contrast to the natural stone.

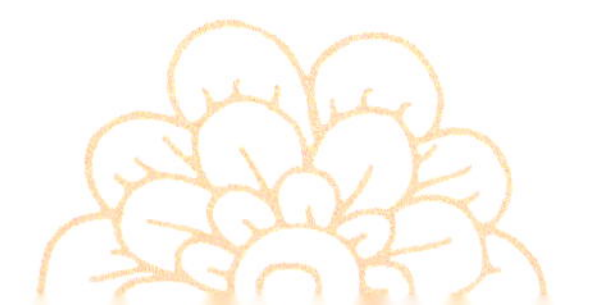

4 Draw contour lines across your design with an extra-fine black liner pen to create a clean and defined look.

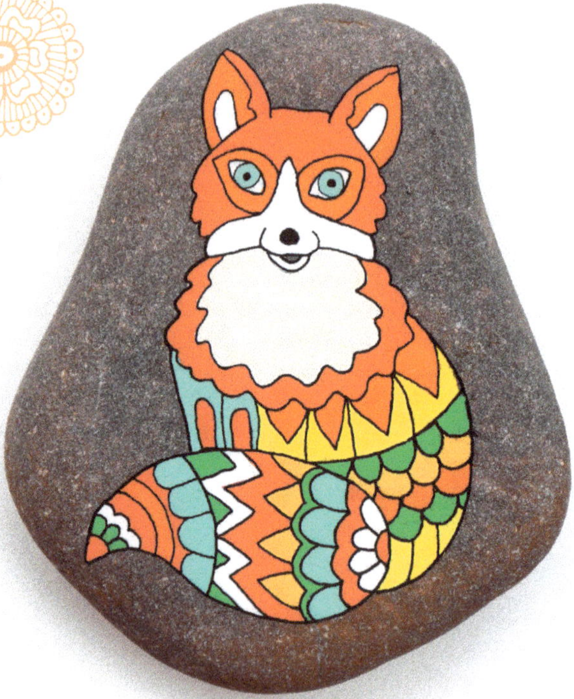

5 Use black liner pens and white paint pens to add a whimsical appearance to your stone by adding extra lines and dots to stylize parts of your design.

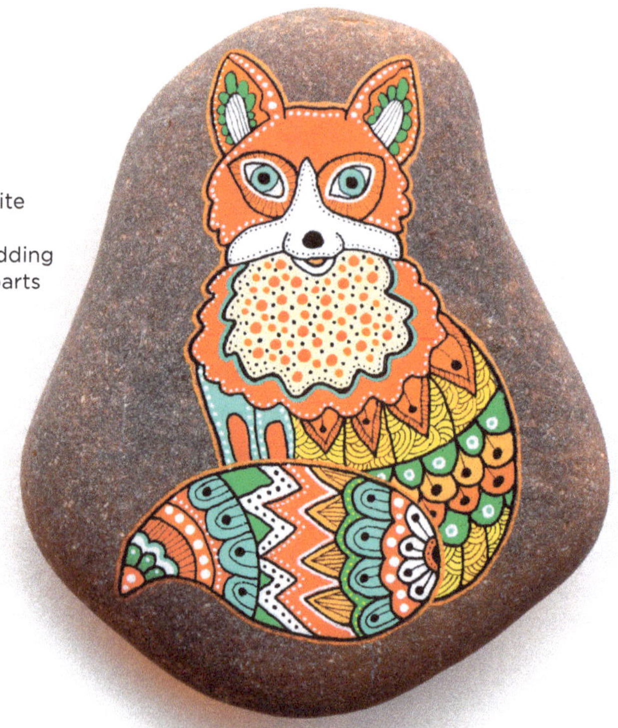

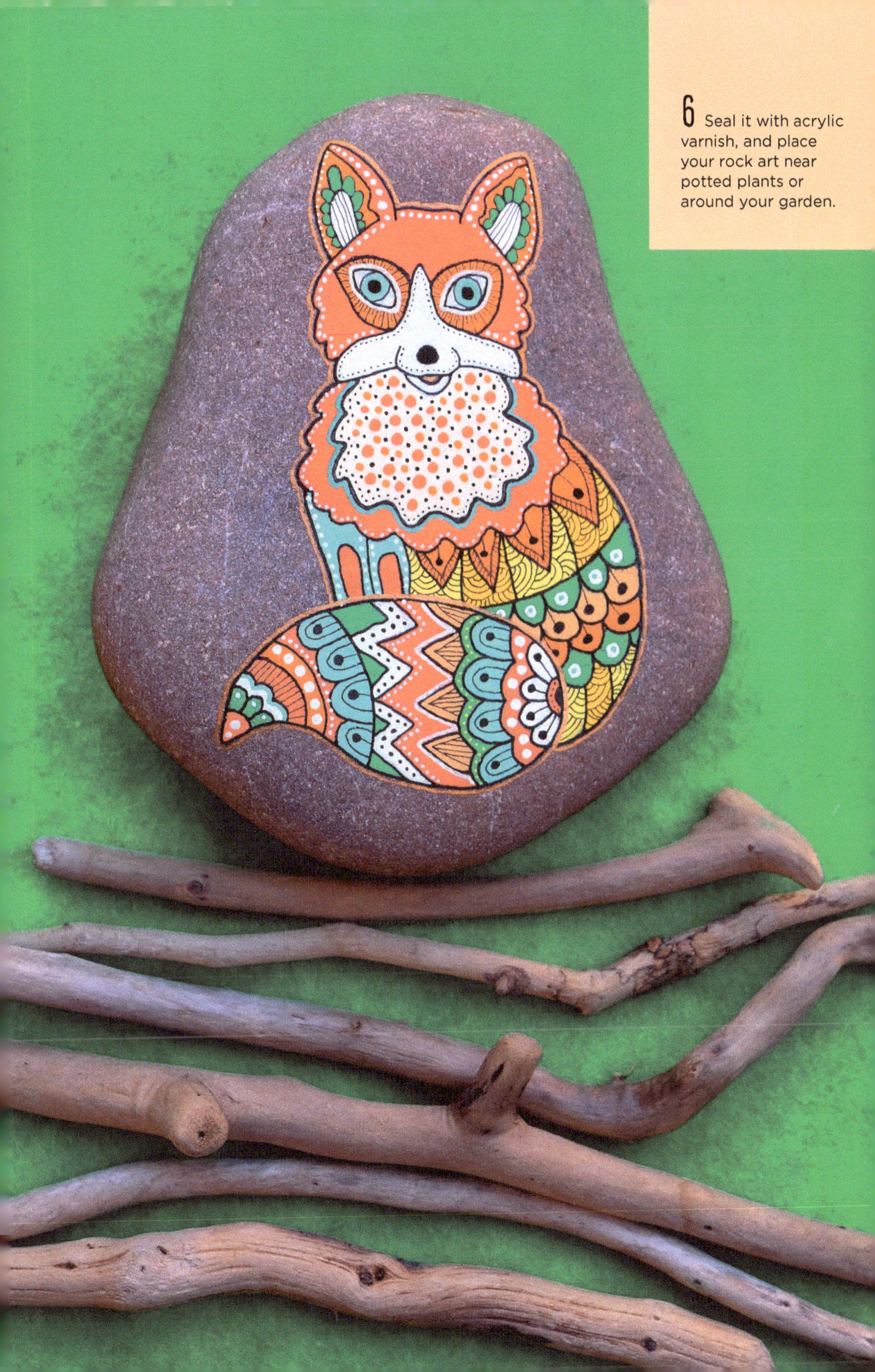

6 Seal it with acrylic varnish, and place your rock art near potted plants or around your garden.

FISH

Fish stones with fresh, bold sea colors will give you a calm, meditative feeling. Try creating a row of fish stones with different colors for a decorative shelf in your home.

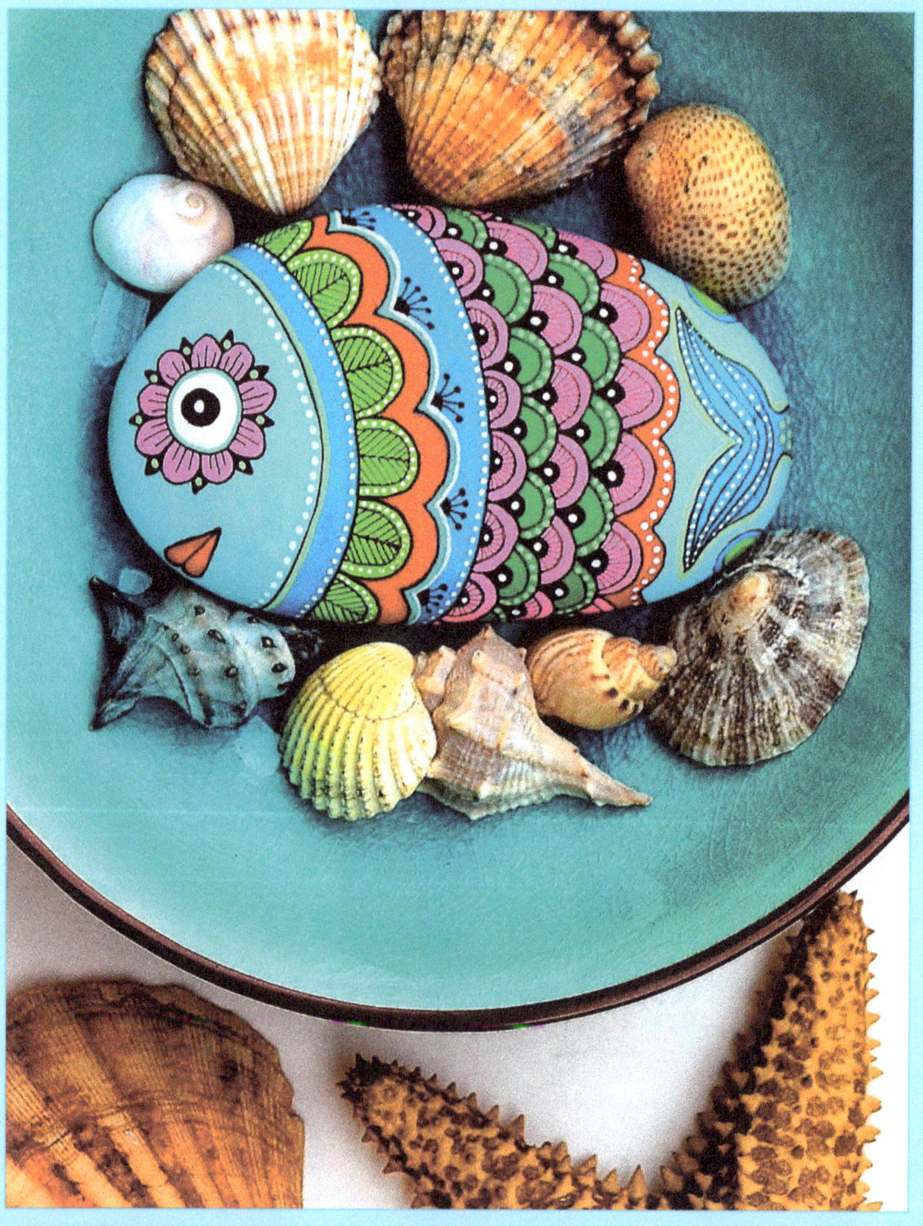

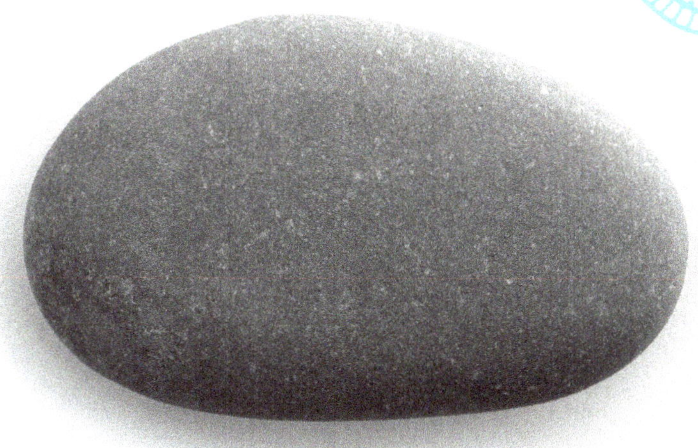

1 Look for a smooth, flat stone with an oval shape that will allow you to work directly on the natural surface of the stone.

2 Start your sketch on the stone. For this fish design, separate the head and body of the fish with vertical, curved lines. Add a flower-shaped eye to the head. For the body, add semiovals to stylize the scales of the fish, and draw a tail.

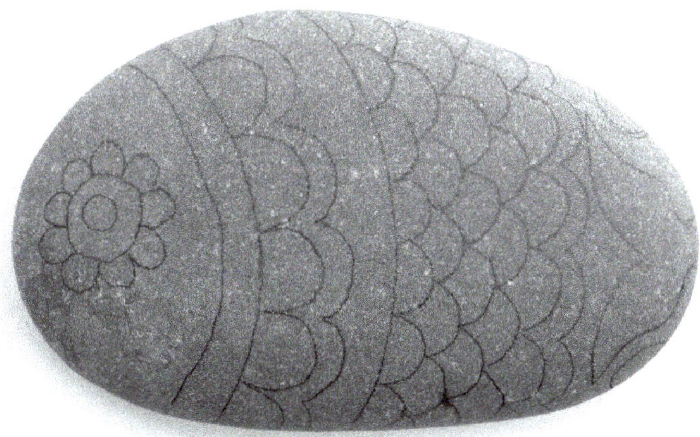

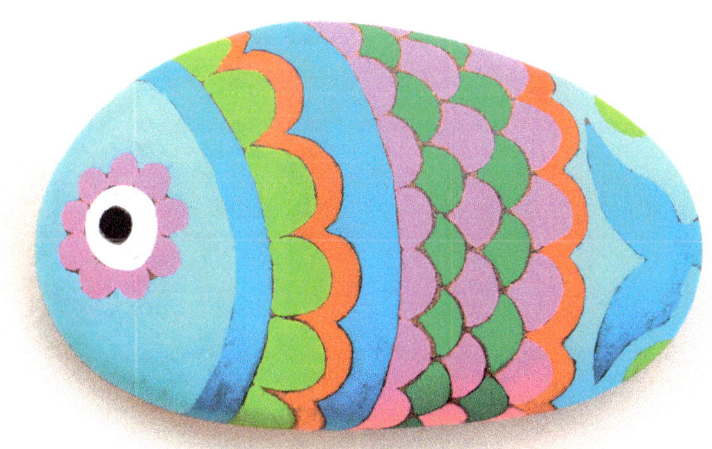

3 Begin to fill your design with color. You can use acrylic paint or inks. Use a thin, round brush to color in small spaces. Choose bright, bold colors that give contrast to your design.

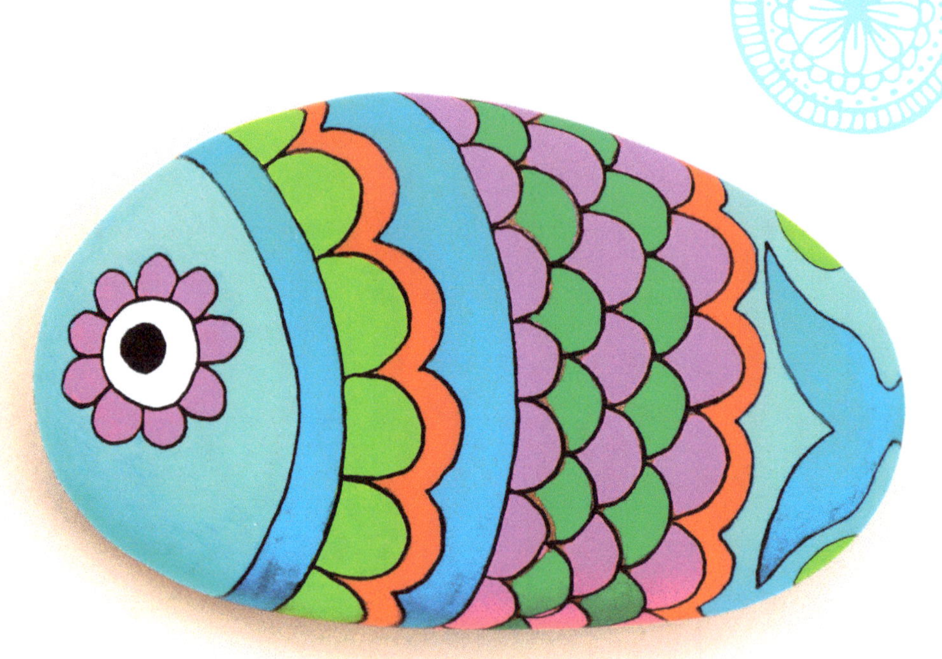

4 Draw contour lines to all parts of your design with an extra-fine black liner pen to obtain a clean and defined look.

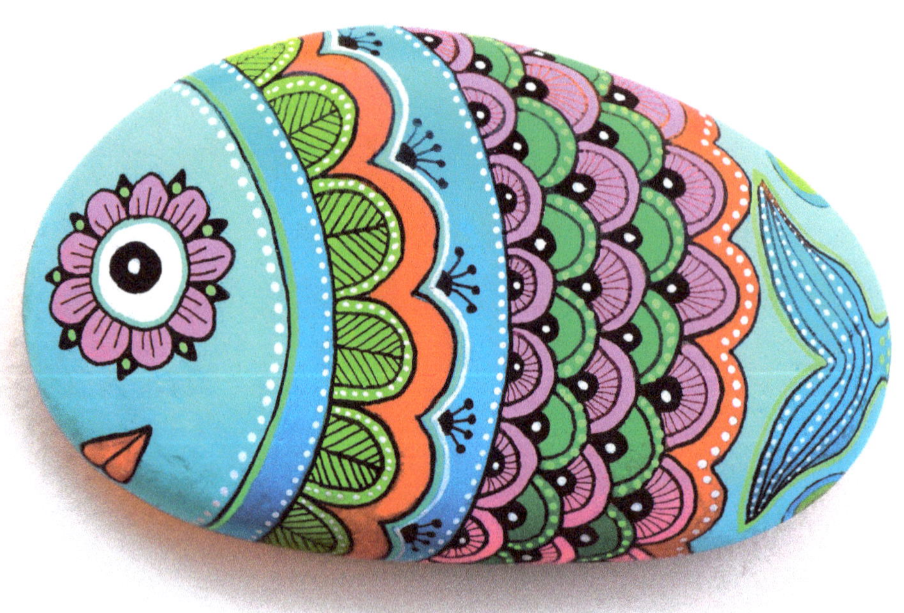

5 Use black liner pens and white paint pens to add extra lines and dots on the eye, scales, and tail.

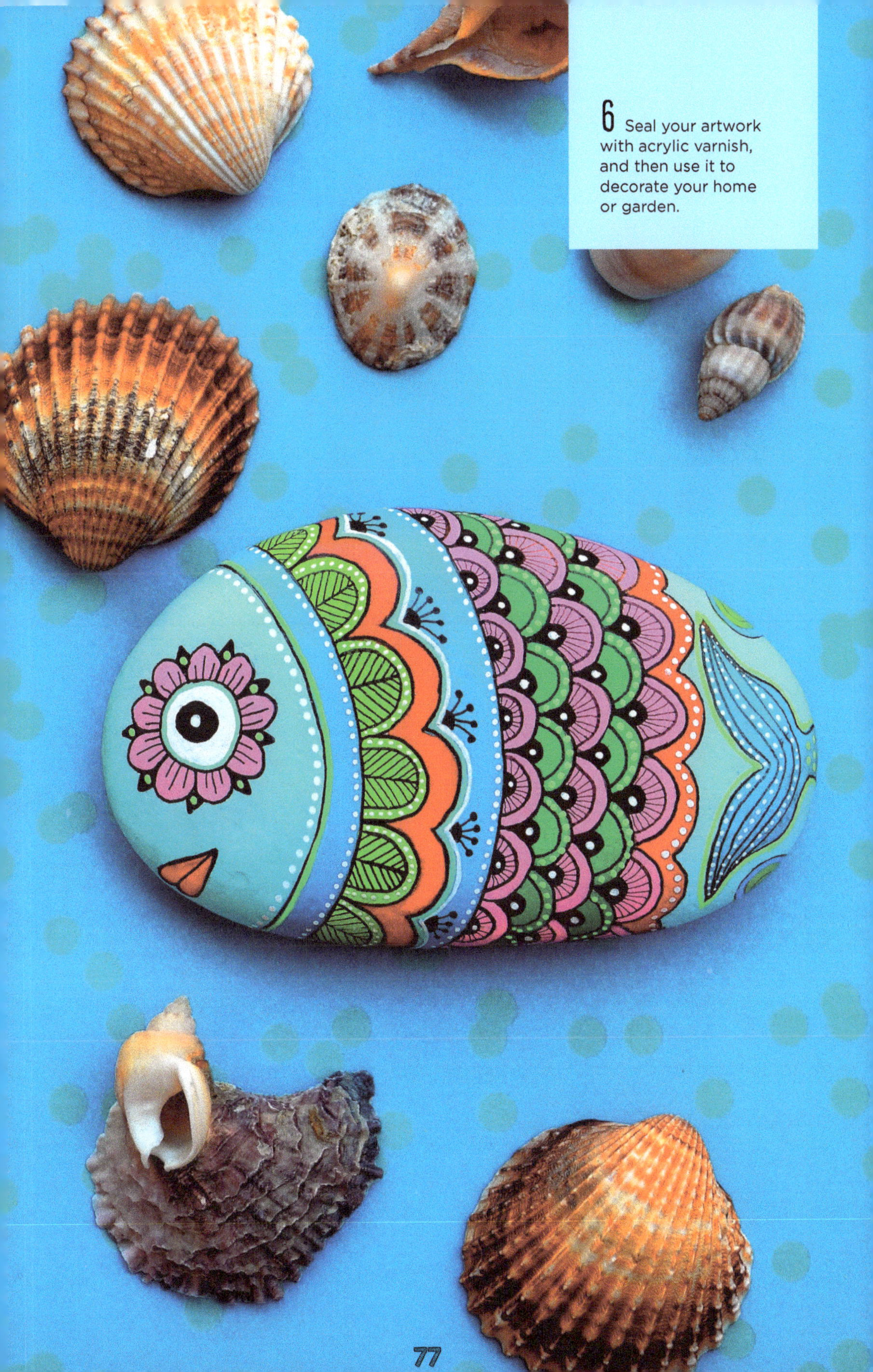

6 Seal your artwork with acrylic varnish, and then use it to decorate your home or garden.

PRACTICE HERE

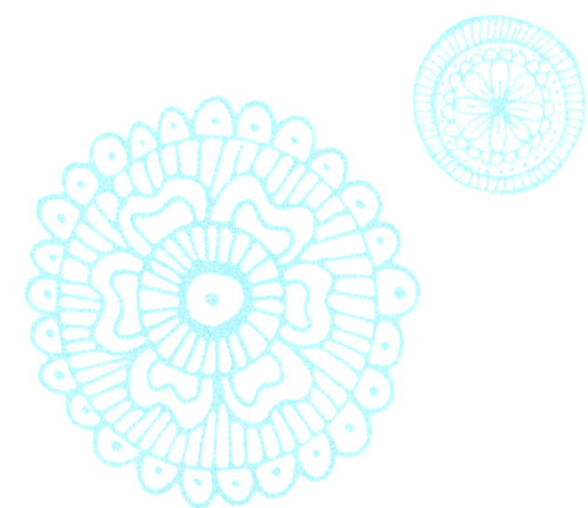

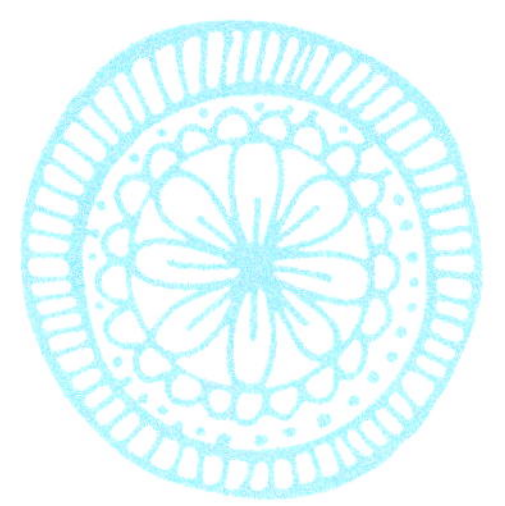

BIRD BATH

Brilliantly colored birds and fish are beautiful to look at and fun to paint. Fish can be adapted to almost any rock, but it's exciting when you discover perfect fish-shaped rocks! The best bird-shaped rocks are round at the head and thinner toward the tail feathers, although simple oval rocks can work as well. When you see how fun and easy these adorable animals are to create, you'll want to make a whole school of fish and an entire flock of birds!

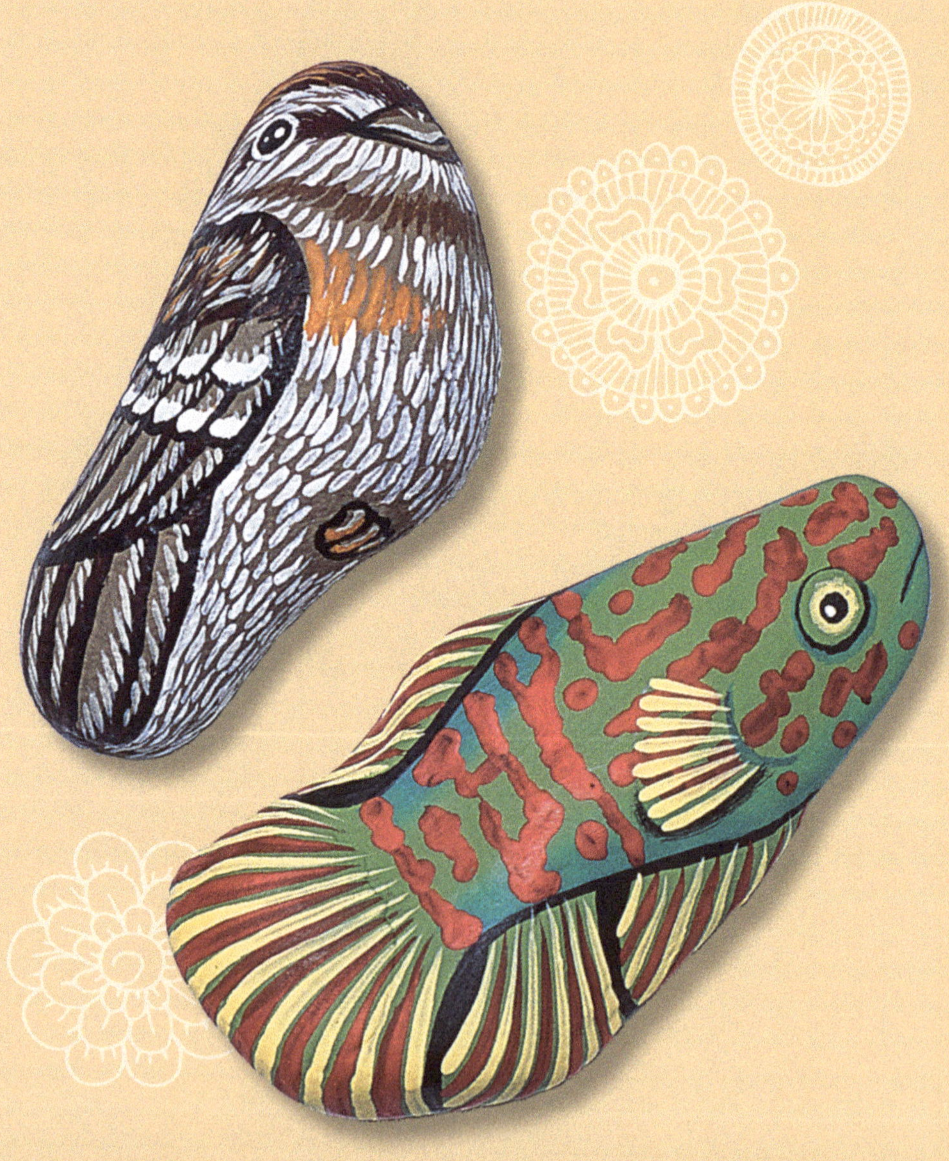

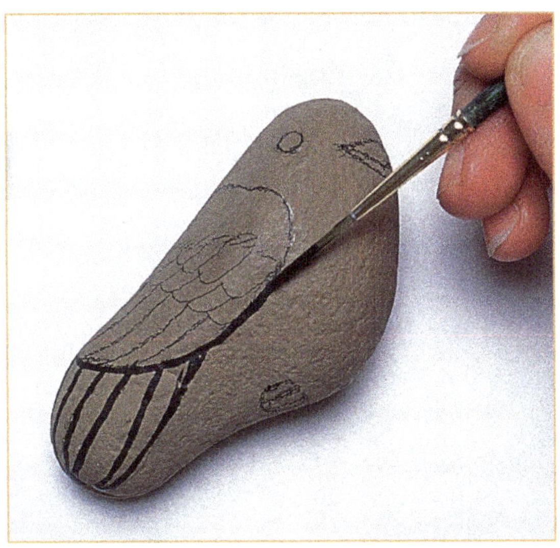

1 The rock shown here is an excellent shape for a sparrow: The back curves slightly, the head is round, and the belly protrudes. Using a wide, flat brush, cover the rock with a beige base coat. When it's dry, lightly draw the sparrow with a colored pencil (or transfer the pattern on page 125). The length of the wings and tail feathers will depend on the shape of your rock, but always keep the eyes and beak fairly close to the top of the head. Using a liner brush and black paint, outline the entire design.

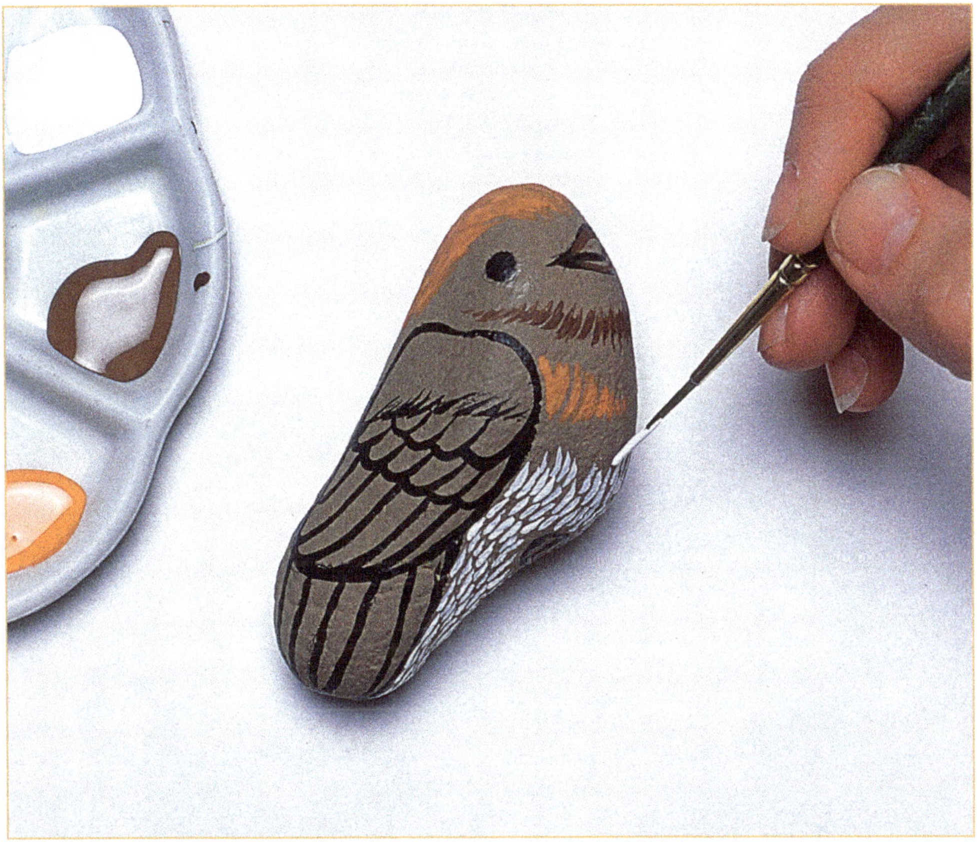

2 Fill in the eye with black. Then use a liner brush loaded with medium brown to paint a thin shadow at the neck of the sparrow with thin, short strokes. Add a fine line inside the upper and lower outlines of the beak. Cover the crest of the head with a bright orange, starting at the middle of the beak and tapering down between the top of the wings. Add a triangular orange patch that extends from each wing into the upper chest. Use white to cover the rest of the chest and head with thin, short strokes, but leave enough space between the strokes for the beige to show through.

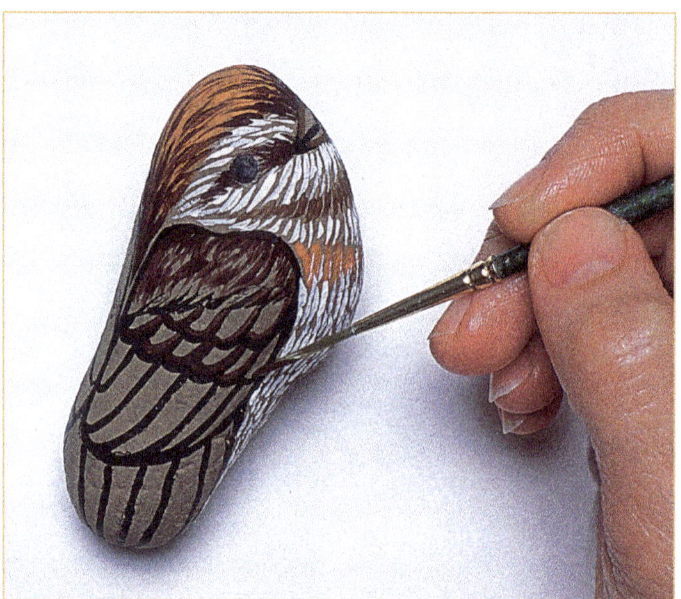

3 Using dark brown, paint feathered strokes into the orange crest, concentrating more at the beak and at the tops of the sparrow's wings. Add a dark brown strip from the beak to the eye, and then taper it just past the eye as it extends toward the back of the head. Add some soft, downy feathers at the tops of the wings with dark brown, and add outlines inside the black throughout the wing feathers.

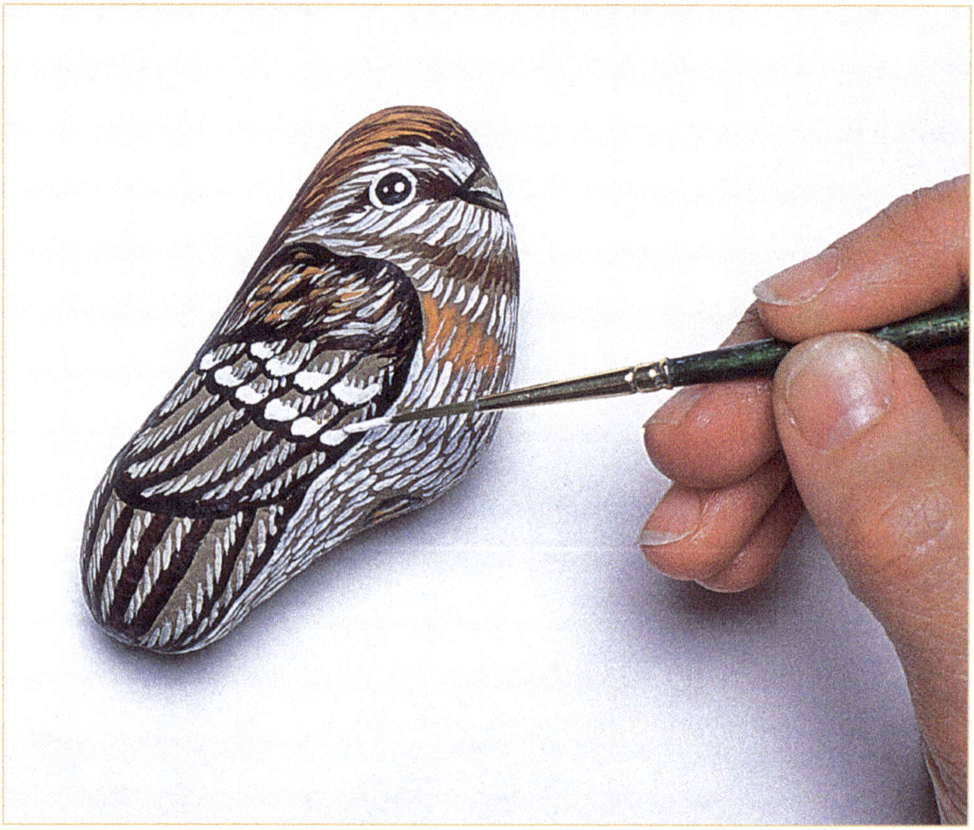

4 With a sand color, highlight the bottom edge of the upper beak and paint the nostrils. Then highlight the middles of each claw and the tops of the wings. Next paint thin, diagonal lines on the side of each feather. Paint a fine white outline around each eye, and highlight each eye with two dots of white. Paint solid white tips on the top two rows of wing feathers, and add a few strokes of orange on the tops of the wings.

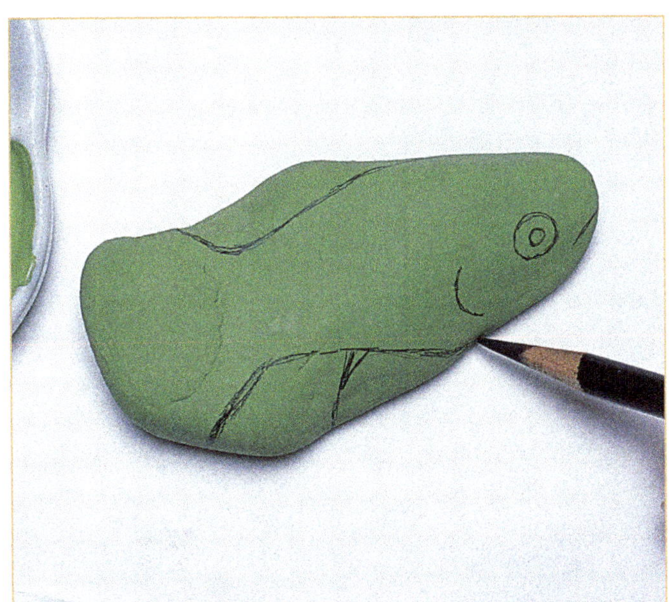

5 For the fish, first cover the rock with a base coat. Let it dry completely, and then sketch the design on your chosen rock with a colored pencil. Use the natural contours of the rock as a guide for your design, and refer to an encyclopedia or the Internet for types of fish to copy.

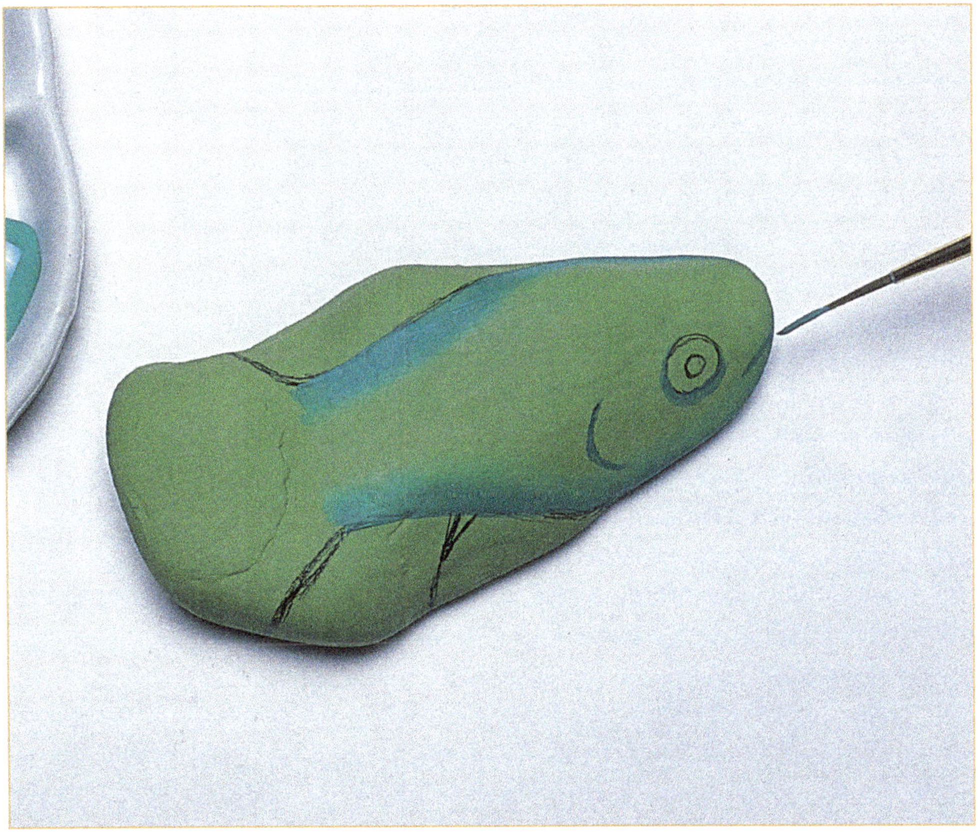

6 Double-load a small, flat brush with medium green and blue-green. Paint a shadow along the top and bottom of the body, flipping the brush so that blue-green is always on the outside. Switch to a liner brush and paint blue-green lines at the gill, the mouth, and around the eye; paint a thicker shadow line under the eye.

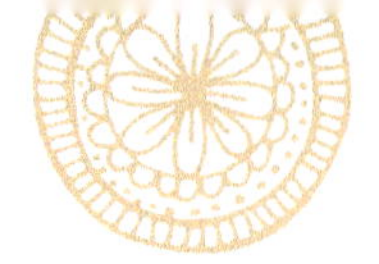

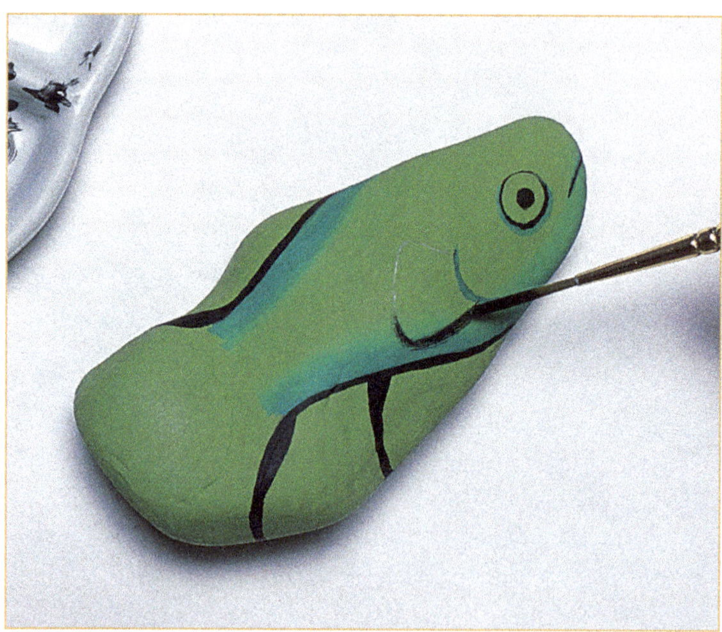

7 Paint black outlines around the fins, and define the top and bottom of the body. Paint black spaces between the fins where they separate. Paint the eyeball black, and define the shadow underneath the eye with a thin, black line inside the blue-green. Lightly pencil in the shape of the side fin, and then drybrush a dark shadow underneath it with black.

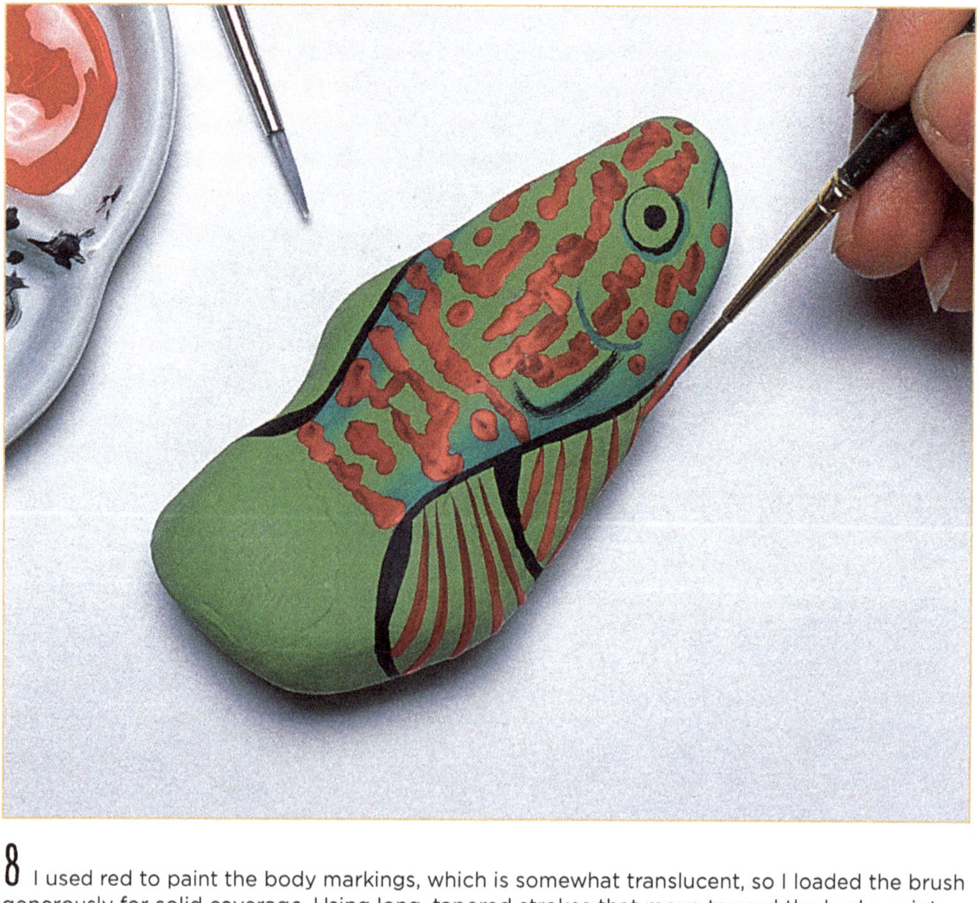

8 I used red to paint the body markings, which is somewhat translucent, so I loaded the brush generously for solid coverage. Using long, tapered strokes that move toward the body, paint red lines on all the fins. Make sure to leave enough room between these strokes for another set of lines.

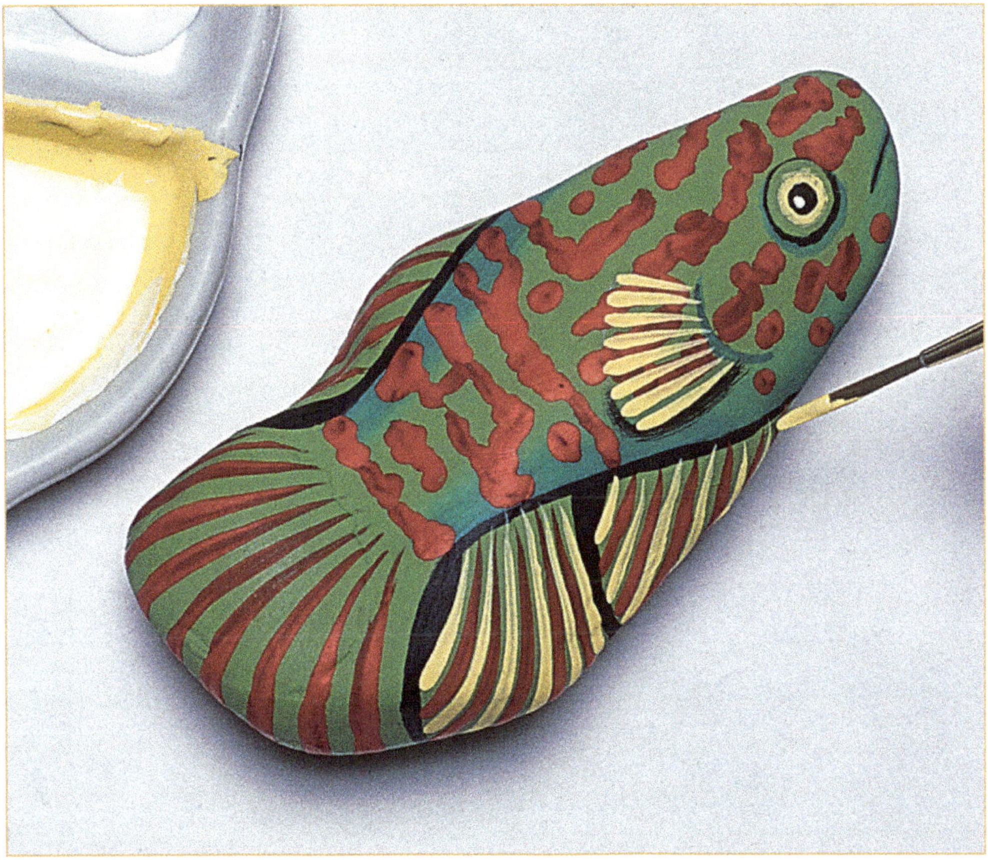

9 With a mix of yellow and white, paint the second set of fin lines between the first red set. Then paint the side fin lines, tapering toward the gill. Paint around the eye with the yellow-white, and add a white highlight to the back of the eyeball.

If the fish rocks will be in water, spray them first with several coats of clear acrylic sealer. (It's also a good idea to seal the bird rocks if they will be displayed outdoors.) Be sure that the sealer you use is safe for animals. Then you can place the fish in a shallow pond or find a special outdoor perch for your new feathered friends! See page 125 for a detailed bird template.

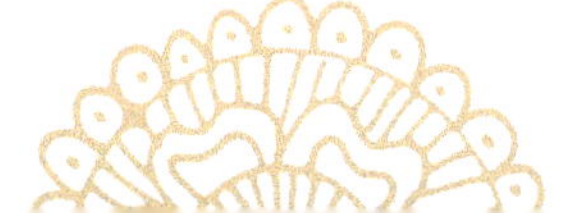

NOAH'S ARK

Tiny animals capture the heart in a big way. To create a cohesive look for Noah and his animals, try to choose very smooth rocks of the same relative size. The key to painting small areas and fine details is to use a light touch with the brush and to simplify the techniques. For this project, there are five miniature creatures, but you can try others as well—after all, the ark supposedly housed them all!

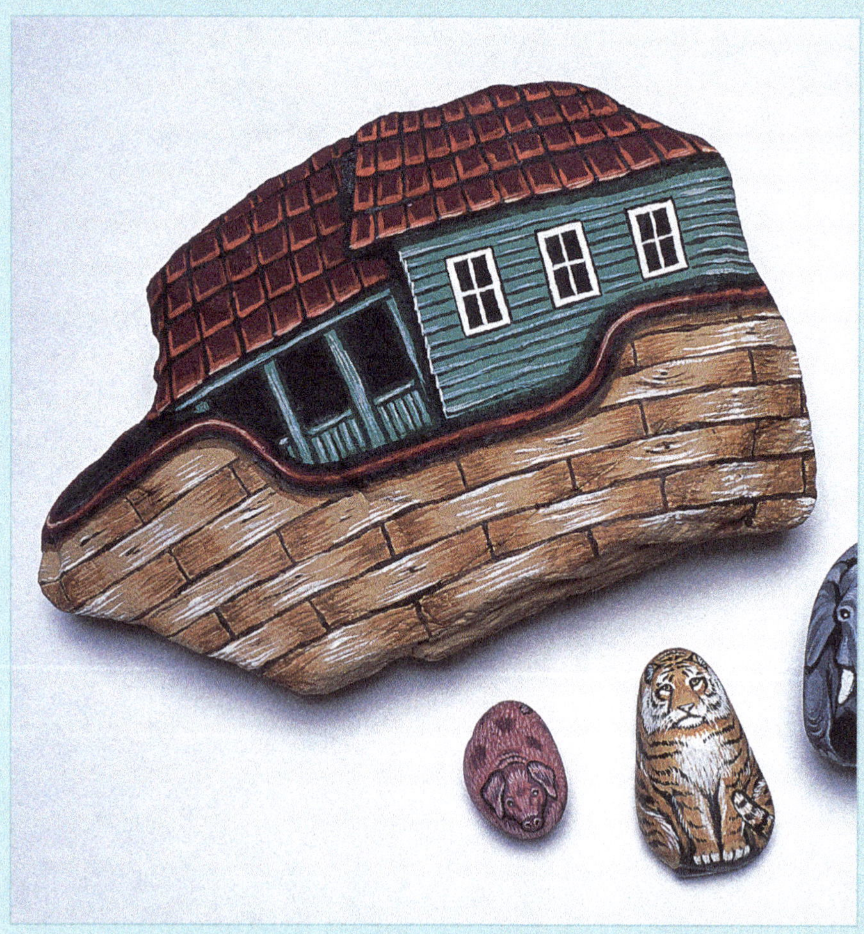

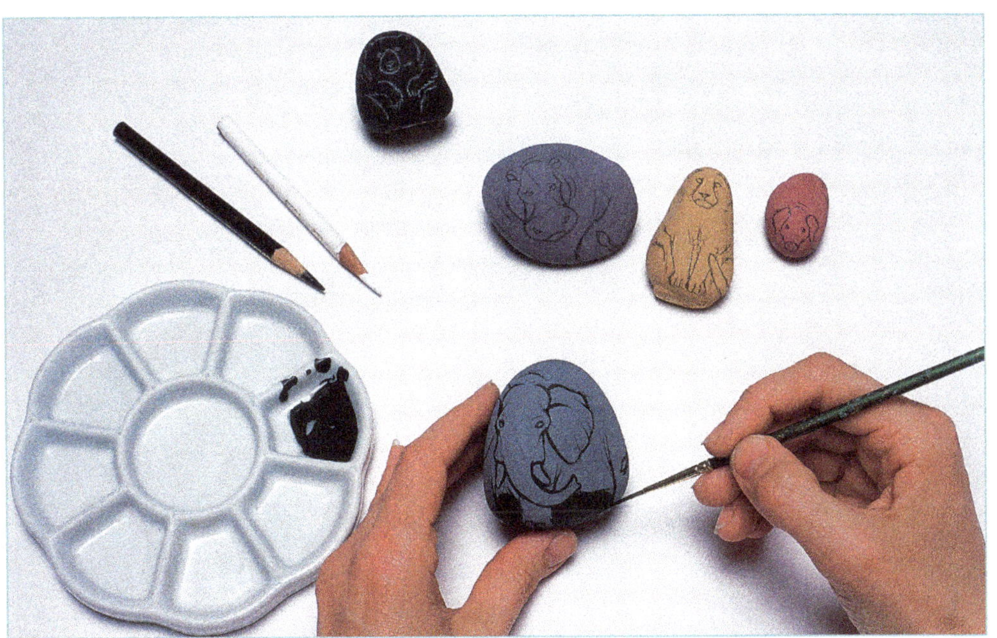

1 Moving clockwise from the top left, you can see the bear, hippopotamus, tiger, pig, and elephant. To begin, paint the base colors on each rock. For the elephant, hippopotamus, and pig, choose a medium color that can be shaded with a darker tone and highlighted with a lighter one. Paint the bear black. For the tiger, use a yellow-orange beige. With the tip of a liner brush and a light touch, paint the black outline designs of all of the animals but the bear. (See the animal templates on page 126.)

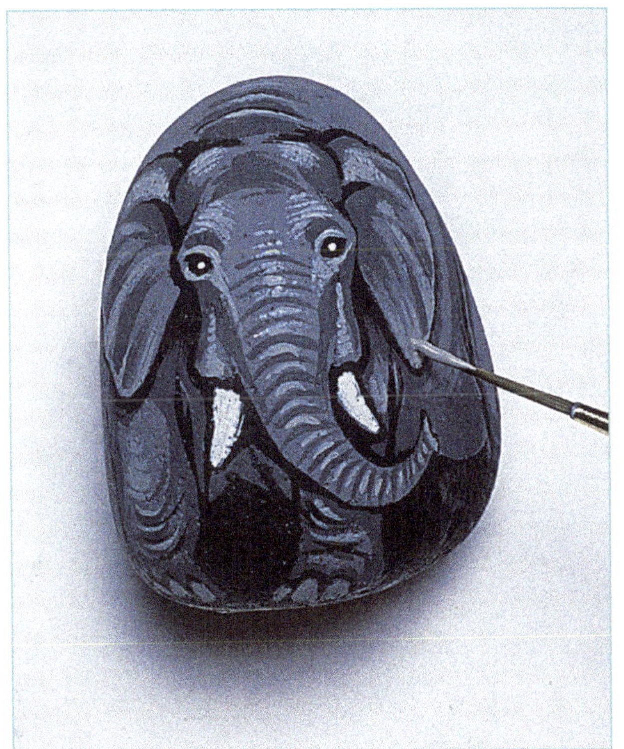

2 Mix a dark gray and paint shadows on the elephant, defining its contours, wrinkling the ears, and rounding the underbelly, legs, and head. Add horizontal wrinkles to the trunk. Mix a light gray and use it to add highlights (including the tail). Paint the tusks white and add a tiny white dot in each eye. Keep your strokes especially light when painting the highlights.

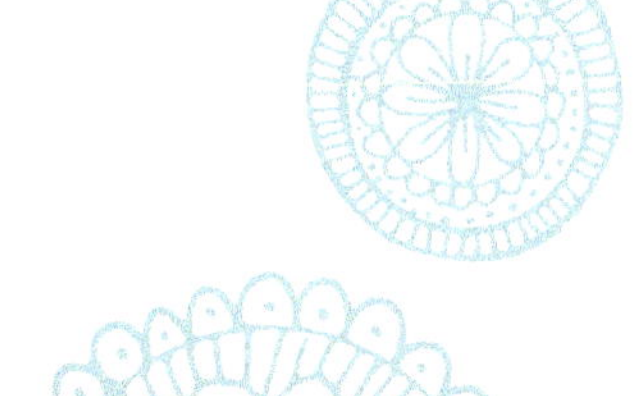

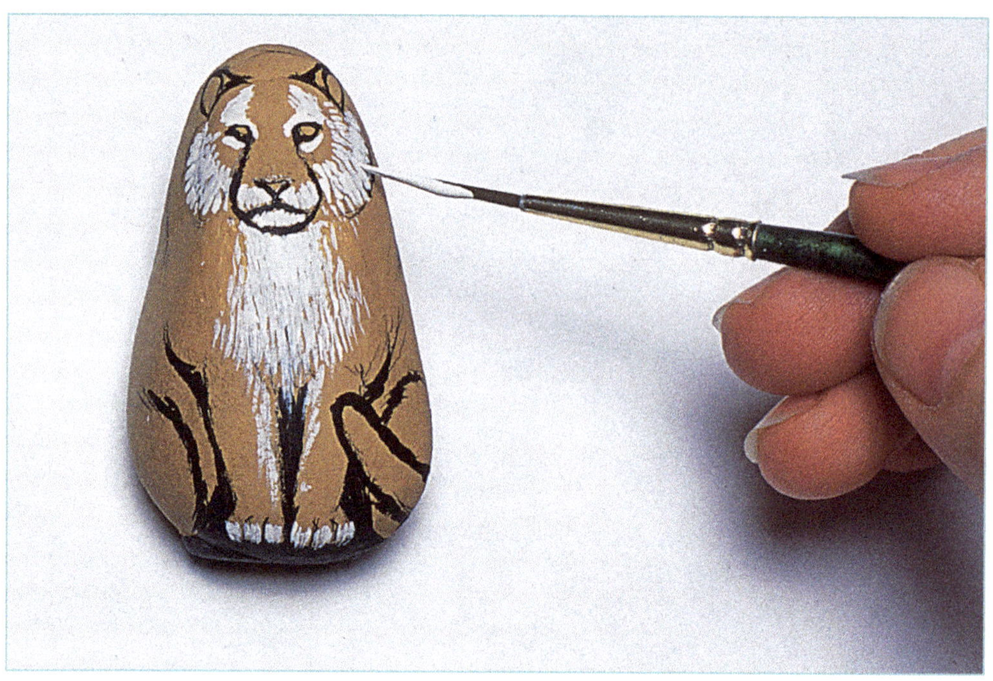

3 Using short, small strokes, paint the white fur on the tiger around the eyes, the muzzle, the sides of the head, the chest, the insides of the front legs, the toes, and the perimeter of the haunches. Add white fur to the insides of the ears and the end of the tail. Be careful not to touch the wet paint as you turn the rock to paint the other side. If you want, use a hair dryer to speed up the drying time.

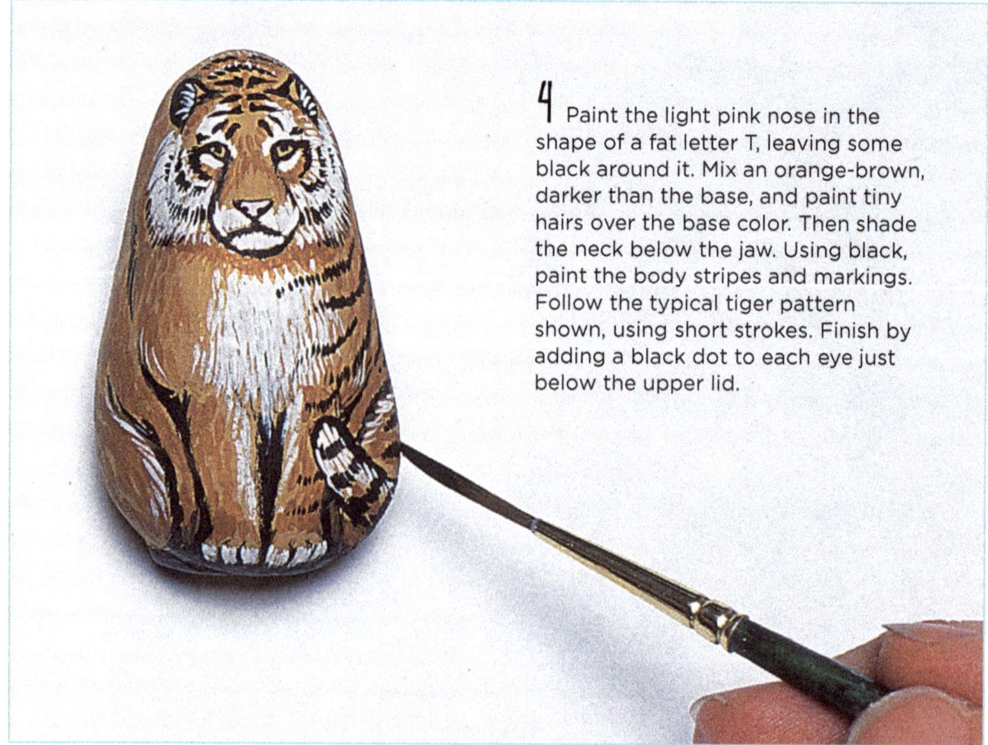

4 Paint the light pink nose in the shape of a fat letter T, leaving some black around it. Mix an orange-brown, darker than the base, and paint tiny hairs over the base color. Then shade the neck below the jaw. Using black, paint the body stripes and markings. Follow the typical tiger pattern shown, using short strokes. Finish by adding a black dot to each eye just below the upper lid.

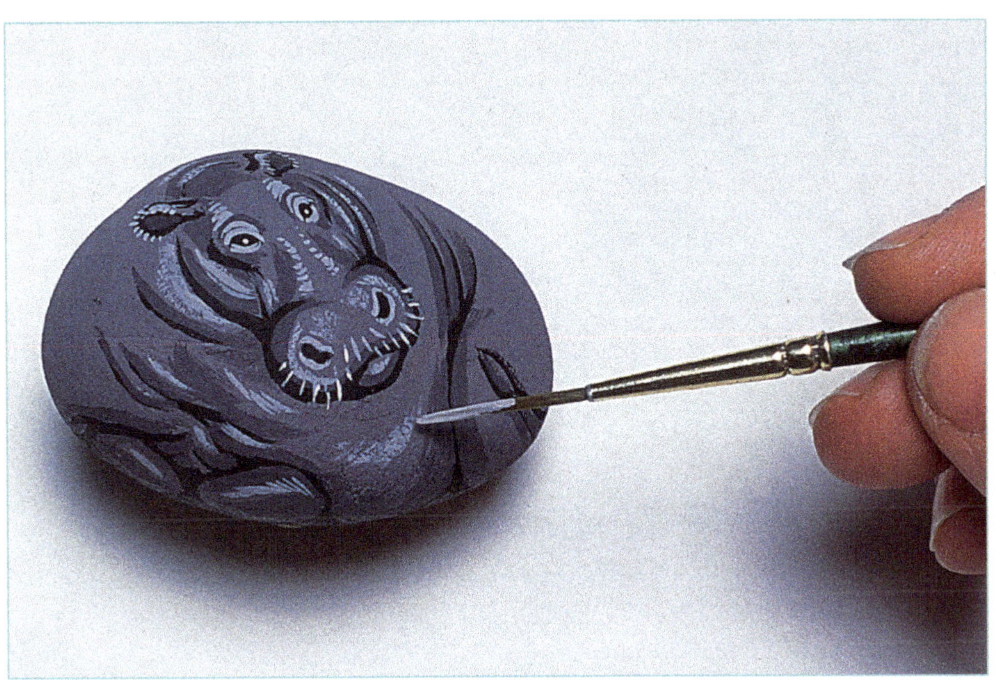

5 Use a brownish-gray for the hippo to differentiate it from the elephant, but the painting technique is the same: Start with dark gray shadows, rounding the body, head, legs, and skin folds. Darken the insides of the ears, and add highlights with a light gray. Next add a tiny white dot in each eye, spiked whiskers on the muzzle, tiny spiked hairs on the ears, and spiked fur on the end of the tail.

6 As you did for the hippo and the elephant, paint the pig's shadows first, mixing a reddish brown in the same tone as the pinkish base. Add spots to the body for interest, and paint them with lines rather than as solid blocks. Mix a lighter shade of the pinkish base for highlights. Carefully stipple in a highlight above each nostril, and highlight the head and body with short, light strokes to represent hairs. Switch to white, and add a tiny dot to each eye, a few hairs at the top of the head, and a few hairs at the end of the tail.

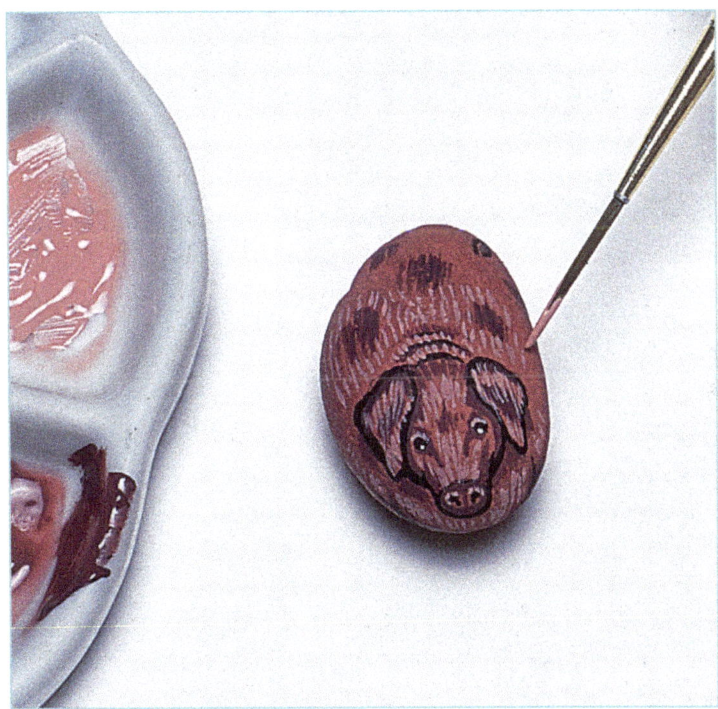

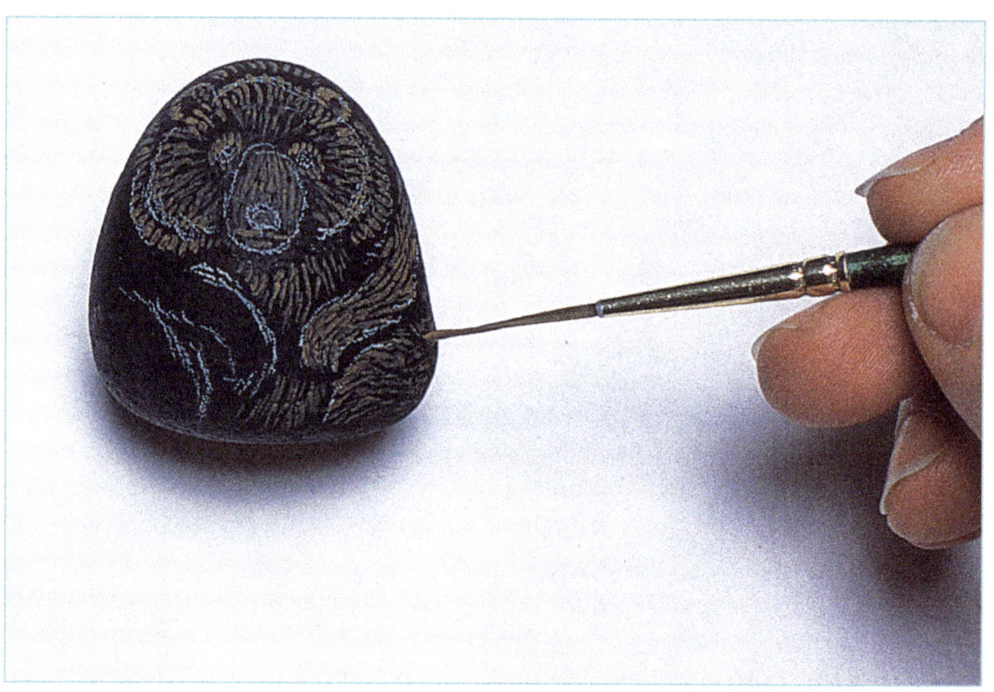

7 Using a medium to light brown, build up the contours of the bear with short strokes. Always stroke in the direction the fur would normally grow. Leave black areas between the body parts, such as the muzzle, eyes, ears, head, and legs. When the paint is dry, either carefully remove the white pencil lines with a kneaded eraser, or paint over them with black.

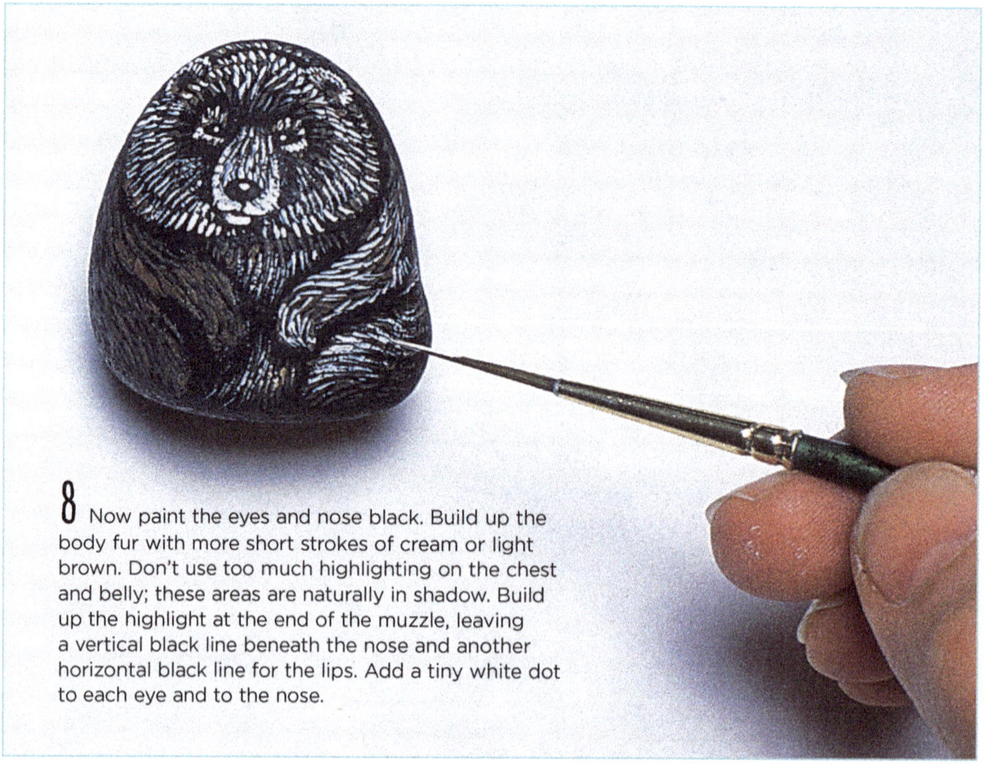

8 Now paint the eyes and nose black. Build up the body fur with more short strokes of cream or light brown. Don't use too much highlighting on the chest and belly; these areas are naturally in shadow. Build up the highlight at the end of the muzzle, leaving a vertical black line beneath the nose and another horizontal black line for the lips. Add a tiny white dot to each eye and to the nose.

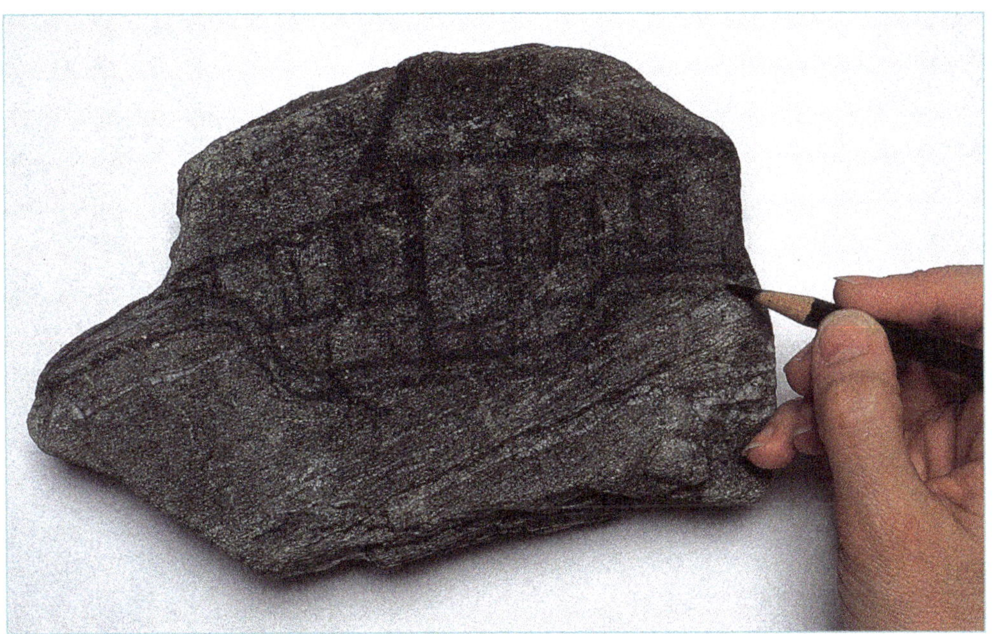

9 The rock shown here has a good ark shape, with a flat bottom for a base. It's a good idea to work out your ark design on paper before sketching it on the rock. Use the shape of the rock as a guide while you're designing, and make sure you include both a house and a barn portion. You may also want to add more animals peeking out from the barn and add trees and flowers for interest.

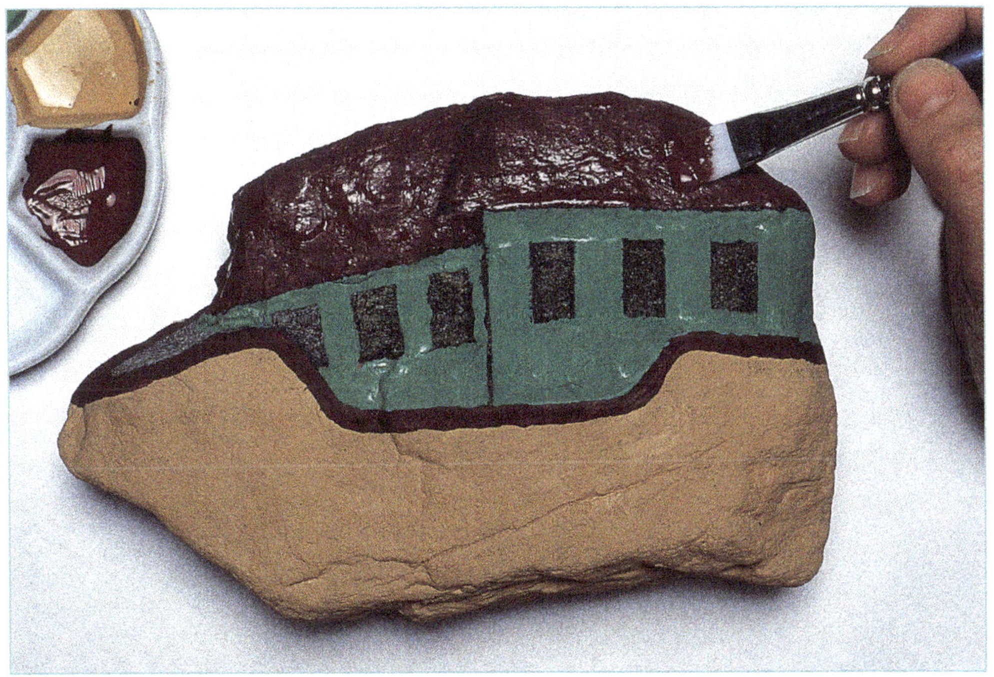

10 Block in the base colors, leaving some space between colors where a guideline is needed. If you are painting both sides, continue the colors around to the back of the rock, but leave the windows unpainted. If you are painting only one side, be sure you paint far enough around the rock so that it can be viewed from the top or the side.

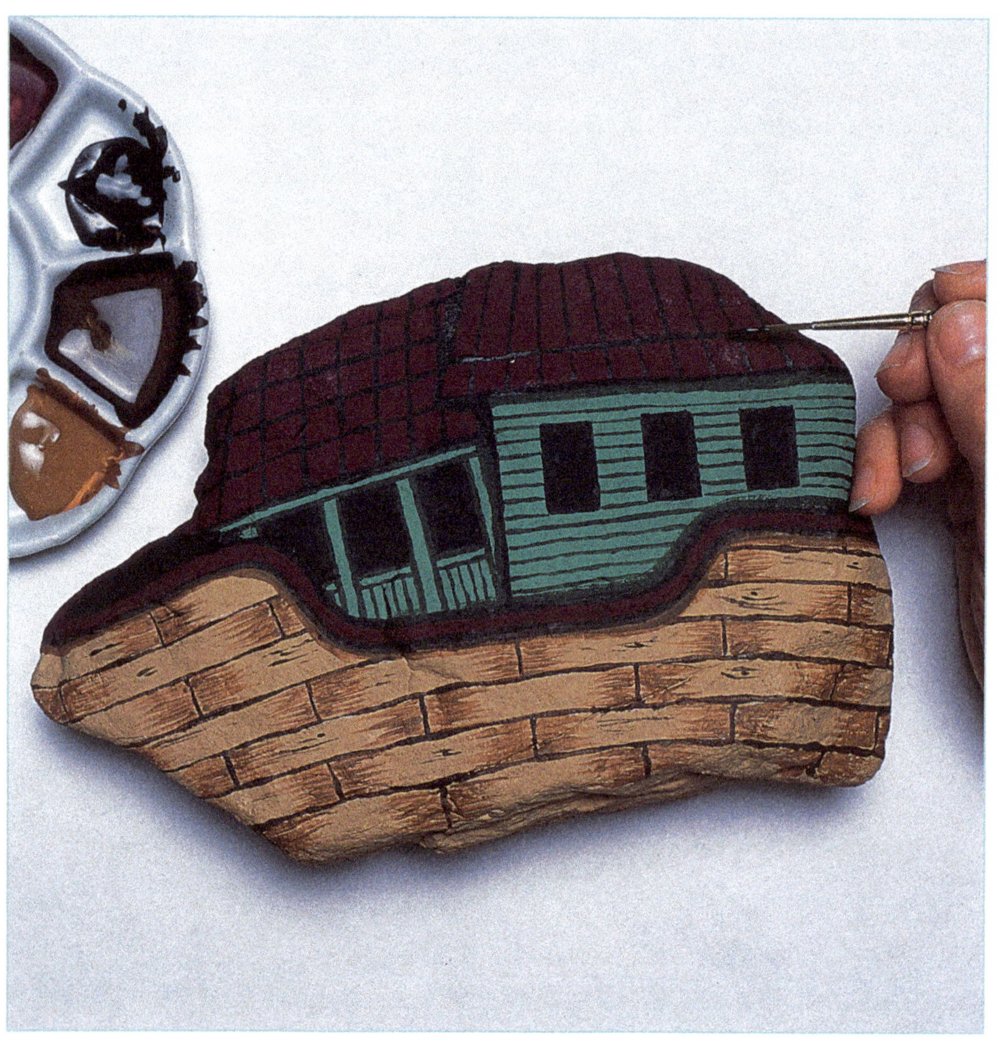

11 Outline the ark features and fill in the windows with black. Paint horizontal lines for the boards with dark brown; then alternate vertical lines for the boards' ends. Don't forget to add a few knot-holes! Using long, tapering lines, apply medium brown to shade the boards on both ends, and add a shadow line under the trim. Use deep green to shade under the roofs and above the trim; then define the house boards and barn. Paint a black checkerboard on the roofs, following the shapes of the rock and the roof.

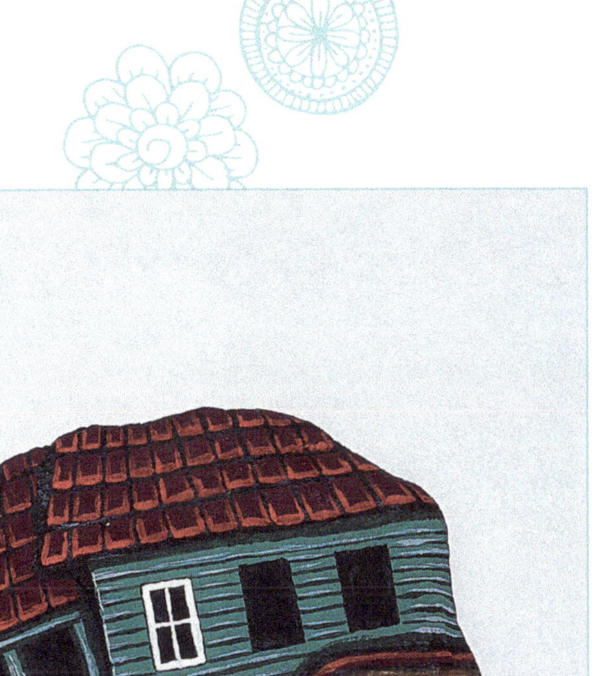

12 Drybrush some cream highlights on the centers of the wooden boards on the body of the ark, following the same horizontal direction. Use red to highlight the trim, and define each of the roof tiles on three sides, tapering toward the tile tops. Highlight the house and the boards of the barn with light sage green lines. Then paint the trim on the windows white, but leave some black showing around the edges. Use soft touches of white to enhance some of the existing highlights, such as at the bottom of the roof line, at the edge of the house, and on spots on the trim.

KITTY CAT DOORSTOP

Cats have a permanent place in the hearts of many humans, and a painted kitty is a welcome addition to any cat-lover's home. Rock cats work perfectly as a doorstop; or you can simply decorate a corner of your home with this lifelike creation. These hand-painted pets require no feeding, and make wonderful gifts to feline fans. Try painting rock pet portraits too!

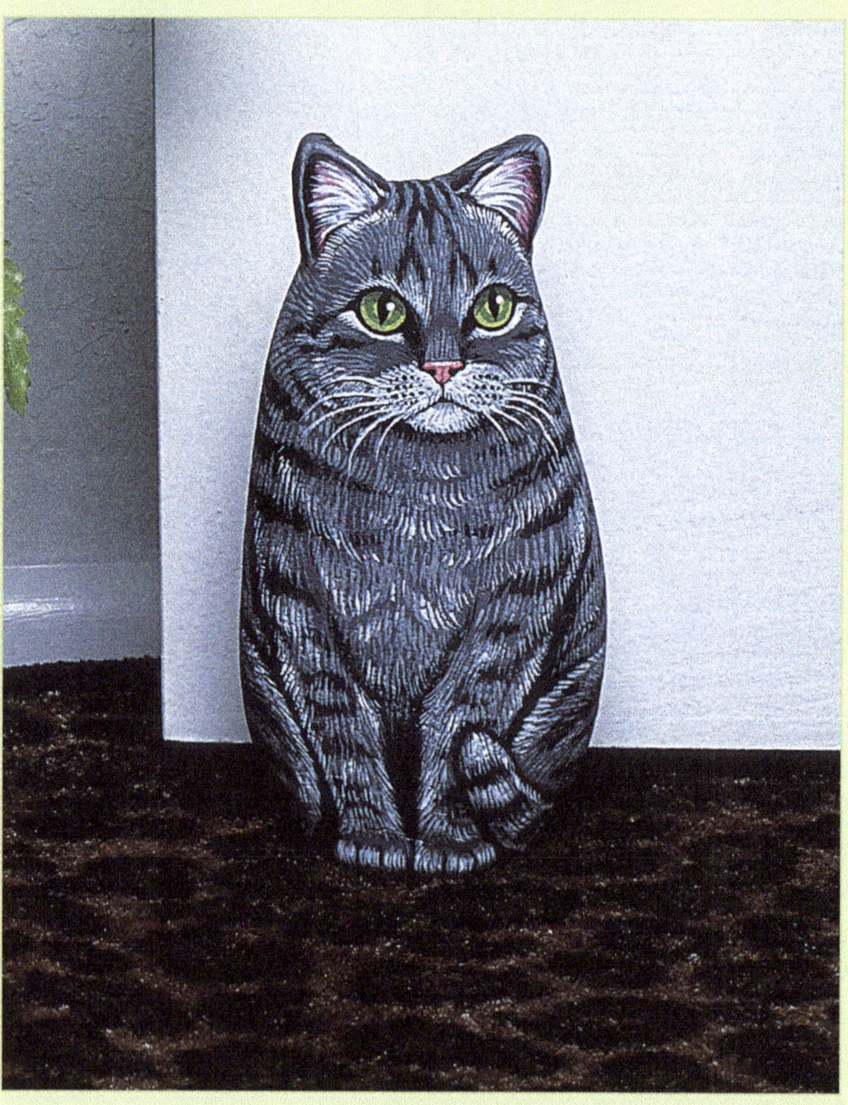

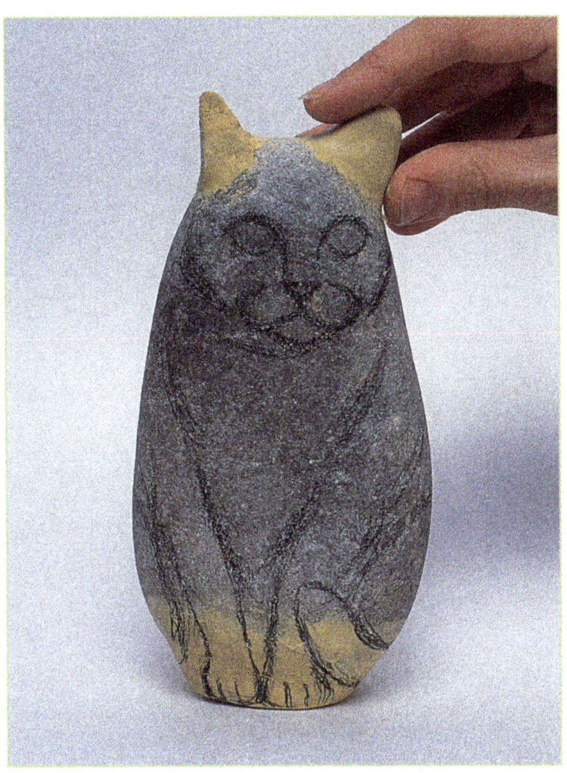

1 Begin by drawing your design on the rock with colored pencil. (See the cat template on page 127.) If your rock does not have a flat base, you can build one with wood filler and let it harden before starting. Next decide where the ears will go; they will be built in two steps to prevent the filler from sagging. When the cones are hard, apply more wood filler over them to mold the final ear shapes.

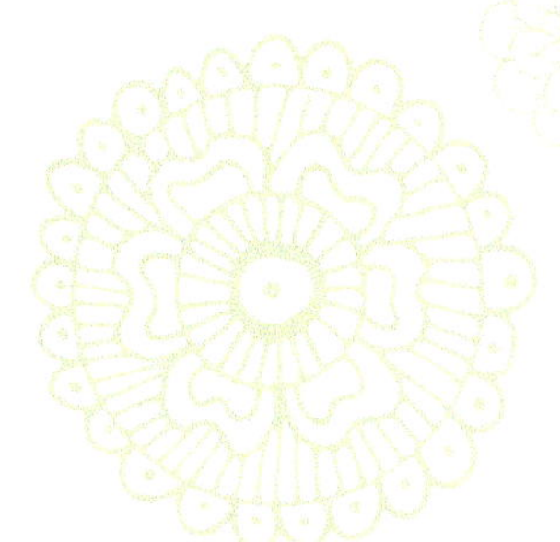

2 When the wood filler is dry, sketch the insides of the ear. Paint the base colors, leaving enough of the pencil lines unpainted to still see the design. Cover the body with medium gray, and paint the insides of the ears magenta or pink. Use light gray for the muzzle, and leave the eyes and the nose unpainted.

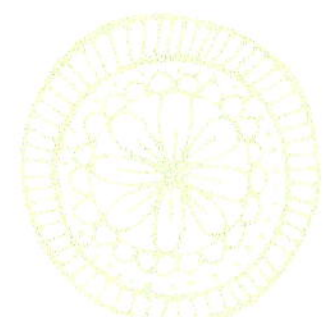

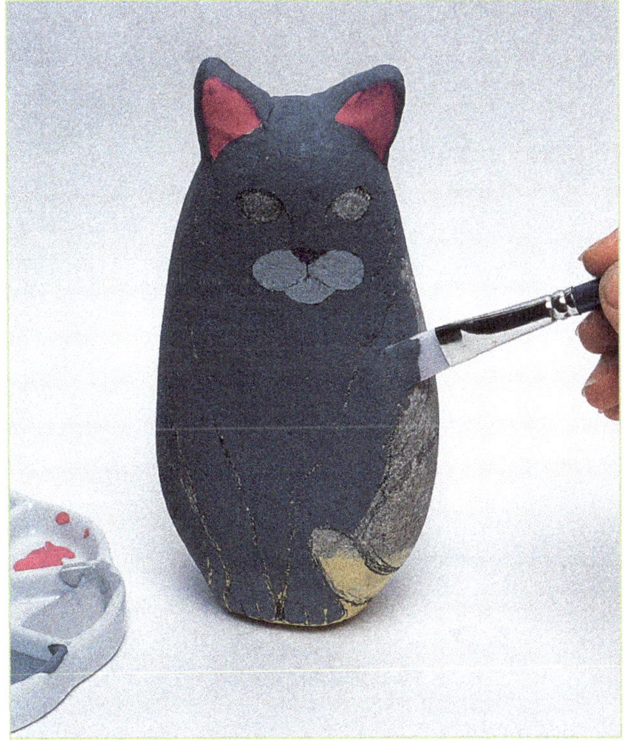

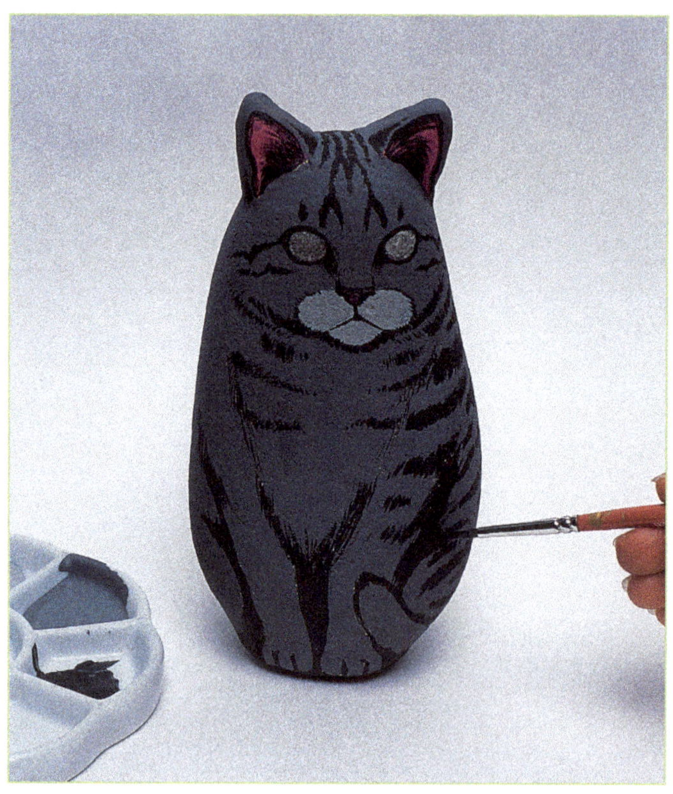

3 Using black, define the design by outlining the ears, eyes, nose, and muzzle with a liner brush. Switch to a round brush, and drybrush the shadows on the edges and centers of the ears with feathered strokes. Define the body contours: the neck, legs, toes, haunches, and tail. Then fill in the shadowed areas—between the front legs, and between the front legs and the haunches. Paint the body markings using light strokes in the direction of fur growth.

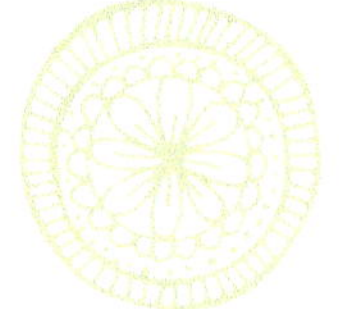

4 Use a liner brush to paint the body fur a light gray. On the face, the fur radiates out from the nose; on the haunches, the fur follows their curves. Paint some hairs lightly over the black body markings, and paint hairs into the black shadow areas to create a furry look. Leave dark areas on the tops of the paws, the bridge of the nose, and under the eyes.

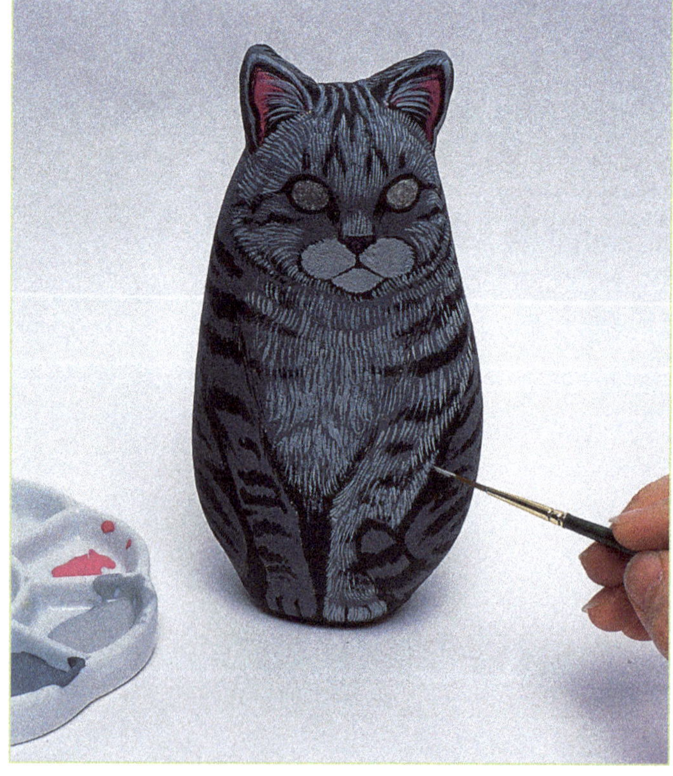

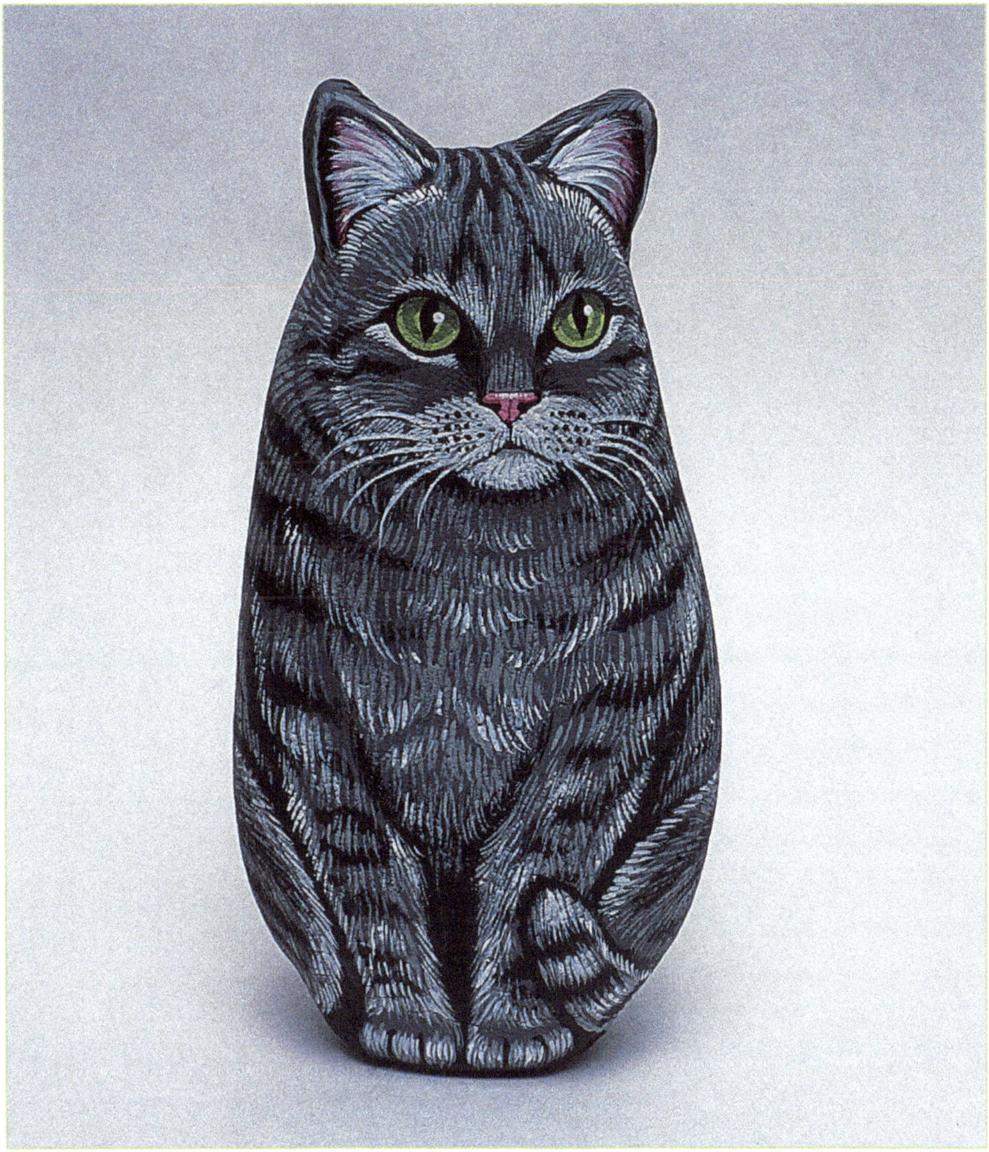

5 Paint the long, soft hairs in the ears with white. Also use white to highlight the following areas: the fur below the ears and around the face, the chest area, the edges of the haunches, the paws, the front legs above the paws, and the tail. Add details to finish the eyes and nose. Then carefully paint the white hairs around the eyes, muzzle, and whiskers.

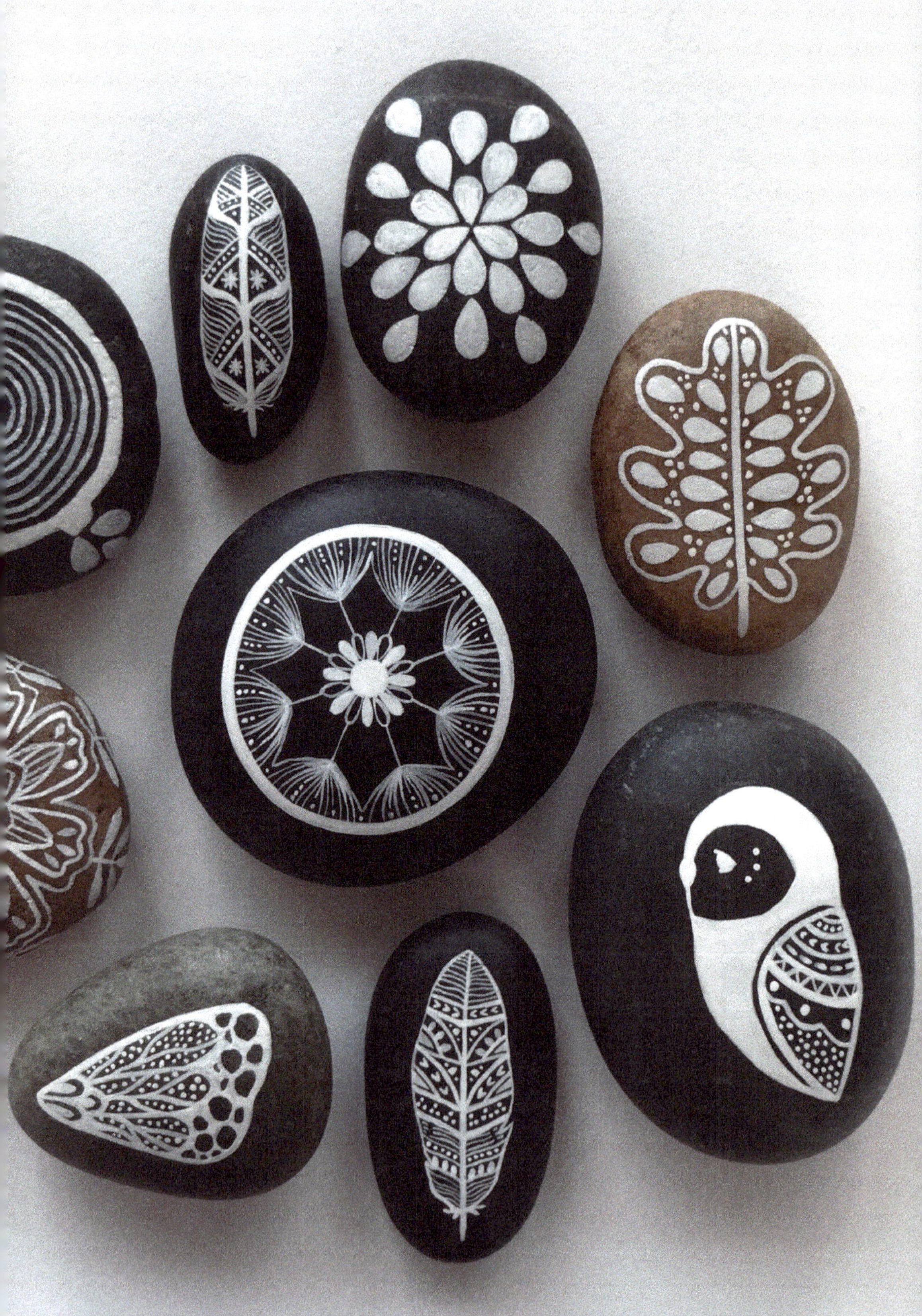

PART IV: MONOCHROME DESIGNS

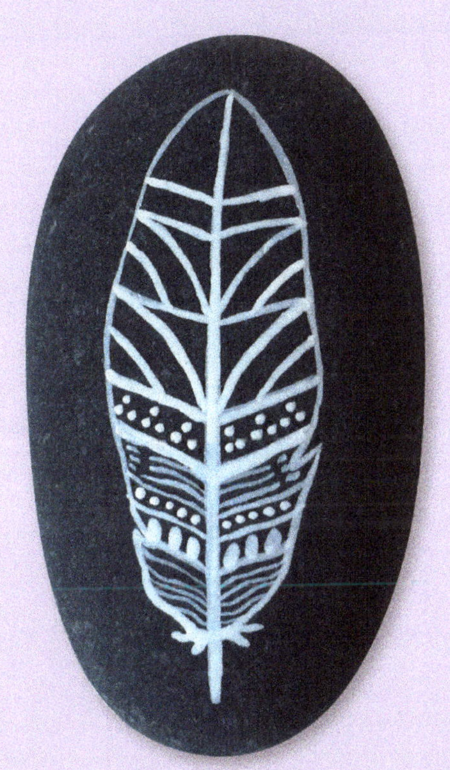

FLOWER

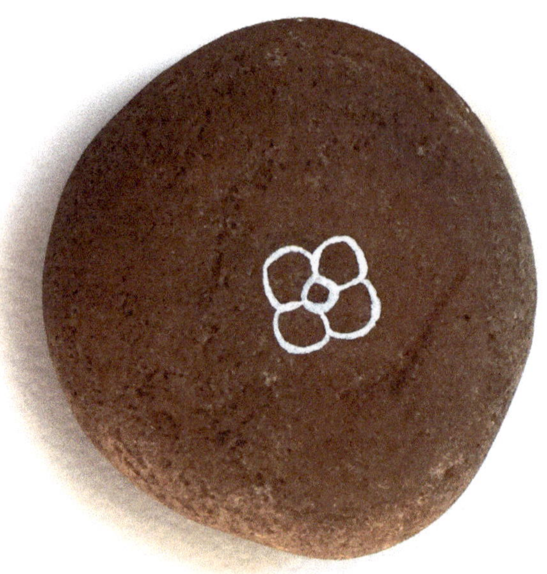

1 Choose a round rock. Apply a thin and even layer of varnish to your rock with a Filbert paintbrush. Once the varnish is dry, begin by painting a small circle in the center of your rock. Add four small flower petal shapes around the circle.

2 Add a little detail to the flower petal shapes, and then add another set of petals between each shape.

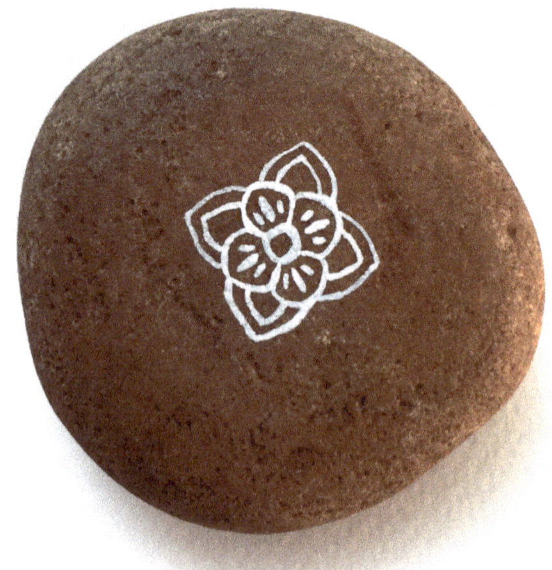

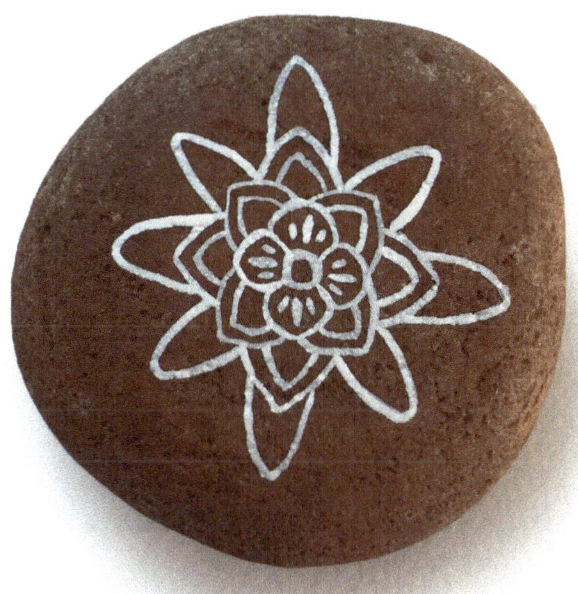

3 Add a second set of flower petals, and then paint long, U-shaped petals extending from the ends.

4 Paint larger flower petals around each U-shape, adding a slight wave to the end of each petal.

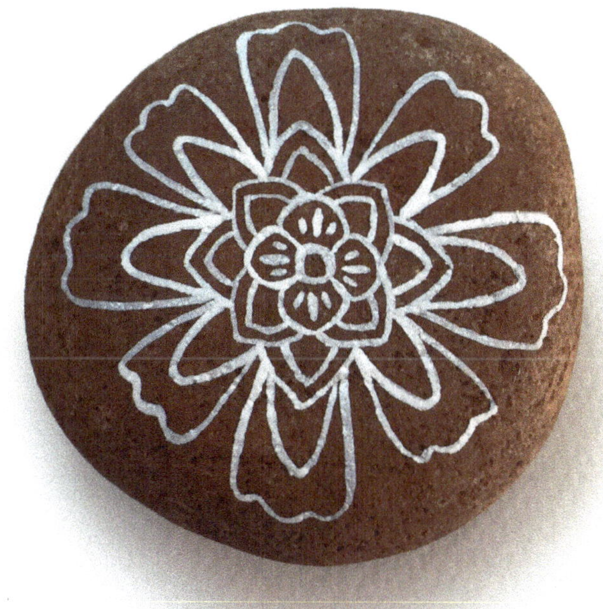

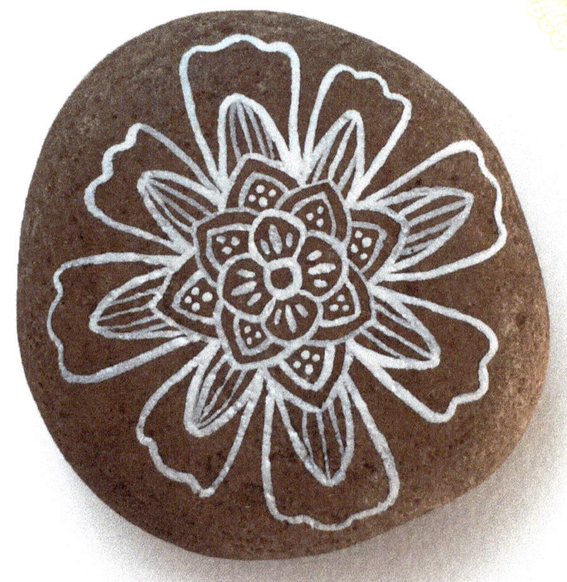

5 Fill the petals with decorative designs, dots, teardrops, lines, or any other shapes you prefer.

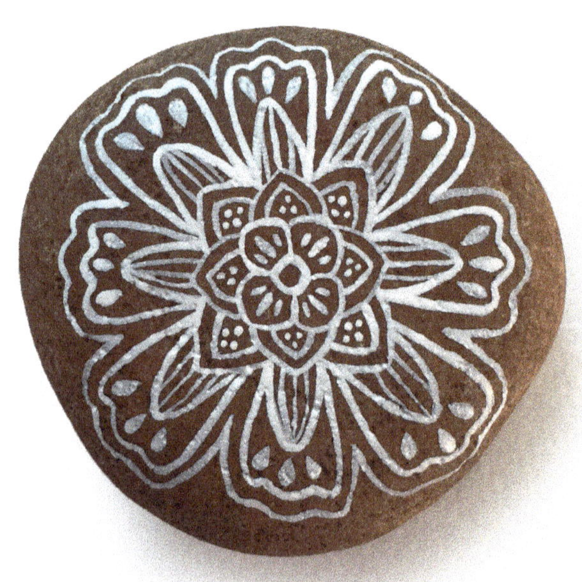

6 Paint a simple outline that borders the entire flower.

7 At the end of each outer petal, paint a small, leafy branch, each with five leaves.

8 Refine the design of your flower wherever necessary. Adding a thin second layer of paint will make the whites brighter and more opaque. Let dry, and apply a thin layer of sealing varnish. Let dry, and add one more thin protective coat of varnish.

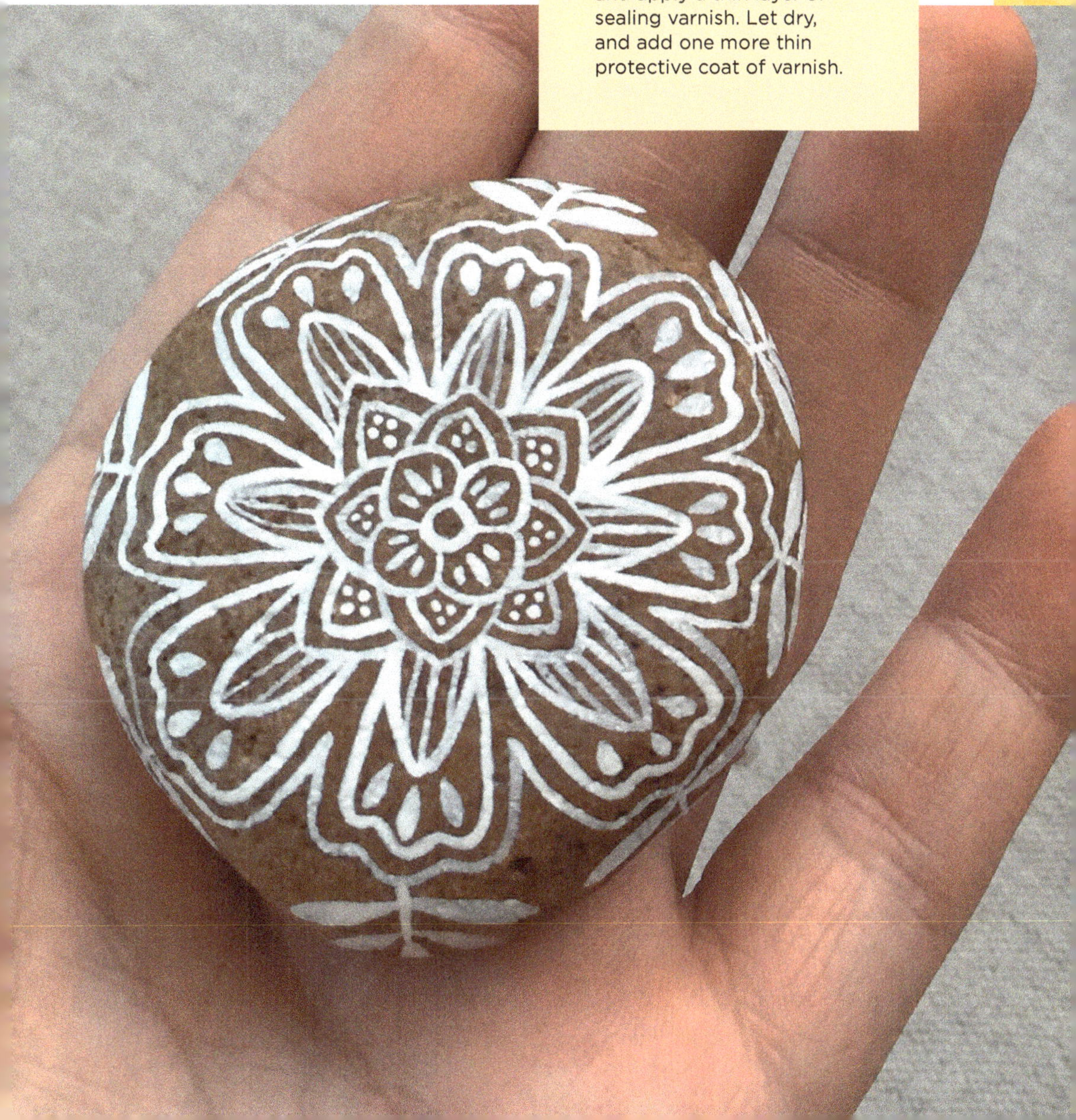

DANDELION

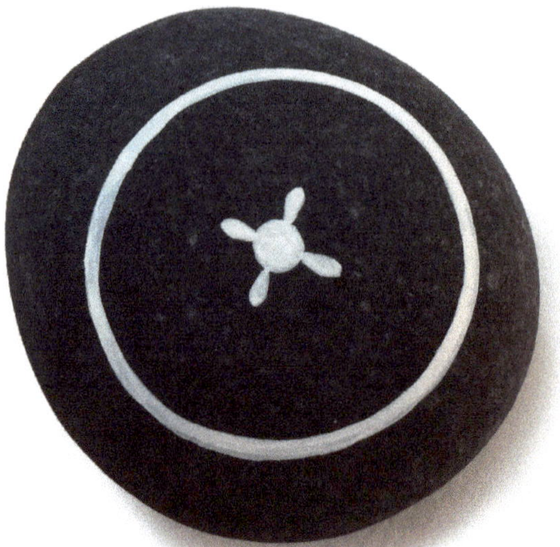

1 Apply a thin and even layer of varnish to your rock with your Filbert paintbrush. Once the varnish is dry, use a pencil to draw a light circle outline on your rock. Paint over your circle outline with a size 1 round paintbrush. Paint a dot in the center of the circle.

2 Begin painting 16 small dandelion spores around the dot with a size 00 paintbrush.

3 Fill every other spore in with paint.

4 Paint a straight, thin line from every other spore toward the outer circle, leaving a small space between the end of the line and the outer circle of the dandelion.

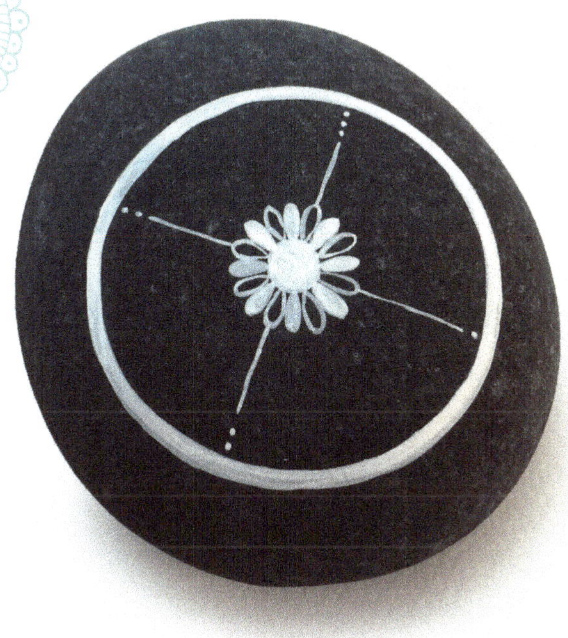

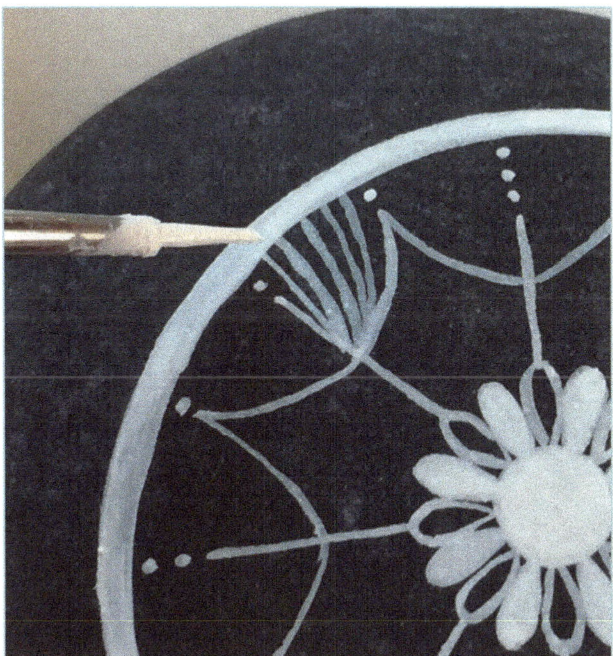

5 Fill the empty space with little dots.

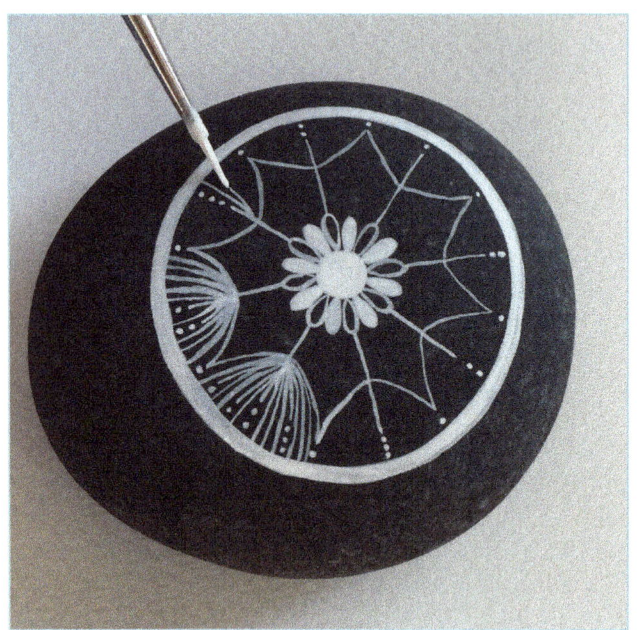

6 Paint a single dot evenly between each line.

7 At the middle of each line, paint a curved line branching up to the outer circle. Repeat this process for each dandelion spore. Add small dot details to enhance your painting.

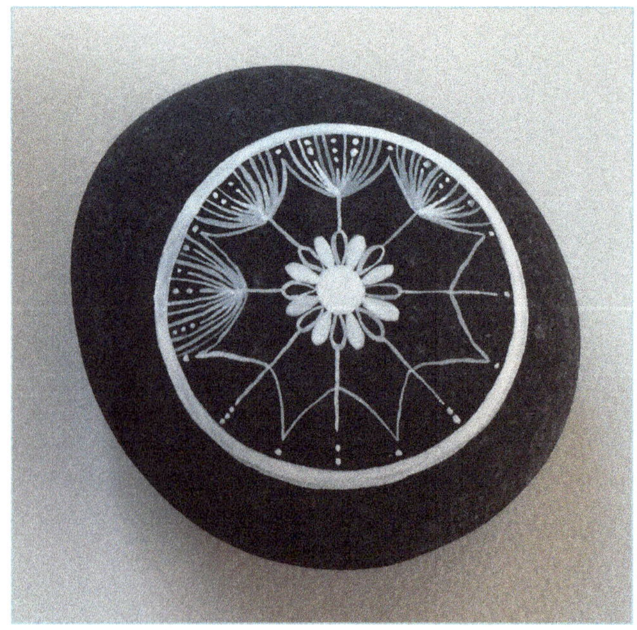

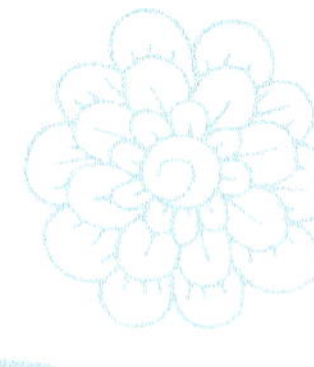

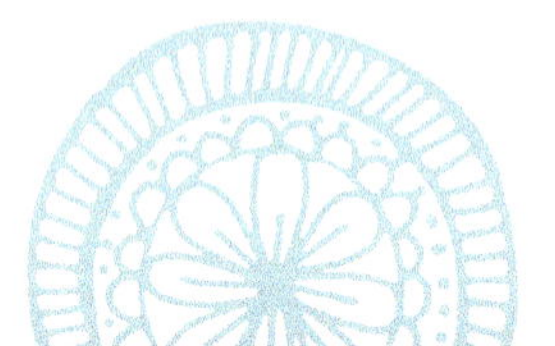

8 Touch up and refine the outer circle border of your dandelion, and anywhere else necessary. When your painting is finished, allow it to dry completely. Apply a thin layer of sealing varnish. Let dry, and add one more thin coat of varnish.

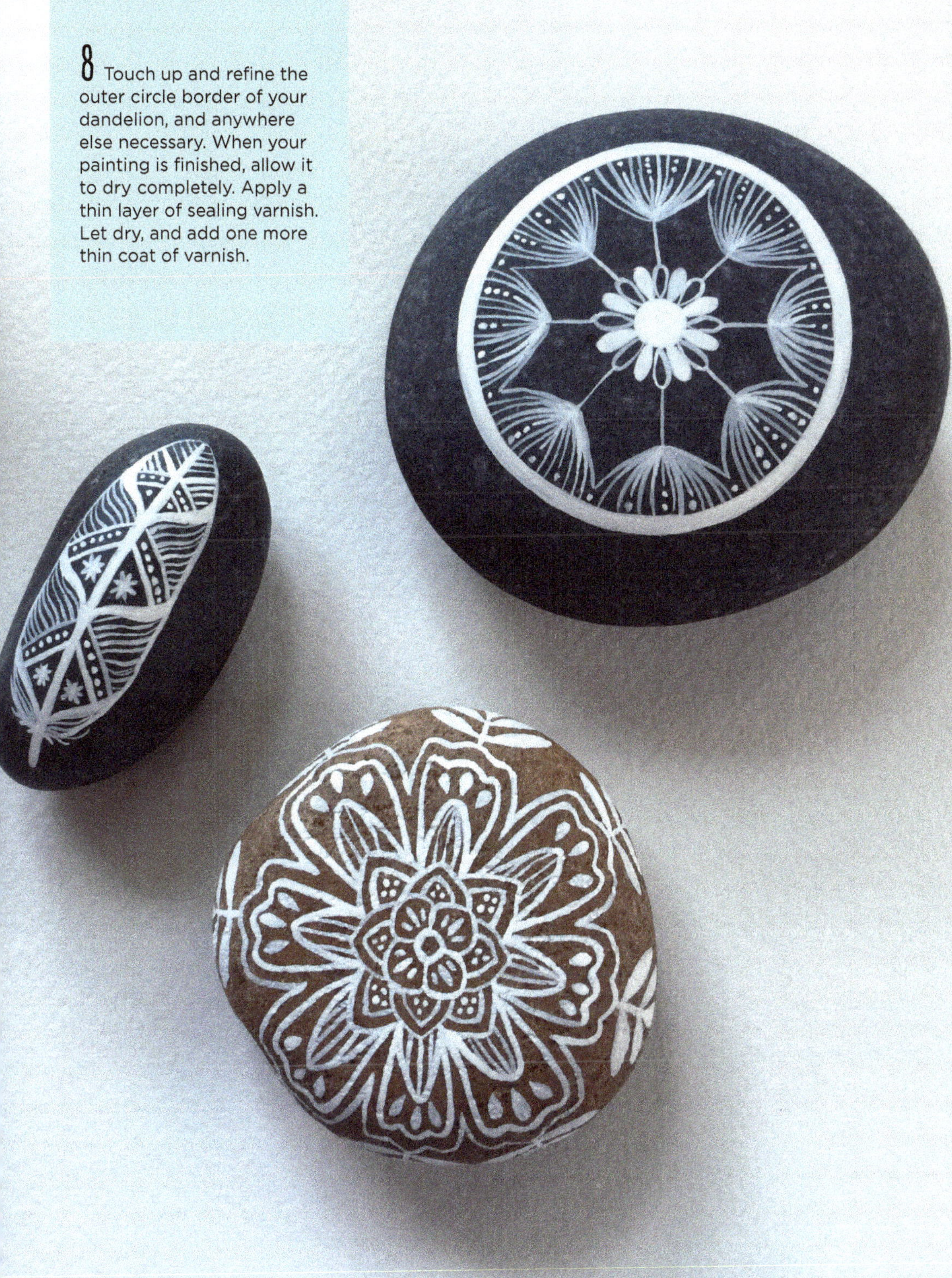

FEATHER

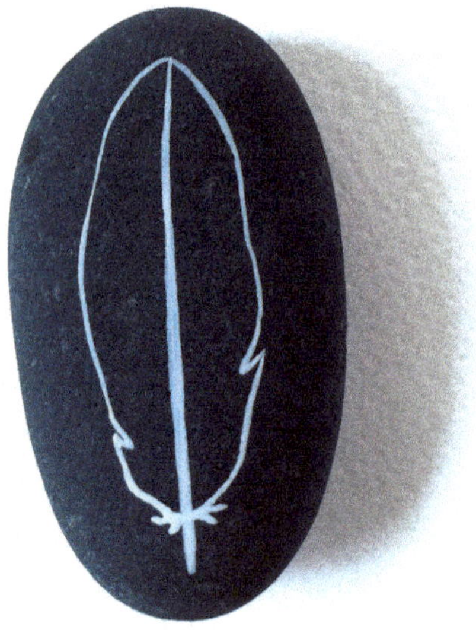

1 Choose an oval rock. Apply a thin and even layer of varnish to your rock with a Filbert brush. Once the varnish is dry, paint a thin, centered line on your rock with the size 1 round paintbrush. Paint a feather outline with a size 00 paintbrush. Use this brush for the remainder of the feather details.

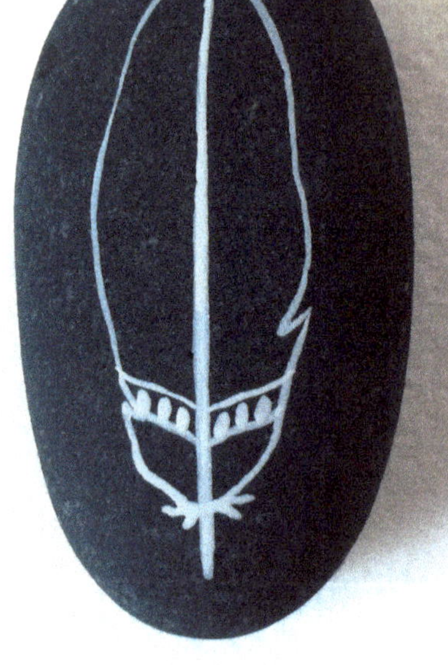

2 Begin your feather details at the base of the feather.

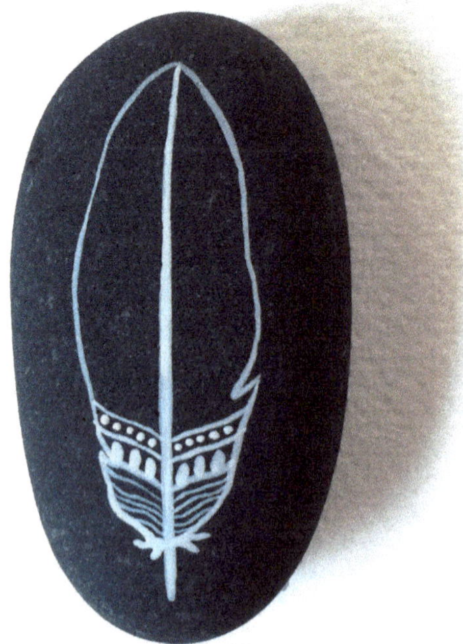

3 Continue to add small, decorative patterns to your feather, divided by sections, and work up to the middle of the feather.

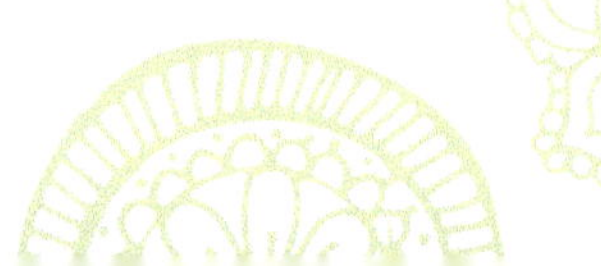

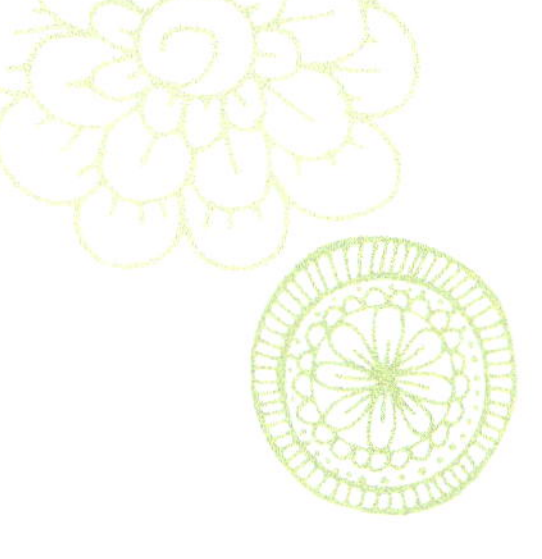

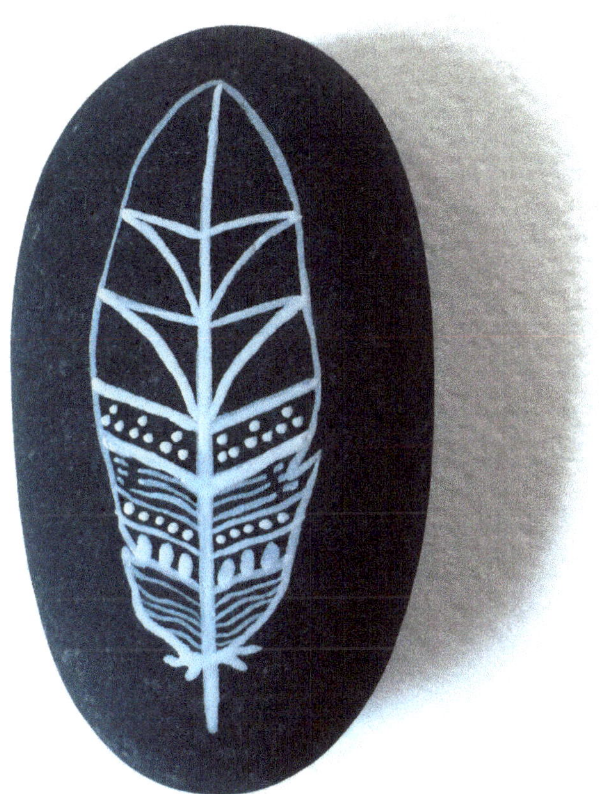

4 Paint two triangular shapes at the center of the feather.

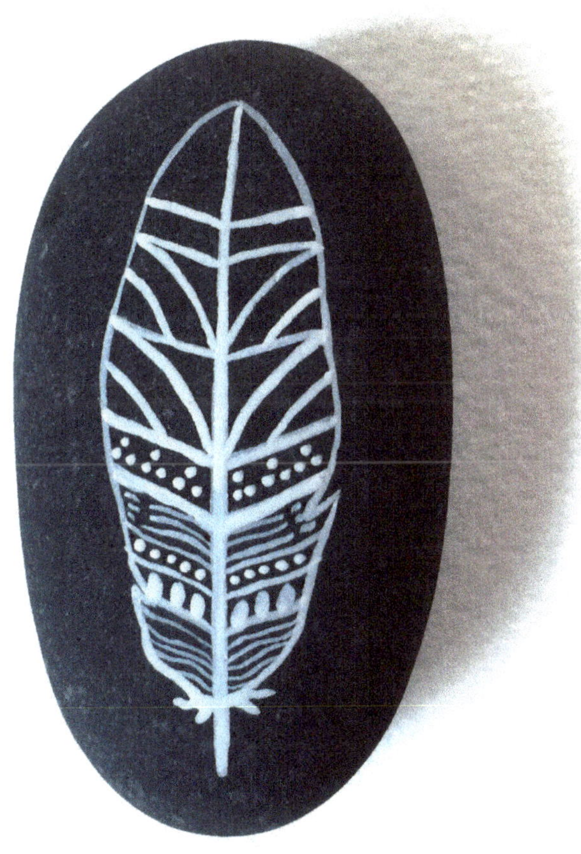

5 Add a few more lines to further divide the triangular shapes into additional sections.

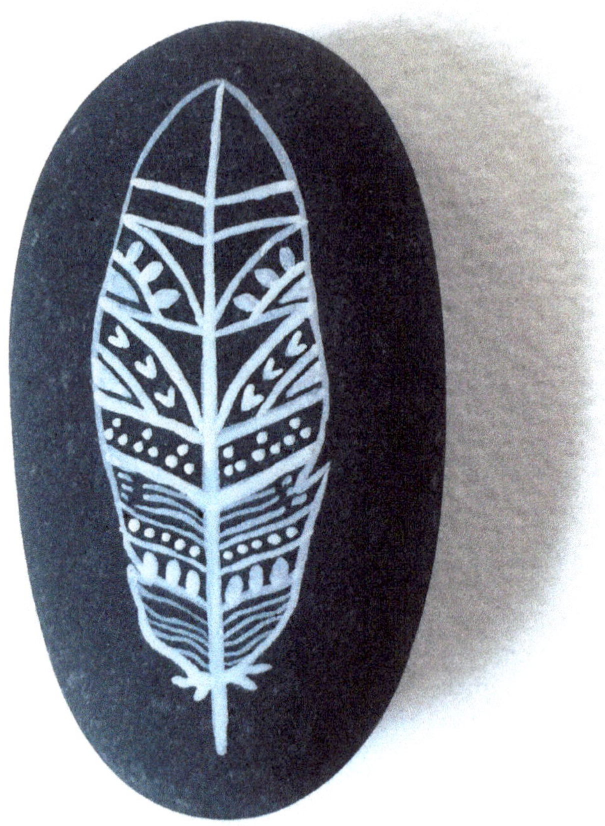

6 Paint decorative details within each section of the design.

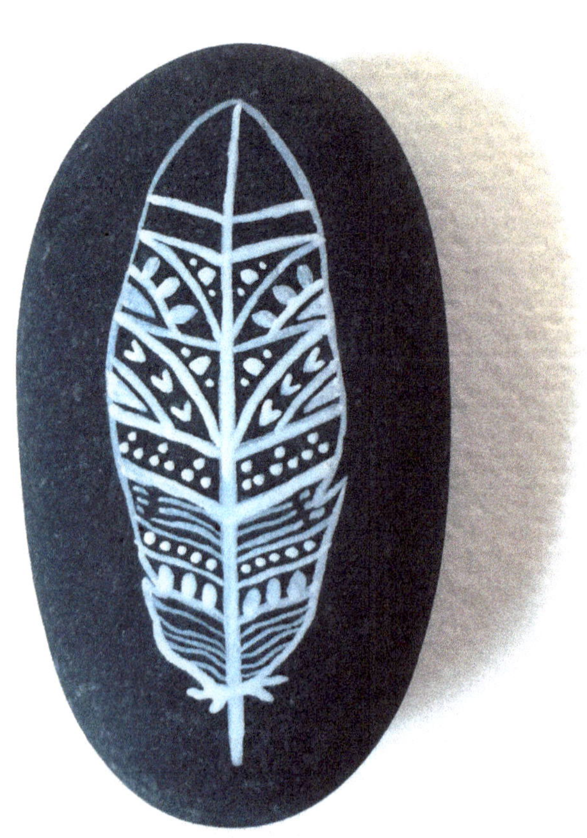

7 Create your own unique feather by using various shapes (dots, triangles, and stars, for example).

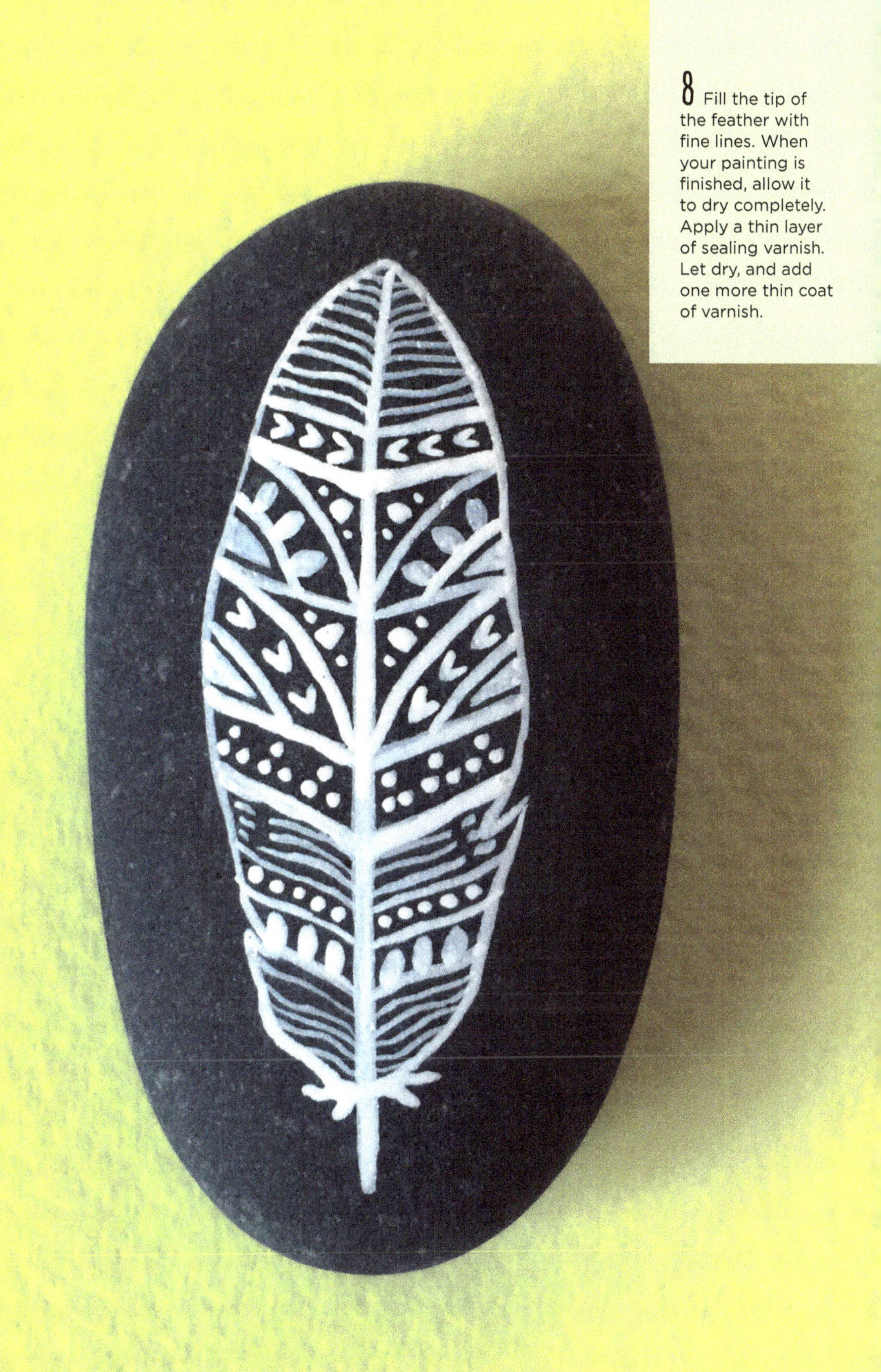

8 Fill the tip of the feather with fine lines. When your painting is finished, allow it to dry completely. Apply a thin layer of sealing varnish. Let dry, and add one more thin coat of varnish.

RAINDROPS

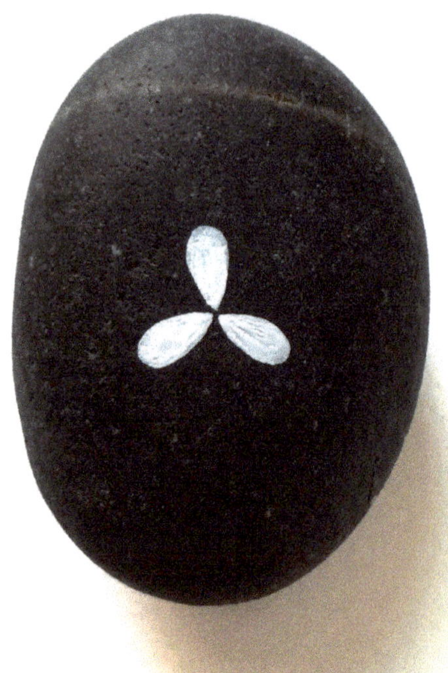

1 Use a Filbert paintbrush to apply a thin and even layer of varnish to your rock. Once the varnish is dry, use a size 00 paintbrush to paint three equally spaced raindrops.

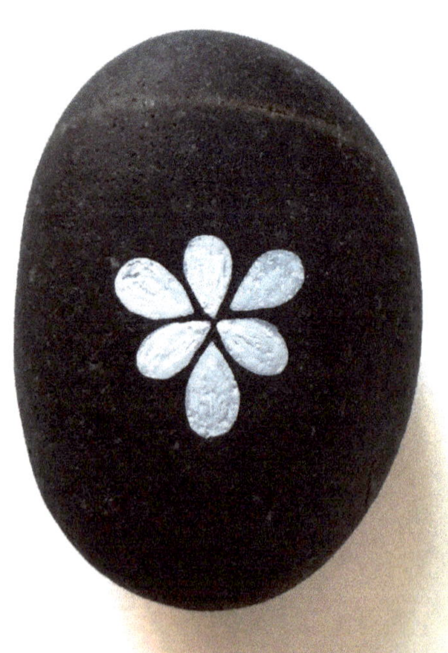

2 In the space between each raindrop, paint another set of three more raindrops.

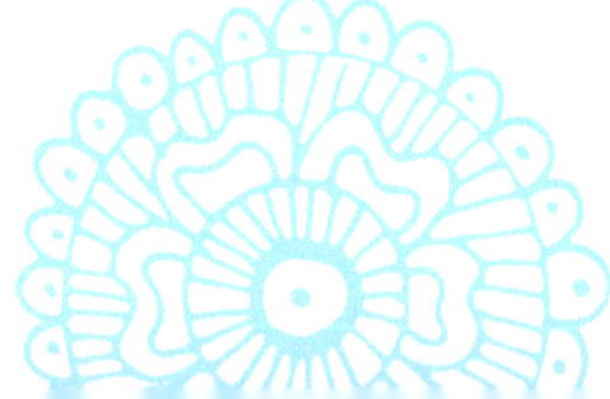

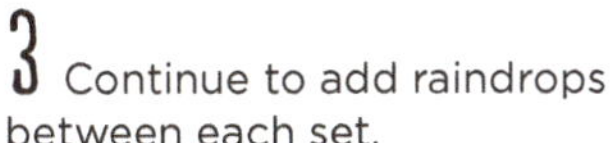

3 Continue to add raindrops between each set.

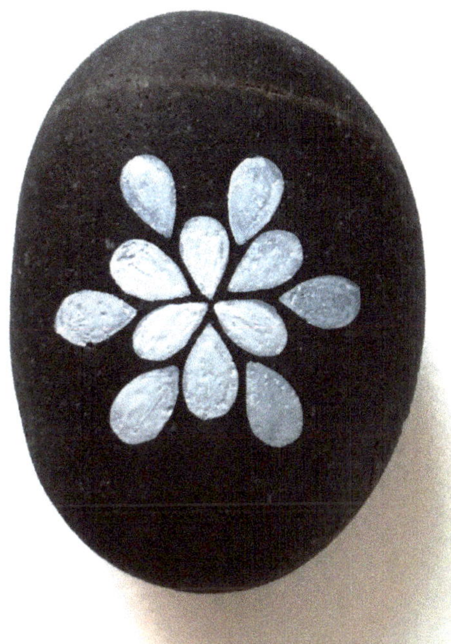

4 Repeat this process three or four times, or more if you prefer to fill the rock.

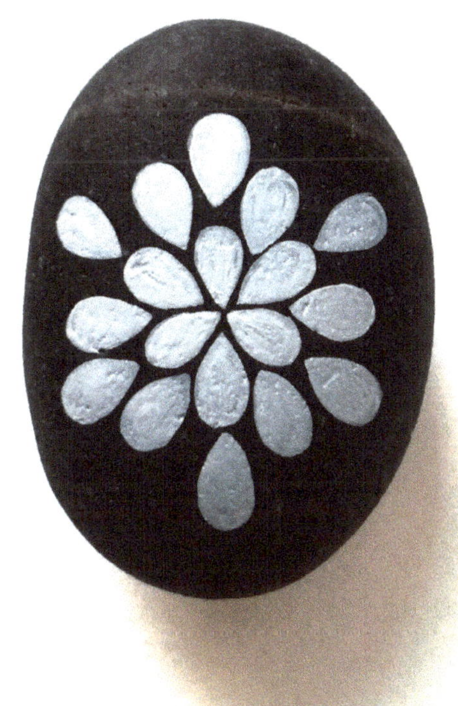

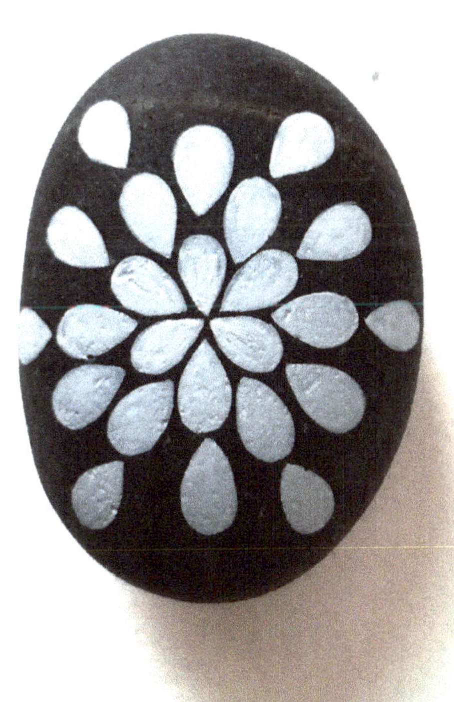

5 Experiment and customize your rock by painting the drops in various sizes. Touch up and refine your painting with a thin second layer of paint. When your painting is finished, allow it to dry completely. Apply a thin layer of sealing varnish. Let dry, and add one more thin coat.

TREE RINGS

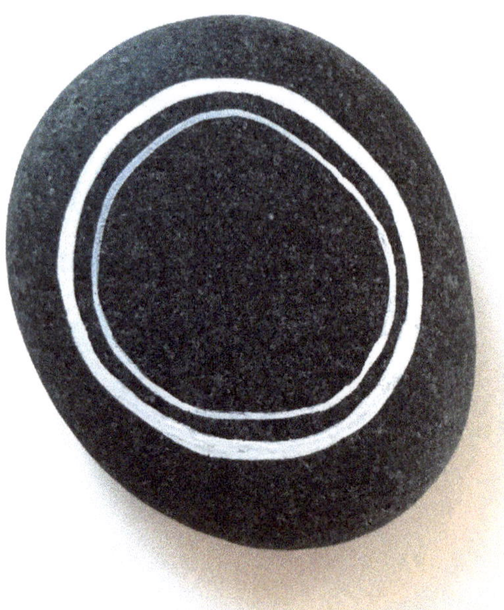

1 Choose a round rock. Apply a thin and even layer of varnish with a Filbert paintbrush. Once the varnish is dry, paint a circle on your rock using a size 1 paintbrush. Leave a bit of space and paint a second circle within the first using a 00 paintbrush.

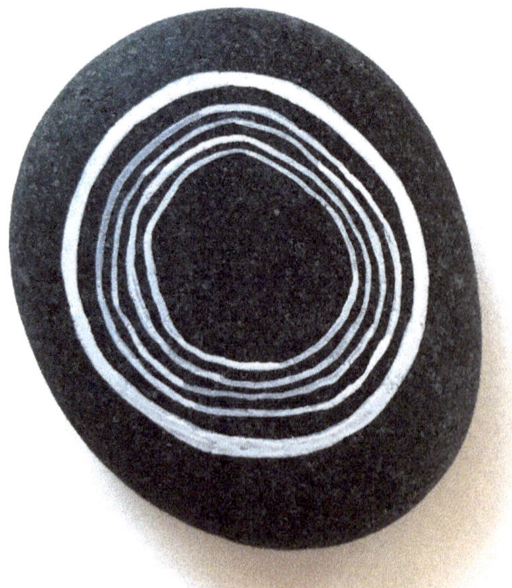

2 Begin to paint circles within circles to look like the rings of a cut tree stump. The tree rings should be close together, but not touching.

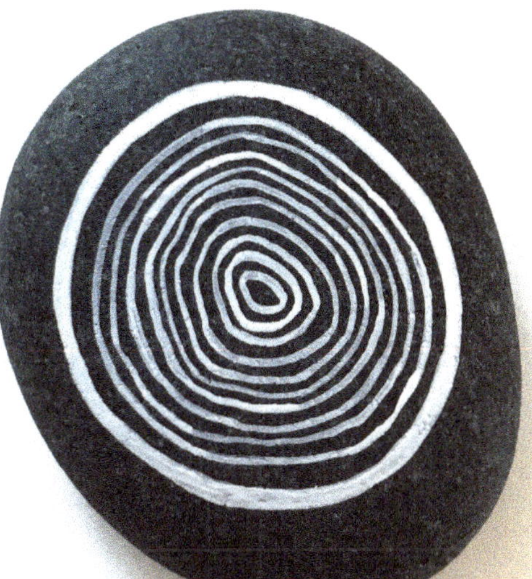

3 Continue to paint circles within circles until you've filled your tree stump with rings.

4 Paint a small branch from the outside of your circle.

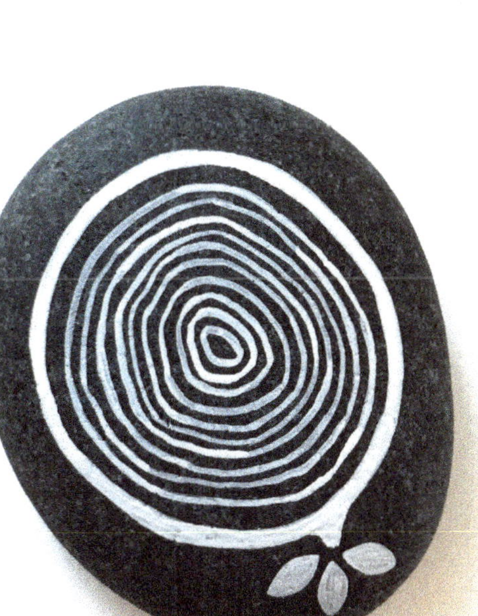

5 Add three small leaves growing from the branch. Touch up and refine the painting with a thin second layer of paint, wherever necessary. When your painting is finished, allow it to dry completely. Apply a thin layer of sealing varnish. Let dry, and add one more thin coat.

LEAF

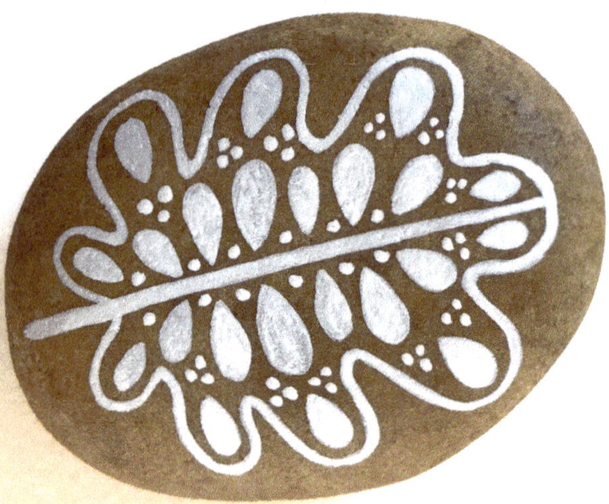

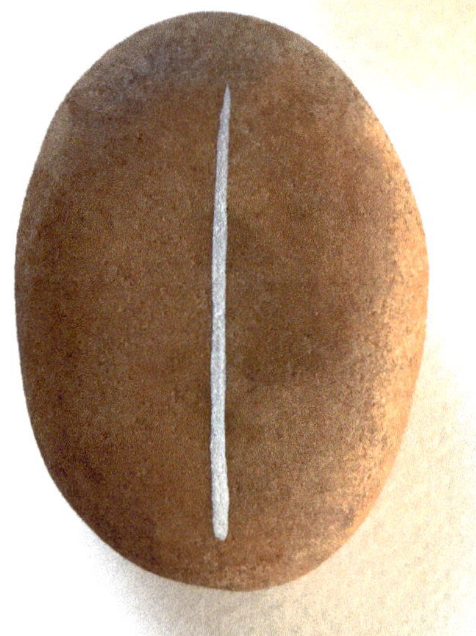

1 Choose an oval rock. Apply a thin and even layer of varnish to your rock with a Filbert brush. Once the varnish is dry, paint a straight line, centered on your rock, with a size 1 round paintbrush.

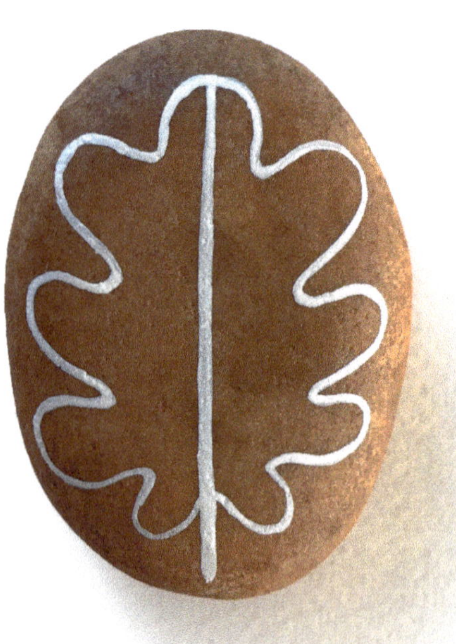

2 Paint a simple, curvy leaf outline.

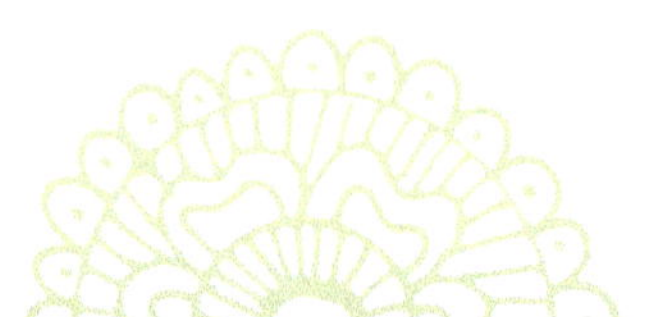

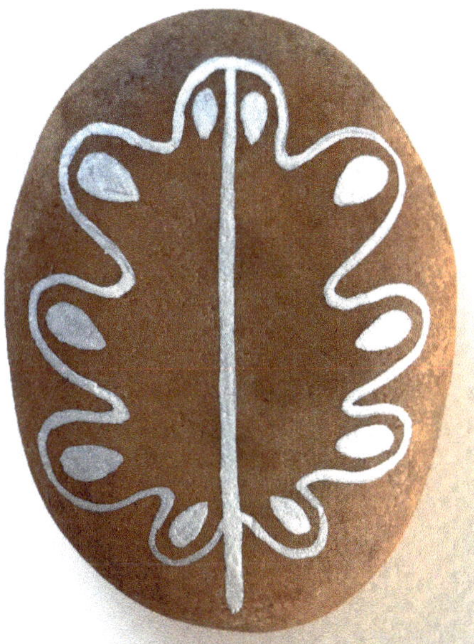

3 Paint five teardrop shapes along each side of the leaf with a size 00 paintbrush.

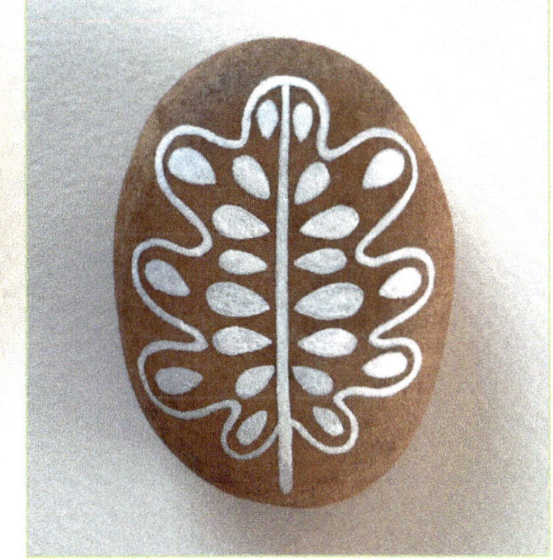

4 Paint six teardrop shapes along each side of the center line of the leaf with a size 00 paintbrush.

5 Fill empty spaces on your leaf with small dots.

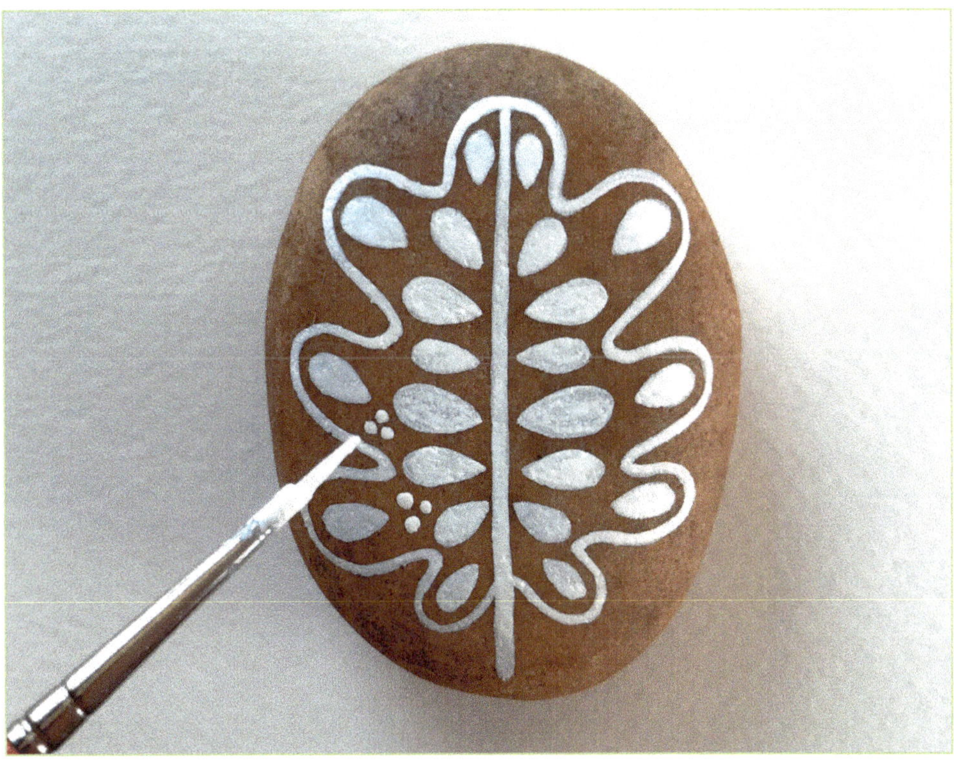

BUTTERFLY WING

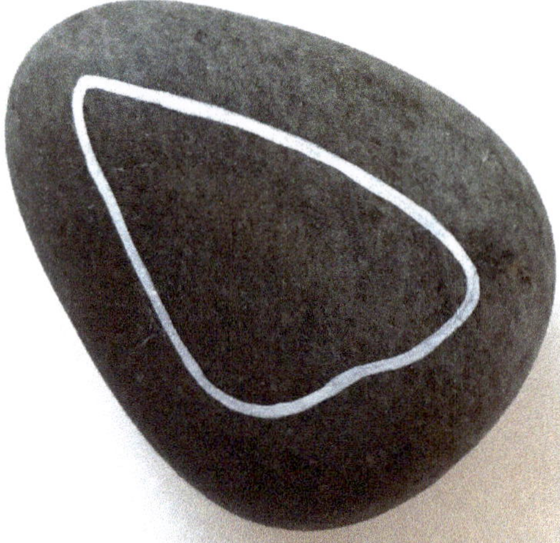

1 Apply a thin and even layer of varnish to your rock with a Filbert paintbrush. When the varnish is dry, use your 00 paintbrush to paint a wing shape.

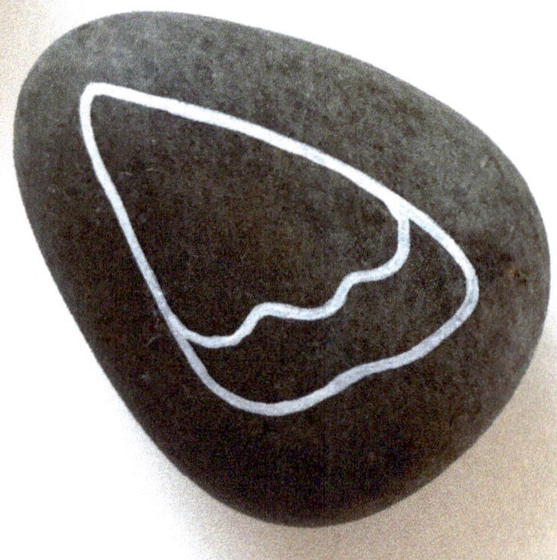

2 Paint a curvy line at the wide end of your wing that has three rounded points.

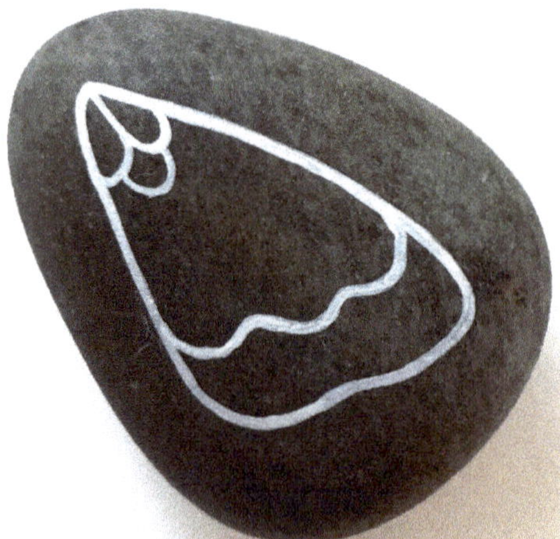

3 Add three small, U-shaped lines at the narrow tip of the wing.

4 Paint two lines down the center of the wing, connecting the tip to the curved line at the wide end of the wing.

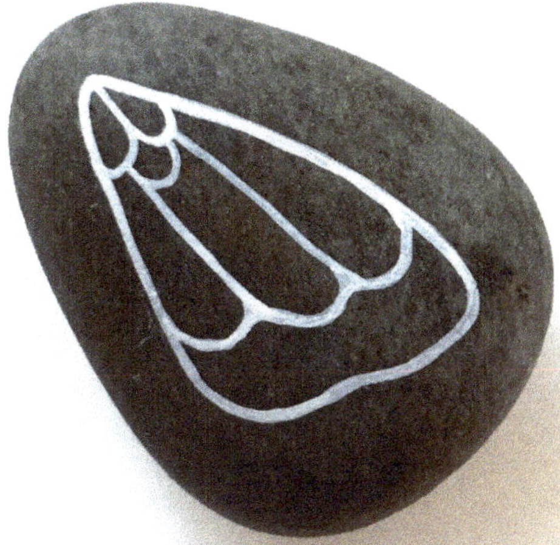

5 Paint circular shapes at the wide end of the wing. Once the space is filled, refine the design as you like.

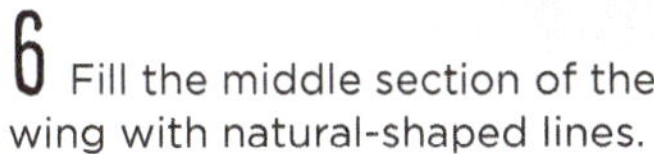

6 Fill the middle section of the wing with natural-shaped lines.

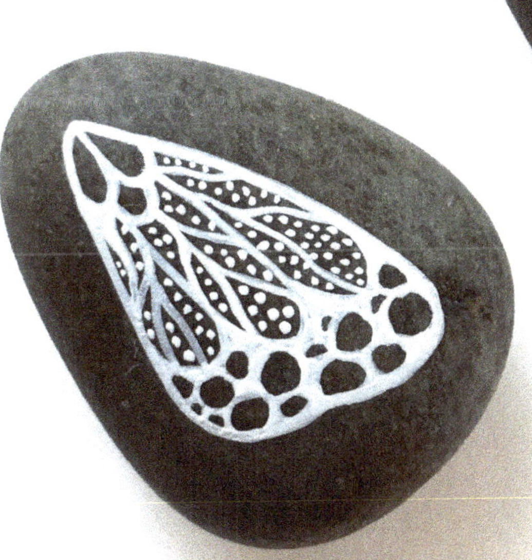

7 Fill the middle section of the wing with tiny dots.

OWLET

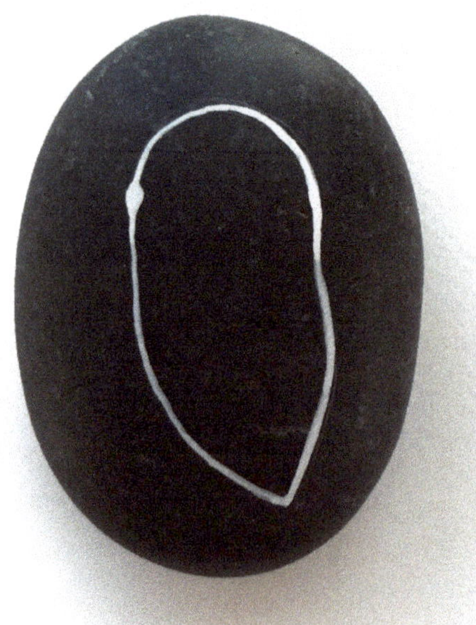

1 Choose a smooth, oval-shaped rock and, after cleaning and drying, apply a single thin coat of varnish. Once the rock is dry, use a pencil to lightly outline your owl shape. Using your smallest round brush, paint over the pencil outline of your owl.

2 Paint your owl's face and wing, as shown.

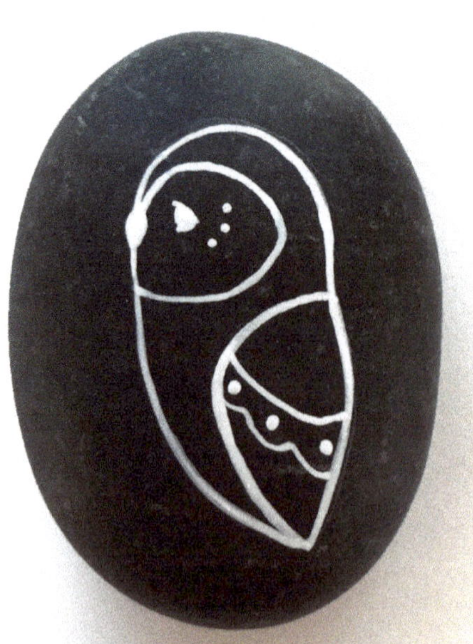

3 Using your smallest brush, take time to paint your owl's eye. Every owl is unique; enjoy creating different expressions with your owl.

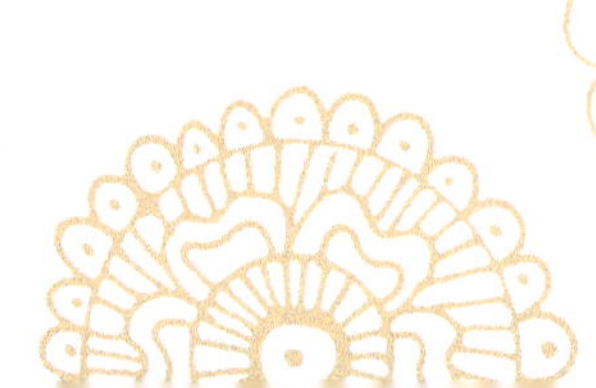

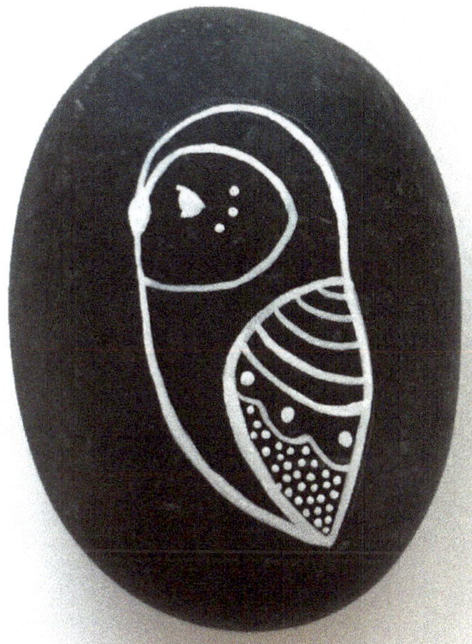

4 Begin adding fine details to your owl's wing.

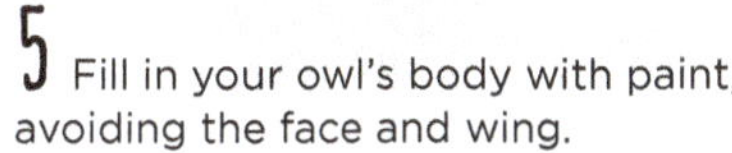

5 Fill in your owl's body with paint, avoiding the face and wing.

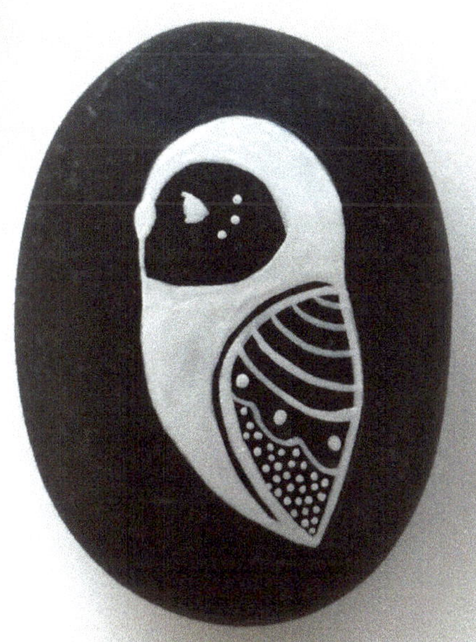

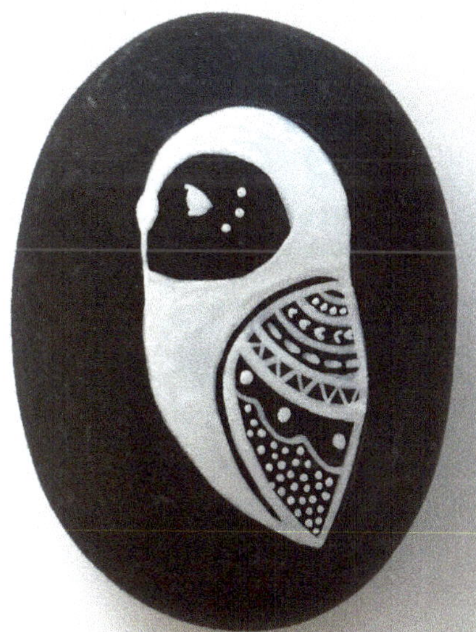

6 Continue adding the final details to your owl's wing. Create your own shapes and patterns and customize them to match your owl's personality.

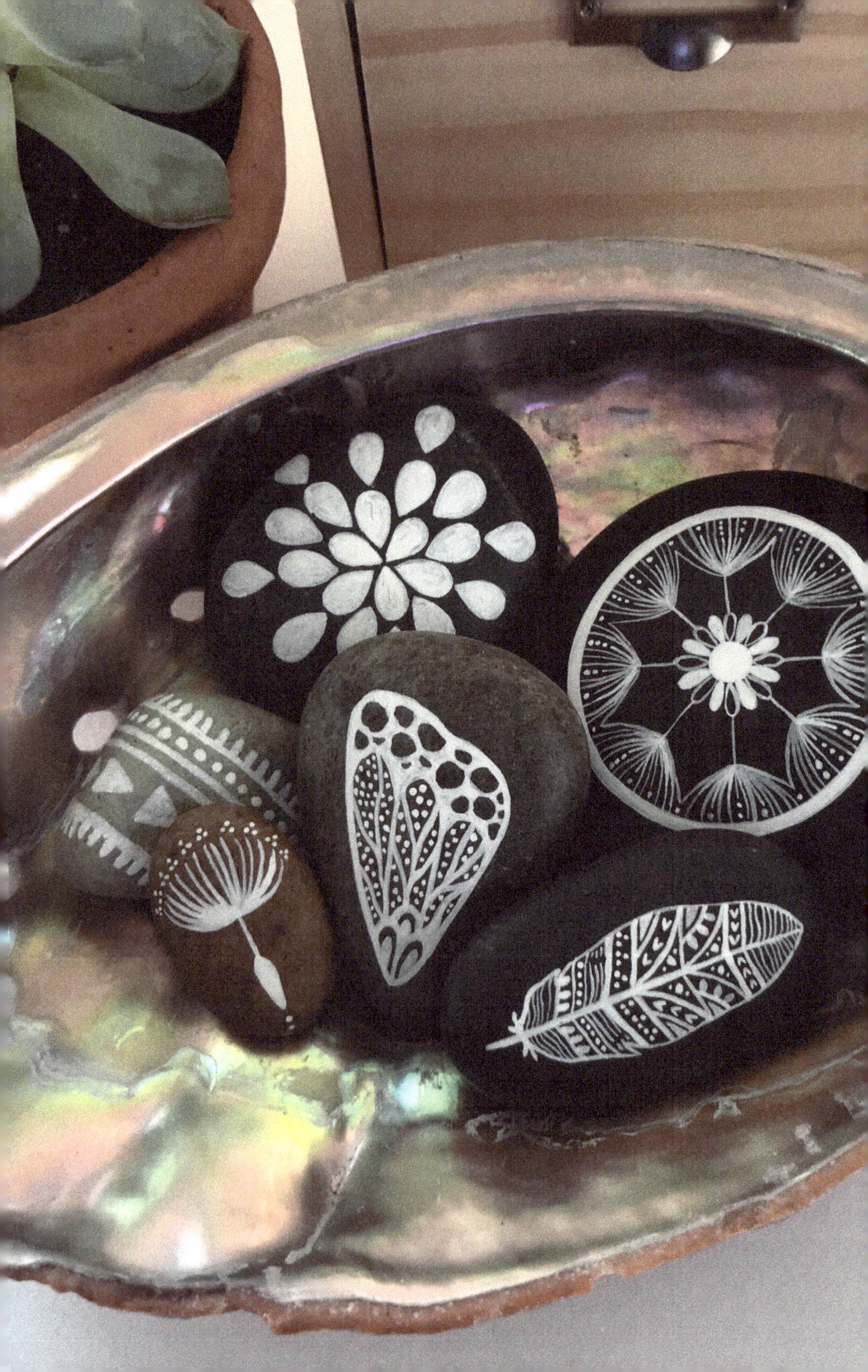

PART V: PROJECT TEMPLATES

Use the templates below for the Zen sponging project on page 16.

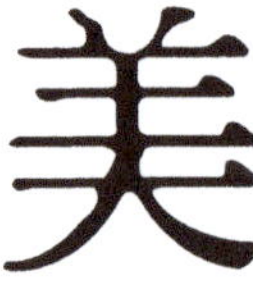

Beauty

安心

Peace

調和

Harmony

恋

Love

繁栄

Prosperity

満足

Contentment

健康

Health

幸福

Happiness

情熱

Passion

Use the template below for the Bird Bath project on page 80.

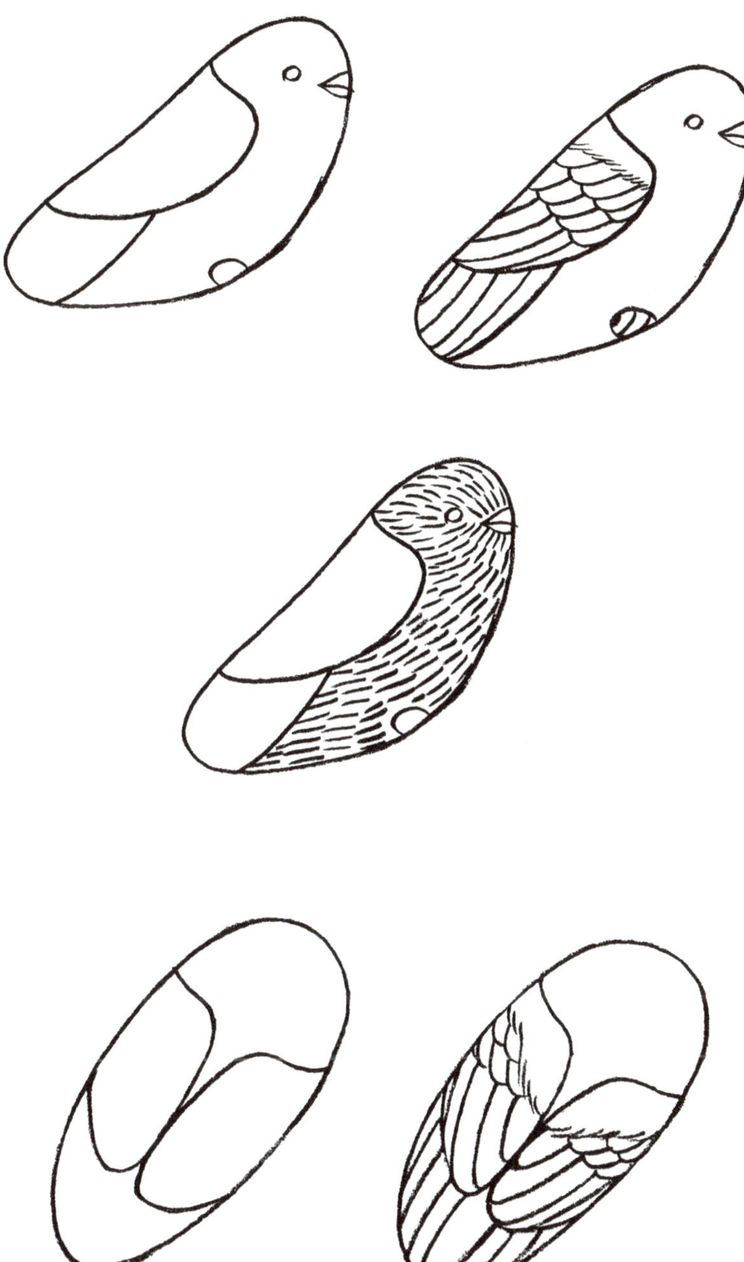

Use the templates below for the Noah's Ark project on page 86.

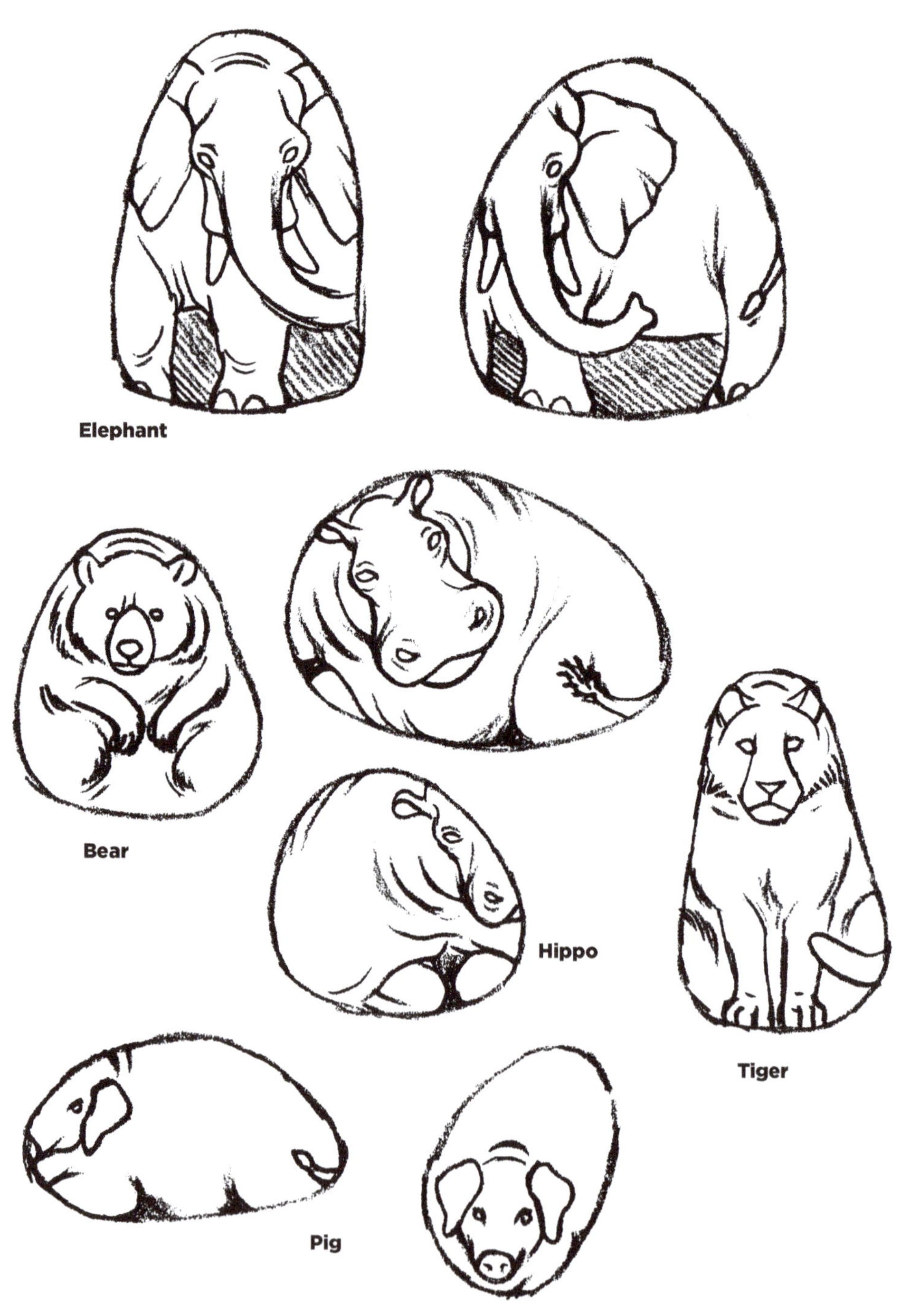

Use the template below for the Kitty Cat Doorstop project on page 94.

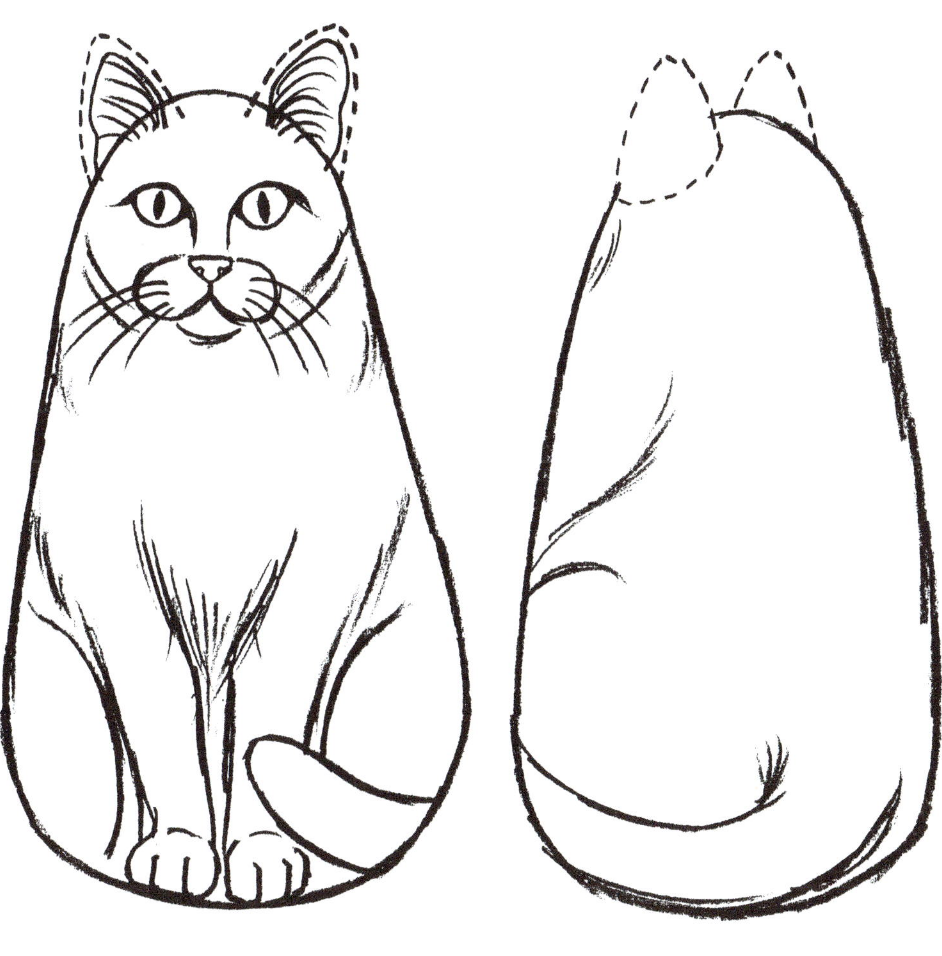

ABOUT THE ARTISTS

F. Sehnaz Bac is celebrated for her radiantly colorful and charming painted stones, which she sells on Etsy as *I Sassi dell'Adriatico* (Adriatic Stones). Her curiosity and imagination inspire her to create very detailed, fine-line drawings and stylized designs inspired from nature. She works with bright and bold colors in a variety of media, including watercolor, acrylic, ink, and marker pens. She currently lives in Alba Adriatica, Italy, a small town on the Adriatic Sea.

Artist and illustrator **Marisa Redondo** works primarily with watercolors and oils. Currently based in Northern California, Marisa is fascinated by nature's creations and the little pieces of life that often go unnoticed, from the fine lines of feathers to the spores of a dandelion. Through watercolor she explores the organic patterns and intricate details impressed on everything from the earth. Learn more at www.riverlunaart.com.

Talented artist **Margaret Vance** paints beautifully vibrant and colorful rock art full of intricate detail and pattern. As in nature, no two painted stones are alike. A simple stone washed downriver becomes a natural and surprisingly fitting canvas. Each stone's size, shape, color, surface texture, and individuality influence the design to create a singular mix of art and nature. Learn more at www.etherealandearth.com.

Diana Fisher studied fine art in New York and computer graphics in Arizona. She is a widely published illustrator currently based in the southwest, where she draws inspiration from the magnificent desert landscapes and wildlife.

ALSO IN THIS SERIES

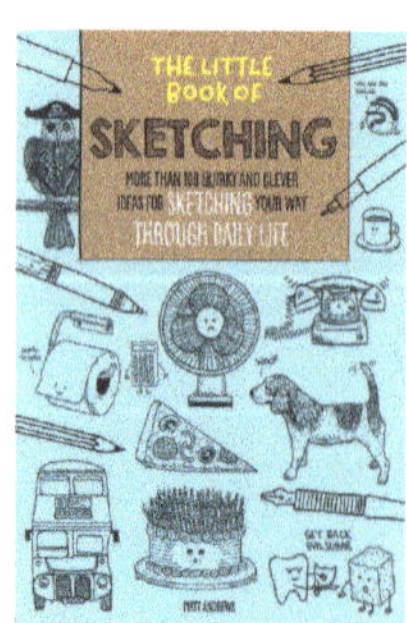

978-1-63322-393-6

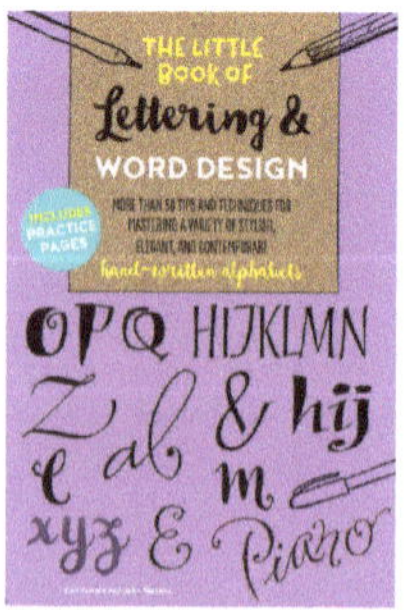

978-1-63322-471-1

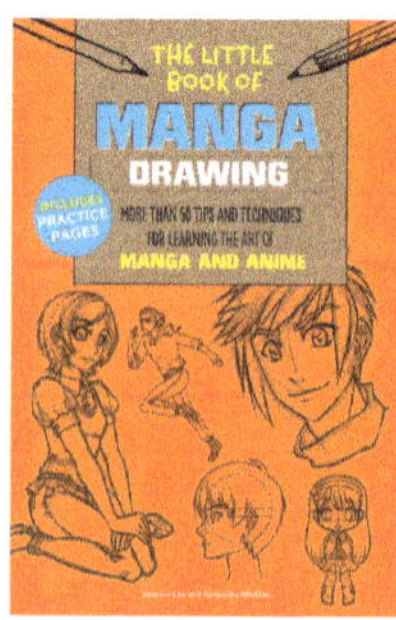

978-1-63322-473-5

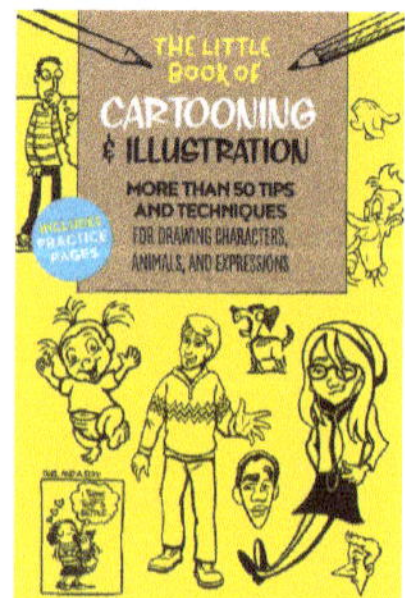

978-1-63322-620-3

Visit www.WalterFoster.com

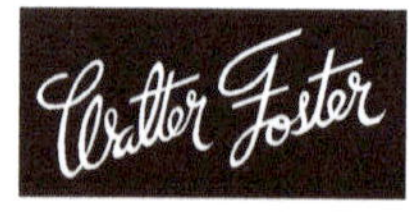

www.ingramcontent.com/pod-product-compliance
Lightning Source LLC
Chambersburg PA
CBHW060855180726
48173CB00002B/2

* 9 7 8 1 6 3 3 2 2 7 3 1 6 *